The Literary Afterlife of
Raymond Carver

Modern American Literature and the New Twentieth Century
Series Editors: Martin Halliwell and Mark Whalan

Published Titles

Writing Nature in Cold War American Literature
Sarah Daw

F. Scott Fitzgerald's Short Fiction and American Popular Culture: From Ragtime to Swing Time
Jade Broughton Adams

The Labour of Laziness in Twentieth-Century American Literature
Zuzanna Ladyga

The Literature of Suburban Change: Narrating Spatial Complexity in Metropolitan America
Martin Dines

The Literary Afterlife of Raymond Carver: Influence and Craftsmanship in the Neoliberal Era
Jonathan Pountney

Living Jim Crow: The Segregated Town in Mid-Century Southern Fiction
Gavan Lennon

The Little Art Colony and US Modernism: Carmel, Provincetown, Taos
Geneva M. Gano

Forthcoming Titles

The Big Red Little Magazine: New Masses, 1926–1948
Susan Currell

The Reproductive Politics of American Literature and Film, 1959–1973
Sophie Jones

Ordinary Pursuits in American Writing after Modernism
Rachel Malkin

Sensing Willa Cather: The Writer and the Body in Transition
Guy Reynolds

The Plastic Theatre of Tennessee Williams: Expressionist Drama and the Visual Arts
Henry I. Schvey

Class, Culture and the Making of US Modernism
Michael Collins

Black Childhood in Modern African American Fiction
Nicole King

Visit our website at www.edinburghuniversitypress.com/series/MALTNTC

The Literary Afterlife of Raymond Carver

Influence and Craftsmanship in the Neoliberal Era

JONATHAN POUNTNEY

EDINBURGH
University Press

Edinburgh University Press is one of the leading university presses in the UK. We publish academic books and journals in our selected subject areas across the humanities and social sciences, combining cutting-edge scholarship with high editorial and production values to produce academic works of lasting importance. For more information visit our website: edinburghuniversitypress.com

© Jonathan Pountney, 2020, 2022

Edinburgh University Press Ltd
The Tun – Holyrood Road, 12(2f) Jackson's Entry, Edinburgh EH8 8PJ

First published in hardback by Edinburgh University Press 2020

Typeset in 10/13 ITC Giovanni Std Book by
Servis Filmsetting Ltd, Stockport, Cheshire

A CIP record for this book is available from the British Library

ISBN 978 1 4744 5550 3 (hardback)
ISBN 978 1 4744 5551 0 (paperback)
ISBN 978 1 4744 5552 7 (webready PDF)
ISBN 978 1 4744 5553 4 (epub)

The right of Jonathan Pountney to be identified as the author of this work has been asserted in accordance with the Copyright, Designs and Patents Act 1988, and the Copyright and Related Rights Regulations 2003 (SI No. 2498).

CONTENTS

Introduction: Authenticity, Craftsmanship and
Neoliberalism in Raymond Carver's Fiction   1

1. 'Bad Raymond': Alcoholism, Education and Masculinity
   in Chuck Kinder's *Honeymooners*   27
2. 'Carveresque Realism': Raymond Carver and
   Jay McInerney   60
3. 'The Transpacific Partnership': Raymond Carver and
   Haruki Murakami   106
4. 'Why Raymond Carver?': Neoliberal Authenticity and
   Culture in Alejandro G. Iñárritu's *Birdman*   148

Conclusion: Willy Vlautin and Diminished Class
Consciousness   182

Works Cited   193
Index   204

For Emma

Introduction: Authenticity, Craftsmanship and Neoliberalism in Raymond Carver's Fiction

In August 1999, a decade after Raymond Carver's death at the age of fifty from lung cancer, *The New York Review of Books* published an extended feature on Carver's place in American letters. The article's author, the critic A. O. Scott, opened by arguing that while plenty of American writers are hyped, imitated, even admired, few have the privilege of claiming, as Carver did near the end of his life in his poem 'Late Fragment', that they are 'beloved'.[1] While at the height of his career in the 1980s, the article argues, Carver's minimalist publications were influential, since his death, he has become an 'international icon of traditional American literary values'. Which is to say, 'His genius – but more his honesty, his decency, his commitment to the exigencies of craft – is praised by an extraordinary diverse cross section of his peers.'[2]

As Scott's generous retrospective suggests, for a writer who only published four major story collections during his lifetime, Carver's cultural impact is remarkably exponential.[3] While he was alive, Carver's influence on the American short story was widely noted, but not so generally known is that since his death Carver's work has continued to have an impact on a number of significant contemporary writers and artists. The list of those who attest to his influence is as diverse as those studied in the forthcoming expository chapters – Jay McInerney, Haruki Murakami, Alejandro G. Iñárritu, Chuck Kinder and Willy Vlautin – as well as others like the filmmakers Robert Altman, Ray Lawrence, Dan Rush and Andrew Kotatko, the writers Salman Rushdie, Stuart Evers and Denis Johnson, the musician Paul Kelly and the photographer Bob Adelman. The admiration of such a multivalent list suggests that Carver's writing, despite its working-class subject matter and its particular Pacific Northwest setting, is not bound by its immediate geographic or cultural context. This book argues that the fundamental reason for Carver's extensive afterlife is that there is a tight and intricate relationship between his texts and his perceived lifestyle and writing practice; that underlying these ideas is the perception that Carver broadly represents a return to what might be best understood as a more 'real' form of literature – what Scott calls 'traditional American literary values' – one that is, Carver's advocates would argue, more authentic than other kinds of recent writing.

Given the aesthetic and formal differences between Carver's writing and those who claim to have been influenced by him, this book argues that Carver's literary afterlife is best viewed as being a social phenomenon, one born out of the social relations, historical circumstances and economic forms that were produced by the shifting paradigms of US capitalism during Carver's lifetime. While he may have struggled to make productive sense of this period, and while Carver may not have directly identified the tenets of the early neoliberal era in which he lived, they affected his life in pointed and particular ways. This book argues that his experience, which is communicated in his writing, becomes a model of how to negotiate, for better or worse, the complex and shifting foundations of this significant socio-economic transition. What's more, while Carver experienced these events at a local level, the expansion of neoliberalism – or similar forms of free market capitalism – throughout the world in the last forty years has meant that his experience, his writing and his influence has a particularly global resonance.

Read within this socio-historic context, this book argues that Carver's realist authenticity embodies a model of retreat from the bewildering world of late capitalism, and becomes a coping mechanism, or a form of consolation, that offers other writers and artists living in similar circumstances a way of navigating a world which seems to exceed the frame of conceptual mapping. In this sense, much of Carver's early work inhabits a zone that explores the differences between the hegemonic narratives of late capitalism – that is, the conventional American dream of equal opportunity, individual freedom and upward socio-economic mobility for all who work hard enough – and the reality of lived experience in this same period. This idea is complemented by Carver's late fiction, which offers a muted oppositional alternative based on the residual values of craftsmanship, which, for those who are influenced by him, provides a distinctive site of resistance to the hegemonic norms of neoliberalism. The chapters that follow this introduction consider how this is the case in relation to a number of contemporary artists who claim to be influenced by Carver and who are also working within countries or cultures that have recently made, or are in the process of making, the transition to neoliberal capitalism.

Thomas Edsall illustrates the substantial changes to the socio-economic conditions in America that occurred during Carver's lifetime by recalling the defeat of the Republican presidential candidate Barry Goldwater in the 1964 election.[4] Defeated by Lyndon B. Johnson in the largest margin in US history, Goldwater's campaign advocated major reductions in federal spending alongside sharp increases in military investment. Sixteen years later Ronald Reagan was elected president on a platform that bore an uncanny resemblance to Goldwater's campaign. Reagan then even persuaded Congress, including a Democratic House of Representatives, to enact fiscal legislation that would have been inconceivable at any time during the previous fifty years.

This significant change in economic and political thought – what has been called the eras of Fordism and post-Fordism, or, now more commonly, embedded liberalism and neoliberalism – had a notably negative impact on the life of the American working-class – those individuals that surrounded Carver for much of his early life and who form the foundation of his fiction – and is best understood in light of a number of important historical crises in the capitalist structures in the 1970s. The first was the dissolution of the Bretton Woods currency agreement in response to the increasing domestic crises of overaccumulation, unemployment and inflation, and also to the loss of control over the global free-flow of US dollars, which, because of their high value, had been deposited en masse into European banks. In 1971 President Nixon announced the suspension of the dollar's convertibility into gold and international currency and exchange rates were allowed to float. Around the same time the effects of the OPEC Oil Shock – which tripled the price of crude oil for OECD member countries – dramatically increased production costs for private corporations. As a way to balance the slow-down in manufacturing, the US put military pressure on Saudi Arabia to recycle its petrodollars through the New York banking system. The banks, it was hoped, could then use their funds to help kick-start the domestic economy, but, precisely because of the poor domestic economic conditions, instead sought profitable outlets in the Global South, and, because of the liberalisation of international credit and finance markets, were free to loan at low risk and in favourable rates designated in US dollars.

These two historical events highlighted the increasing autonomy in the financial services industry. Since President Roosevelt had passed the Glass-Steagall Act in his first hundred days in office – a bill designed, in Roosevelt's own words, to 'safeguard against a return of the evils of the old order', that is, the intricate relationship between business and politics that preceded the Great Depression – federal law had demanded the separation of investment and commercial banking. Federal insurance had also been provided on all bank deposits, and the federal government, through Keynesian intervention, remained in control of the private banking sector.[5] But in the 1970s there began to be a power shift. This point is again illustrated by the Bretton Woods agreement, which was signed in 1944 with the conspicuous absence of bankers and financiers. Giovanni Arrighi sums the situation up well when he writes that at that moment 'Washington rather than New York was confirmed as the primary seat of "production" of world money.'[6] But with the introduction of the floating exchange rate and the excessive petrodollar recycling in the 1970s, the federal government began to lose its control over the financial sector. Sensing the opportunity, the business community turned to lobbying and policy think tanks. A 'new' kind of free market liberalism based on the ideological principles of the Mont Pelerin Society was touted by key economic institutions, and the static regulatory flaws of Keynesian economics fast became unpopular. By the late 1970s, and especially in the 1980s, Washington's corporate lobbying community had become so infiltrated by the business community that New York banks began to gain a level of influence on par with those in the 1920s. What made this acquisition of power so remarkable is that the business community achieved its goals without any broad public mandate.[7]

While signs of neoliberalism can be traced back to the early 1970s, it is broadly recognised that Paul Volcker's decision as Chair of the Federal Reserve to raise interest rates by 20 points on 6 October 1979 symbolised the beginning of the neoliberal era. The swing to neoconservative politics and the election of Reagan in 1980 cemented its impetus. Built on a system of laissez-faire economics, neoliberalism holds to libertarian free market principles and Adam Smith's hidden hand as a guide for the demand and supply of free market goods. Within this framework the neoliberal state has two clear objectives. The first is to prioritise the creation of a business climate in which capital can accumulate. The second is that when financial crises appear, the state must favour business interests over its citizens. Of course, there are times when political pragmatism predominates and the state cannot follow neoliberal orthodoxy, but the overall impact of neoliberal policy over the last forty years has been an augmented wealth gap, a decrease in the manufacturing industry, an increase in temporary service sector labour and the retraction of social privileges such as universal health care, public education and pension rights for the working class.

To argue that there is an important connection between this historical circumstance and Carver's writing is to position oneself in line with critics who view Carver's fiction as being, on some level, a response to his working-class experience. Many of these critics also suggest that Carver's writing is a class-conscious commentary on American life that stands in as a synecdochic example for the socio-economic struggles faced by many Americans during this same period. Irving Howe typified this opinion when, in a review of Carver's fourth collection *Cathedral*, he wrote that 'Mr Carver is showing us at least part of the truth about a segment of American experience few of our writers trouble to notice.' He continued by writing that critics often 'charge him with programmatic gloom and other heresies, but at his best he is probing, as many American writers have done before, the waste and destructiveness that prevail beneath the affluence of American life'.[8] The particular American life that Howe refers to is the negative space behind the ideological common sense of neoliberalism; between the American dream of individual freedom and equal opportunity, on the one hand, and the reality of inequality and social immobility, on the other. Carver and his first wife, Maryann, married after they graduated from high school and employed an orthodox American protestant work ethic as a means to realise their ambitions, but the financial burden of two young children, a lack of secure long-term employment and a marriage complicated by alcohol addiction and infidelity undermined any hope of social mobility. Writing about his experience in 'Fires', an essay published in 1982, Carver recalls when he realised that his long-term plans for upward socio-economic mobility were little more than fantasies. 'We had great dreams, my wife and I', he wrote. 'We thought we could bow our necks, work very hard, and do all that we had set our hearts to do. But we were mistaken.'[9] In the essay Carver recounts the 'exact' moment of realisation – while washing his children's clothes in the laundromat, a setting of almost uncanny Carveresque banality:

> At that moment – I swear all of this took place there in the laundromat – I could see nothing ahead but years of more of this kind of responsibility and perplexity. Things would change some, but they were never really going to get better. I understood this, but could I live with it? At that moment I saw accommodations would have to be made. The sights would have to be lowered. I'd had, I realized later, an insight. But so what? What are insights? They don't help any. They just make things harder.[10]

Carver's resignation in the face of failed hegemonic narratives points towards the broader affect of capitalism's ideological efficacy. Mark Fisher's popular short book *Capitalist Realism* seeks to illustrate the famous statement, nominally attributed to Fredric Jameson, that it is easier to imagine the end of the world than the end of capitalism.[11] Jodi Dean – whose work has been concerned with a leftist retreat of oppositional alternatives to neoliberal hegemony – draws on Fisher's book when, in conversation with him, she argues that Fisher's term 'designates a general ideological formation ... wherein all illusions and hopes of equality have been shed'.[12] In this sense neoliberal ideology operates in two distinct ways. The first is the acceptance and propagation of the belief that neoliberalism cannot be fought. And the second is the notion that adapting to neoliberal domination is just a question of pragmatic survival. These two ideas combine to produce a depressive resignation, an affective dimension in which it becomes 'common sense' to follow the dominant neoliberal line.

In *The Enigma of Capital*, David Harvey echoes this idea when he argues that the past and future evolution of capitalism is contingent on its concomitant ability to evolve what he calls 'mental conceptions of the world' (that is, 'knowledge structures and the cultural norms and beliefs consistent with endless accumulation') in line with more conspicuous developments in technological production, labour processes and institutional arrangements. Harvey theorises seven 'activity spheres' within the evolutionary trajectory of capitalism (one of which is 'mental conceptions of world'), in which each sphere develops on its own, but always in dynamic relation with the other spheres.[13] The effect of this idea, to use Harvey's own example, is that adaptions in mental conceptions will have a consequential effect on the very social relations, labour processes and institutional arrangements which dominate life in neoliberalism and which, in turn, serve to uphold and support neoliberal hegemony. Capital, Harvey postulates, cannot circulate or accumulate without touching these 'activity spheres' (to the extent that if any of these areas limits or restricts accumulation then capital must overcome it). The result is that the formation of a belief system in support of neoliberal capitalism (whether that be a positive affirmation or, more likely it seems, a resigned acceptance) is vital to capitalism's development and survival.

Carver's story 'The Student's Wife' illustrates the fictional transposition of this kind of resignation in the face of neoliberal common sense. Nan's recollection of a camping trip she took with her husband, Mike, just after their wedding – like Carver and Maryann, they too were married after high school graduation – symbolises, it seems, a time of youthful innocence. Their heavy blankets in the tent, which are so thick 'she could hardly turn her feet under all the weight', appear indicative of the protective hegemonic narrative of hard work as a route to socio-economic security and prosperity. But Nan's sentiments are countered by Mike, who reminds her, with a definite sense of resignation, that 'that was a long time ago'. Time and experience in late-capitalism has changed things for Mike. 'What he did remember', Carver writes, 'was very carefully combed hair and loud half-baked ideas about life and art, and he did not want to remember that.'[14] Mike, then, appears to have settled for the reality of their impoverished situation, helplessly caught, as he is, amongst the folds of American experience, in a new society without the support of conventional working-class narratives of conscious rebellion, and where state support is moving towards neoliberal hegemony.

In an attempt to help her sleep, he asks her to make a list of her likes and dislikes. The 200-word monologue that follows – what amounts to a conspicuous anomaly in Carver's writing – embodies her desire for social mobility. 'Most of all', she concludes, 'I'd like us both just to live a good honest life without having to worry about money and bills and things like that.'[15] Nan's concern for what might be pragmatically called a reasonable standard of living overtly mirrors Carver's own situation in the 1960s. In her monologue Nan recounts her desire for a social life, a nine-to-five existence, a fixed residence and clothing for her children. In an interview with Gordon Burn, Carver described his early married years in the following way:

> In those days I always worked some crap job or another, and my wife did the same . . . Time and again I reached the point where I couldn't see or plan further ahead than the first of next month and gathering enough money, by hook or by crook, to meet the rent and provide the children's school clothes.[16]

In 'The Student's Wife' Nan's dreams are eventually, and devastatingly, undermined, when, sitting at the kitchen table later that same night she notices the sunrise, and it dawns on her – perhaps for the first time – the hopelessness of her situation. In what might easily be seen as a continuation of Edward Hopper's artistic impressions, Carver writes, 'She had seen few sunrises in her life . . . and none of them had been like that. Not in pictures she had seen nor in any book she had read had she learned a sunrise so terrible as this.'[17] The ending to Carver's story – the explicit way in which Nan learns or realises the reality of her situation – neatly corresponds with his own laundromat epiphany. It is a moment of shameful failure and personal inferiority, and a moment reminiscent of Carver's – and other Americans' – experience during that era. In short: Nan's insight only makes her struggle harder.[18]

Considering the parallel experience depicted in stories like 'The Student's Wife' and Carver's own personal essays, it is unsurprising that many critics see the class crises of Carver's early life as being the source for much of his fiction.[19] It is, as Ben Harker argues, the precise 'creative struggle to narrate apparently inexplicable social experiences', along with the conjuncture of Carver's 'socioeconomic disempowerment and diminished class-consciousness', that is the essential component of his fiction.[20] Stephen Groarke argues that Carver's fiction, while often linked to his nominal literary ancestors, is better viewed as emanating from the socio-economic situation of his familial, relational and financial circumstances. He argues that it was the necessary banalities of the laundromat, childcare and low-wage employment that impacted his writing most readily. Martin Scofield, in two separate publications, also views Carver's life as being the basis for his fiction, and he praises Carver's ability to mix the reality of that socio-economic context into the fiction of his writing. While the relationship may not be as unmediated as it seems, it does provide, Scofield argues, the foundation upon which Carver is able to operate empathetically at close quarters with his characters.

For many readers and reviewers, then, a large part of Carver's appeal – and many would argue, a large part of his commercial and literary success – is that his realism has the definite ring of authenticity. It is this idea that denotes Carver's right to cast a light on a very particular type of American working-class experience. By the end of his life, some critics even felt he had been successful in promoting this cause. Writing in *The New York Times Book Review*, Marilynne Robinson, in a review of *Where I'm Calling From*, goes as far as saying that Carver's fiction has transformed the nation's perception of the rural working class. Carver, she wrote – with a not insignificant amount of sentimentality – has 'turned banality's pockets out and found all their contents beautiful'.[21] Mark Helprin, in *The New York Review of Books*, argued that Carver's fiction gave dignity to the forgotten 'working people [who] seem to be backed up against the northwest coast, as far away from the centres of Anglo-American literary tradition as they can get'.[22] The idea even extended beyond the borders of America. Writing in the *London Review of Books*, Michael Foley calls Carver a kind of 'literary Rocky – janitor, delivery man, sawmill operator, service-station attendant, an uneducated alcoholic no-hoper who rises to Major Writer status'. He adds, 'One can tell Carver is genuine because he makes nothing of it.'[23] The obituaries and short biographies that appeared after his death from lung cancer at the age of fifty only cemented these perceptions. Many link the harshness of his early life (and that of other Americans) with the content of his fiction. *The New York Times* summarised Carver as the chronicler of 'the working poor', before reminding readers (lest they forget) that 'Carver came from the hardscrabble world of the down-and-out blue-collar characters in his stories.'[24] And while it is important to note that claims of authenticity have a tendency to be overblown – in Carver's case his persistent self-identification as 'a paid-in-full member of the working poor', which the facts of his later life patently contradict – it is this rather mythic representation of Carver as an authentic artist that seems to persist most readily in the final years of his life.[25]

Since my argument about Carver's afterlife rests on the assertion that other writers and artists find his work to be useful for making sense of a post-Fordist, neoliberal context, it is important to be clear about the characteristics of Carver's work that enable this to happen. I want to suggest, therefore, that Carver's influence can be read in two ways. The first, as I have already suggested, is that later artists find in Carver's work a powerful way to handle the distinction between hegemonic narratives and lived experience. Examples of this are most conspicuous in his personal essays, which explicitly recount the travails of his socio-economic disempowerment bought on by his working-class background, as well as his early fiction, which, for many, is drawn directly from that same experience. The second aspect that appears to resonate with others is Carver's retreat from the hegemonic narrative of neoliberal work – that is, as I will argue later, short-term, flexible, competition-based work – towards an artisanal form of craft and non-alienated labour. Of course it was Karl Marx who famously argued that the adjustment of labour processes to enhance capital accumulation alienates the worker, but in the neoliberal era, an age which has seen the systematic dismantling of labour unions, the reduction of state intervention, the mass-migration of labour through globalisation, the de-skilling of workers in the name of technological automation, and the increasing dominance of age-management in corporations, there appears to have been an intensification of its impact. The fragmentation of these institutions in recent years has led, as the ethnographer Richard Sennett makes clear in *The Culture of New Capitalism*, to large groups of working-class and even middle-Americans feeling cast adrift, or, to use Marx's term once more, alienated. The result is a widespread sense of personal inferiority and failure for many Americans during the last half-century – a fact accentuated by neoliberal hegemony which denies the very existence of the working classes.[26]

Carver's writing, then, appears to offer a muted oppositional alternative to this dominant ideology. It is a narrative of personal belief based on what Raymond Williams famously called residual values, 'experiences, meanings, and values which cannot be verified or cannot be expressed in terms of the dominant culture, [but] are nevertheless lived and practiced on the basis of the residue – cultural as well as social – of some previous social formation'.[27] In the context of late-capitalism or, more specifically, the move from embedded liberalism to neoliberalism, the residue operates outside of the laissez-faire economics linked to free market principles, and in Carver's work in particular, the residue is also one that is localised to his Northwest setting and operates outside of the political realm. In this sense, Carver's writing projects an alternative, deeply personal form of non-incorporated culture that is distinctive from, say, larger political oppositional solutions and yet – and this is, perhaps, what makes Carver's work so intriguing – it still provides a distinctive, and even powerful, site of resistance to the hegemonic norms of late capitalism.

To develop this point a little further, Carver's anti-political, ground-level resistance might be classed as being part of a wider trend of oppositional movements that have emerged since 1980. In his popular history of neoliberalism, David Harvey argues that the impact of these types of movements has been to shift the terrain of political organisation away from traditional party politics towards a less focused, yet powerfully broad, dynamic social action across the whole spectrum of civil society. He concludes by writing, 'What such movements lose in focus they gain in terms of direct relevance to particular issues and constituencies. They draw strength from being embedded in the nitty-gritty of daily life and struggle.'[28] Carver's fiction then, which to borrow Harvey's term, is heavily invested in the 'nitty-gritty of daily life', lends itself to a similar kind of ground-level resistance. What it loses from not being tied to political orthodoxy, it gains in relevance, applicability and immediacy. I will analyse in more detail the specifics of Carver's commitment to an atypical political formation, his residual retreat from neoliberalism, and its impact on others in my upcoming chapters, but for now, and as a way of illustrating my point, I want to provide a few brief examples from Carver's work.

In 'Kindling', a posthumous story published in *Esquire* in 1999, Myers, the story's protagonist, finds solace from his peripatetic life through the act of splitting logs for the couple he is lodging with. This activity seems to be a deliberate refracted reflection of the rural past, and the more Myers involves himself in the work the more its significance is heightened. Carver writes, 'He decided that he would cut this wood and split it and stack it before sunset, and that it was a matter of life and death that he do so.'[29] Although Carver does not explicitly state it, the emphasis placed on the importance of Myers's physical action suggests the notion of craftsmanship. Writing in *The Craftsman*, Sennett argues that craftsmanship 'names an enduring, basic human impulse, the desire to do a job well for its own sake', and this idea and principle is a notable trope of characters' attitudes to work in Carver's late-life fiction.[30] It also, importantly, stands in opposition to the neoliberal common sense and the dominant ideology of economic-based, flexible labour. Elsewhere, in *The Culture of New Capitalism* Sennett argues that 'The emerging social order militates against the ideal of craftsmanship, that is, learning to do just one thing really well; such commitment can often prove economically destructive.'[31]

Sennett's analysis is useful to the extent that it alludes not only to the cultural dependency of craftsmanship's opposition to neoliberal economic determinism but also its continuing disposition which stands in line with historic conceptions of alternative living. In American literature, these oppositions find their source in the notions of Emersonian self-reliance found in Thoreau's thought experiments and Whitman's poetry and continue through to the Arts and Crafts Movement at the turn of the twentieth century and the modernist work of Sherwood Anderson, Alfred Stieglitz and, perhaps most applicably for Carver, in Hemingway's *mot juste*. During the modernist age in particular, the desire for therapeutic, joyful and useful labour stems from the increasing rationalisation of economic life in the organised structures of capitalism. As T. J. Jackson Lears points out in *No Place of Grace*, for white-collar clerks and professionals, despite the relative security that modernist labour patterns granted, working life seemed relatively insubstantial. Indeed, he continues to argue more particularly, 'the new bureaucratic world of work often fragmented their labor and reduced their sense of autonomy: more important, it isolated them from the hard, substantial reality of things'. The result was a 'yearning to reintegrate selfhood by resurrecting the authentic experience of manual labor'.[32] Carver's own retreat from neoliberal hegemony towards residual craftsmanship echoes these sentiments and stands in the roots of this modernist fascination. And while these tenets find themselves to be particularly visible in Myer's overtly physical action in 'Kindling' they are equally present, if in a divergent form, in other characters in Carver's late-fiction too.

In another story, 'Menudo', the protagonist, who has been having an affair with a neighbour, finds solace and a peculiar satisfaction in raking leaves. Carver writes:

> It's light out – light enough at any rate for what I have to do. And then, without thinking about it any more, I start to rake. I rake our yard, every inch of it. It's important it be done right, too. I set the rake right down into the turf and pull hard. It must feel to the grass like it does whenever someone gives your hair a hard jerk.[33]

Like the work undertaken by Myers in 'Kindling', Carver's protagonist in 'Menudo' places an emphasis on doing a job 'right', that is, to take Sennett's terminology, 'to do a job well for its own sake'. The task itself (raking leaves) seems particularly significant in that it is the pulling up of dead matter, a not entirely pleasant process – 'It must feel to the grass like it does whenever someone gives your hair a hard jerk' – but a necessary one for providing the light and oxygen necessary for organic growth. In this sense, the action of raking becomes a route to personal character development. As the mid-twentieth-century sociologist C. Wright Mills argued:

> The craftsman's work is thus a means of developing his skill, as well as a means of developing himself as a man. It is not that self-development is an ulterior goal, but that such development is the cumulative result obtained by devotion to and practice of his skills. As he gives it the quality of his own mind and skill, he is further developing his own nature; in this simple sense, he lives in and through his work, which confesses and reveals him to the world.[34]

In Carver's story, then, the action speaks more broadly towards the protagonist's own domestic situation, that in the act of cleaning his lawn, he is also cleaning up his own domestic 'mess'. After his own yard, he moves across the road to his neighbour's yard, a movement that suggests that craft leads towards a muted kind of collectivism. When the Baxters, the homeowners, come out to see what he's doing, he stops. 'I've finished here anyway', Carver writes. 'There are other yards, more important yards for that matter. I kneel, and, taking a grip low down on the rake handle, I pull the last of the leaves into my bag and tie off the top.'[35] Having completed his task to a gratifying level, his mind turns to others – especially, it seems, to the neighbour he has been sleeping with – which suggests the possibility of spreading the effect of craftsmanship, that, like the action of tidying the leaves, he might be able to 'tie off' the loose ends of his extra-marital relationship.

The idea that craftsmanship extends to the area of social collectivism or personal development is reinforced in 'Elephant', another late story in which the protagonist's walk to work becomes a time of social craftsmanship, a moment to reflect and cultivate his familial relationships, even if the reality of his social situation appears, initially at least, far more constrained than the end of the story actually suggests. The allusion to social craftsmanship underlines the idea that, in Carver's fiction, craft stretches beyond its natural territory of manual labour. Craftsmanship, after all, focuses 'on objective standards, on the thing in itself', as Sennett argues in *The Craftsman*, and therefore the ultimate example of craftsmanship in Carver's work is the presentation of his own writing practice, which becomes itself an example of sharing or providing a model for non-alienated labour.[36] This, again, is an idea that I will develop in more detail later when I discuss the influence of John Gardner and Carver's own teaching philosophy in relation to McInerney in Chapter 2, but to briefly indicate the nature of this argument, Carver wrote in his essay 'On Writing', 'In the end the satisfaction of having done our best, and proof of that labour, is the one thing we can take into the grave.'[37] Carver's essay places a strong emphasis on craft and skill over the idea of sudden inspiration or innate, untrained talent. In his later-life fiction and personal writing Carver depicts work done for enjoyment and self-worth, a space where the ultimate aim is not the accumulation of capital or the accomplishment of an arbitrary numerical target, but rather the accumulation of dignity, personality and experience – an idea that, again, stands in sharp contrast to the transient, adaptable and ephemeral labour processes of both embedded and neoliberal capitalism.

Carver's poem 'Shiftless' reinforces this idea by emphasising creative activity, and what might be read as his own creative expression, as being firmly outside of the sphere of economic activity. He writes, 'I never liked work. My goal was always to be shiftless.' He continues later in the poem, 'I liked the idea of sitting in a chair in front of your house for hours, doing nothing', perhaps just, 'Making things out of wood with a knife'. 'Where's the harm there?', Carver asks.[38] The poem clearly places a preference on a type of artisanal – what might be understood as pre-Fordist or even pre-capitalist, and certainly residual – type of work, where the aim of adhering to the dominant ideological logic of work and consumption depicted earlier in the poem (by the 'painted houses', 'flush toilets' and cars 'whose year and make were recognizable') is replaced by the more simple aim of wood whittling. It is not that Carver is against work in and of itself, but he is against a certain *type* of work. In the conveniently titled poem 'Work', for instance, Carver talks about the 'Love of work. The blood singing in that. The fine high rise of it into the work.' And later, in reference to

Gardner's unflagging early-morning writing process, he alludes to 'The fullness before work', before concluding by writing, in a phrase that echoes his thoughts in 'On Writing', 'And work . . . The going to what lasts'.[39] These poems, then, emphasise the writing process as being one which is fulfilling and purposeful only when it resides outside of the norms of the capitalist labour process. It is a clear example, as Harker argues, of 'anachronistic craftsmanship seemingly outside or pre-dating the alienating processes whereby things and people are re-produced'.[40] And while a political analysis might be inferred from these poems, its emphasis is subtle compared with that placed on the craftsman-like action, suggesting that Carver's residual response is rather more consolatory than it is critical.

If it is a twofold foundation of Carver's afterlife – that, first, his writing represents a zone that explores the difference between hegemonic narratives and lived experience, and second, that his work presents a consolatory retreat towards residual craftsmanship – that attracts others to his writing, then, given this book's propensity to influence, the question that follows is: does this idea fit into a larger critical or operative framework? As a preliminary to this discussion it is worth pointing out that, broadly speaking, literary history is constituted by a favourable view of influence. In this sense, writers typically seek to embed themselves amongst their literary predecessors by calling into practice allusions, affinities and kinships with earlier authors. This, for example, was something that Carver was apt to do. In 'On Writing' he situates his own work within a broader canon of past short story writers from Isak Dinesen to Anton Chekov, Evan Connell, Flannery O'Connor and V. S. Pritchett, and while Carver was sometimes rather coy about his own influences – when one inquiring interviewer tried to pin his work to Hemingway's, Carver replied, 'I don't write fishing stories' – generally Carver was keen to cement himself as a member of the short story canon.[41]

It is worth noting that Carver's allusion to other writers echoes Mark McGurl's recent formulation of post-war influence in *The Program Era*. In his account of American post-war literature's relationship with the rise of creative writing programmes, McGurl presents a model of influence that, in some ways, reflects Carver's own thoughts on the topic. In his book, McGurl argues for a twofold approach to the influence of creative writing programmes. The first is that they impart what McGurl calls a 'traditionally textual' influence through their teaching syllabi. 'Consider the stylistic afterlives of Faulkner and Hemingway', McGurl writes, 'who spent little time in the classroom but have been "teachers" to so many.' The second, more associative with the creative writing programme itself is, 'the influence of the teacher at the head of the table, the professional author who, in his or her spare time, authors marginal comments on apprentice fictions'.[42] This is an idea, McGurl makes clear, that has its precursor in the relationship between editors and writers, such as Stein and Hemingway, or Pound and Eliot. In many ways Carver exemplifies something of what McGurl is arguing for. He learnt to write, for instance, at several higher education institutions but also claimed the influence of non-institutionalised precursors such as Chekov and Dinesan. What's more, Carver reciprocated the effect when he later taught at a plethora of universities in the 1970s and 80s.

McGurl's ideas on influence are reinforced by a more general interest in the topic, and the proliferation of critical models of literary influence in the last century – in the criticism of T. S. Eliot, F. R. Leavis, Ihab Hassan, Harold Bloom and Christopher Ricks – suggests an equally broad critical interest in the topic. The most noteworthy – and certainly controversial – in this list is Bloom's theory of influence outlined in *The Anxiety of Influence*, in which Bloom argues for an individualist reading of authorial influence that is heavily mediated by his idealist view of literature. Bloom relates this to literary influence by asserting that literary history is 'indistinguishable from poetic influence' since writers make literary history by misreading their precursors in an attempt to 'clear imaginative space for themselves'.[43] This misreading, or what Bloom calls 'poetic misprision', is best understood as a twofold psychological action. First the later writer falls in love with a precursor's text with a Longinian passion, which results, secondly, in a psychological imprisonment. The anxiety of influence which is produced out of this complex act of misreading draws heavily on Freud's family romance in which the later writer is locked in a struggle that takes place at the level of the psyche with their precursor. Consequently, a battle occurs between both writers, a battle which is, above all, an individual one, independent of external circumstance, enacted in the later writer's own private mind against their precursor until the precursor is eventually, if the later writer is to escape the anxiety of influence, effaced.

It is worth dwelling on Bloom's theory, not only because it is perhaps the most widely recognised theory of literary influence in the last few decades, but because Bloom, in his introductory series for Chelsea House Publishers, applies his theory to Carver's writing. In it Bloom writes that he has an 'imperfect sympathy' for Carver's fiction, arguing, in an allusion to Irving Howe's book review, that Carver is 'a master within the limits he imposed upon himself'. These limits are what Bloom perceives as the restrictions of a Hemingwayean literary realism:

> So overwhelming was Hemingway's influence upon Carver's earliest stories that the later writer wisely fended Hemingway off by an *askesis* that went well beyond the elliptical style practiced by the author of *The First Forty-Nine Stories*. In his own, final phase, Carver began to develop beyond an art so largely reliant upon leaving things out.[44]

To explain, just briefly, what Bloom means by this I want to first turn to his definition of *askesis* in *The Anxiety of Influence*. The shortened definition given for this penultimate revisionary ratio is that it is a 'movement of self-purgation which intends the attainment of a state of solitude . . . [the later artist] yields up part of his own human and imaginative endowment, so as to separate himself from others, including the precursor'.[45] In other words, the later artist yields up part of their creative freedom, and in this process of self-sacrifice, individuates themselves. *Askesis* is, on a simple level, a curtailment. The later artist makes themselves smaller than their precursor – or in Bloom's violent lexicon, 'wound himself *without further emptying himself of his inspiration*'.[46]

While Bloom's assessment of Carver is provocative, he fails to give a single example of how or why Carver might have done this. The only clue he provides is his reference to Carver's 'final phase', in which he proposes that Carver 'began to develop beyond an art so largely reliant upon leaving things out', an idea that only reiterates what other critics, like Ewing Campbell for example, had previously argued regarding the evolution of Carver's writing.[47] Bloom's intimation seems to be – and this is reinforced by his critical focus on Carver's late stories in the book – that Carver's early fiction, specifically his first two story collections, were unable to circumnavigate the anxiety of influence posed by Hemingway's fiction. However, through a curtailment of his minimalism – which in practice, perhaps rather counter-intuitively, means a formal expansion – Carver was able to overcome Hemingway's influence. Which is not to say that Bloom necessarily counts Carver's late fiction as being particularly successful in and of itself. For Bloom closes his analysis by suggesting that one of Carver's most anthologised stories, 'Cathedral', is actually indebted to D. H. Lawrence's 'The Blind Man', and argues that Carver, who he suggests must have known of Lawrence's story, produces a weaker work of art. Bloom concludes by revealing his Gnostic tendency, 'There is a reverberation in Lawrence's story that carries us into the high madness of great art. Carver, though a very fine artist, cannot carry us there.'[48]

The problem with Bloom's formulation in relation to Carver's work is that his idealism fails to accept the role of any external circumstances in the creation (and subsequent reading and interpretation) of Carver's text. From a historical point of view, it is now widely understood that Carver's development (which was nominally thought of in terms of a broadening of literary style in line with his own personal victory over alcohol addiction) has more to do with an increased editorial independence in the 1980s than any type of stylistic development or even – to indulge Bloom just a little – psychological battle with Hemingway's fiction.[49] Likewise Bloom's accusation that Carver's 'Cathedral' is indebted to Lawrence's 'The Blind Man' fails to take account of the broader biographical background in the formation of Carver's narrative, which is now recognised as being based on a real-life meeting between Carver and Tess Gallagher's blind friend Jerry Carriveau.[50]

Bloom's theory then, while stimulating, appears to fall short of providing a definitive route into analysing Carver's influence. Alan Sinfield provides a useful summary of the opposition when he argues that typically literature is seen as '"rising above" its conditions of production and reception; as transcending social and political concerns'. The argument most often cited as evidence for this is, Sinfield continues, 'that great art has endured the test of time'. But, Sinfield usefully concludes, 'the "art" of other times and places that we "appreciate" is, *ipso facto*, that upon which we can gain some kind of purchase from our own time and place, mediated through our particular institutions'.[51] While Sinfield's former point highlights the type of idealism that underpins Bloom's theory of influence, his latter point is helpful in developing an understanding of how Carver's texts operate on those who are influenced by them. Despite some admirers' protestations, I hold that Carver's texts, to borrow Sinfield's phraseology, do not transcend the social, political or historical circumstances in which they were produced, and therefore must not be studied independently of those realities. Raymond Williams summarises this position in *Problems in Materialism and Culture* when he argues that literature and art cannot be separated 'from other kinds of social practice in such a way as to make them subject to quite special and distinct laws'.[52] Likewise, my exploration of Carver's influence in the following chapters suggests that Carver's influence is most pronounced when those who are influenced by him find in his writing a way of gaining some kind of purchase on their own reality. I have already tried to show something of this in the way in which the institutionalisation of Carver as an authentic artist in the media came to be the dominant view of his writing and persona, and the following chapters will more fully develop a number of specific examples – such as the impact of Carver's stylistic changes in the late 1980s, which seem significant for Murakami as he tries to respond to the twin tragedies of the Kobe earthquake and Tokyo gas attack in 1993, and Kinder's admiration for Carver's working-class sensibilities within his own context of the academic establishment.

While there has been useful and stimulating work surrounding the topic of literary influence, this book is concerned with something that is more political and global than critics like Bloom or McGurl allow; it seeks to push beyond the boundaries of the higher education institution to suggest that while one important aspect of Carver's literary afterlife is the socially constructed framework in which his writing was produced, another, which in a way precedes this concept, is that what is of real interest is the way in which the socio-economic reality of those who are influenced by Carver affects their reading and understanding of his work. This book argues, therefore, that it is through this lens that Carver's writing becomes, to quote Sinfield one final time, 'powerful stories working in and beyond their initial historical moment'.[53] To repudiate the idealist position in this way is not to diminish the consequence of Carver's texts; rather, to see them in this way frees them to multiple interpretations, none of which need be bound by geographic, political or historical exclusivity, meaning that it is possible to read Carver's literary afterlife across a number of significant geographic, cultural and historical boundaries.

The following chapters, which are presented in, broadly speaking, chronological order, provide a detailed exploration of Carver's afterlife in the work of five distinctly individual writers and artists. While it has been inevitable that personal preference has played a role in my selection, it is also true that each fulfils a basic criterion. The first is that each produced work after Carver, and the second is that each admits to being influenced by, or at least having an affiliation with, Carver's work. Admission, of course, is not a condition of influence, but it did help narrow down what was otherwise a long shortlist of candidates.[54] Similarly, it is worth highlighting the male exclusivity of this selection, which does not, of course, discount the importance of Carver's work on recent female authorship, but which does highlight a certain working-class masculinity – one founded on the authenticity of his rough early-life experience and the craftsmanship of his respectable later life – which seems to lie at the heart of Carver's literary afterlife. Perhaps the final thing to say in justification is that these are also artists in whom I am interested and whose work raises stimulating and important questions for the study of Raymond Carver and contemporary literature and film more generally.

Chapter 1 is more biographical in nature and records Carver's early adult life, his peripatetic search for literary education and success at institutions like the Iowa Writers' Workshop, and his relationship with writers like Chuck Kinder, William Kittredge and John Cheever. Summarised by Carver as his Bad Raymond years, the chapter will centre its early discussion around Carver's relationship with higher education and will close by analysing Kinder's 2011 novel *Honeymooners*, which is a fictional retelling of this period, and argue that Kinder's portrayal of Carver over two decades after his death recasts Carver's life and work through the lens of American working-class masculinity, which only solidifies the notions of authenticity and craft already connected with his work.

Chapter 2 documents the relationship between Carver and Jay McInerney, from their initial meeting in Greenwich Village in 1980, to McInerney's relocation to study under Carver at Syracuse University, and his decision to publish his debut bestseller *Bright Lights, Big City* (1984) alongside Carver's own collection, *Cathedral*, in Gary Fisketjon's Vintage Contemporaries Series. The chapter analyses Carver's pedagogical impact on McInerney, which emphasised the principles of craftsmanship, and argues that many of these residual ideas proved particularly enabling for McInerney's early career. The chapter closes by arguing that the pinnacle of Carver's influence is found in McInerney's novel *Brightness Falls* (1992), which, through parody and satire, signals a retreat from postmodern experimentation towards a more Carveresque form of literary realism.

Chapter 3 similarly chronicles Carver's relationship with the Japanese writer Haruki Murakami, from Murakami's first encounter with Carver's fiction in 1982, to his decision to translate and publish all of Carver's fiction in Japanese, and his visit to Carver's home in Port Angeles, Washington on the International Visitor Program in 1984. For those familiar with Murakami's longer novels, his admiration of Carver's short fiction may come as a surprise; this chapter, therefore, documents the close relationship between the two writers while arguing that Murakami's early short fiction published in *The Elephant Vanishes* (1993), like Carver's own early work, charts the destructive affect of failed hegemonic capitalist narratives. The chapter moves on to explore two concomitant turning points in both writers' lives (Carver's newfound sobriety and Murakami's rise to literary celebrity) and argues that Carver's retreat towards residual narratives of social craftsmanship helped facilitate Murakami's own residual spiritual narrative in his collection *After The Quake* (2002).

Chapter 4 proceeds on slightly different lines to the previous chapters in that it considers Carver's afterlife in the diegetic world of Alejandro G. Iñárritu's 2014 Oscar winning film *Birdman* (2013).

The chapter charts Iñárritu's critique of multinational capitalism in his early trilogy before arguing that he makes Carver the focal point of his film because Carver has come to represent a version of artistic authenticity that can transcend the ephemerality of neoliberal culture. Through analysis of key scenes, the chapter assesses the portrayal of Carver's work and persona in the film and argues that the film's principal characters, Riggan Thomson and Mike Shiner, hold two radically divergent opinions on Carver's legacy. The chapter concludes by arguing that the film's critical discussion of Carver's afterlife has deeper implications for the creation of authentic artwork in the neoliberal era.

I will conclude my study of Carver's literary afterlife by arguing that thirty years after his death, Carver's legacy is as resonant as ever. My conclusion presents a short case study of the American novelist Willy Vlautin, who did not have the kind of relationship with Carver as those studied in the main chapters, but who nonetheless claims to be influenced by Carver, and whose work still appears to have the hallmarks of Carver's afterlife, particularly in its propensity to chronicle the life of white working-class individuals in the neoliberal era. The book concludes by arguing that the recent political spotlight on the plight of the white working-class means that Carver's work is as important as ever. I will argue that Carver's writing reveals the negative space behind neoliberalism, and, in his depiction of the American working class, also reveals a way of American life that has long been overlooked by the political mainstream. *The Literary Afterlife of Raymond Carver* closes by suggesting that Carver's sympathetic portrayals may hold the key to unlocking a new view of the American working-class that could have important implications for contemporary American national identity.

Notes

1. Carver, *All Of Us*, p. 294.
2. Scott, 'Raymond Carver's Enigma', p. 52.
3. I count Carver's four major story collections as: *Will You Please Be Quiet, Please?*, (McGraw-Hill 1976), which was nominated for a National Book Award; *What We Talk About When We Talk About Love* (Knopf 1981); *Cathedral* (Knopf 1983); and *Elephant*, a six story collection published by Collins Harvill in the UK in 1988 and included in *Where I'm Calling From*, published by *Atlantic Monthly* the

same year in the US. Carver, of course, was also a prolific poet and published a number of poetry collections, chapbooks, one screenplay and also some non-fiction essays, but this book is particularly interested in his story writing because, I think it can be reasonably argued, that this is what Carver is most known and celebrated for.

4. Edsall, *The New Politics of Inequality*, p. 15.
5. The Glass-Steagall Act was eventually repealed by President Clinton in 1999 when the Financial Services Modernization Act was passed into law, although it is worth pointing out that Roosevelt's bill had been bypassed by loopholes and lenient regulatory interpretations for decades. Roosevelt, 'Inaugural Address', 4 March 1933. Available at <https://fdrlibrary.org/inaugurations> (last accessed 19 April 2019).
6. Arrighi, *The Long Twentieth Century*, p. 288.
7. Edsall, *The New Politics of Inequality*, p. 107.
8. Howe, 'Stories of Our Loneliness', p. 43.
9. Carver, *Collected Stories*, p. 737.
10. Carver, *Collected Stories*, p. 739.
11. In his introduction to *The Seeds of Time*, Jameson writes, 'It seems to be easier for us today to imagine the thoroughgoing deterioration of the earth and of nature than the breakdown of late-capitalism.' Jameson, *The Seeds of Time*, p. xii.
12. Dean and Fisher, 'We Can't Afford To Be Realists', in Shonkwiler and La Berge (eds), *Reading Capitalist Realism*, p. 26.
13. The other six are: 'technologies and organizational forms; social relations; institutional and administrative arrangements; production and labor processes; relations to nature; the reproduction of daily life and of the species'. Harvey, *The Enigma of Capital*, pp. 123–4.
14. Carver, *Collected Stories*, p. 95.
15. Carver, *Collected Stories*, p. 97.
16. Burn, 'Poetry, Poverty and Realism Down in Carver Country', in Gentry and Stull (eds), *Conversations with Raymond Carver*, p. 119.
17. Carver, *Collected Stories*, p. 99.
18. In their study of working-class life in Boston in the 1960s and 70s, *The Hidden Injuries of Class*, Richard Sennett and Jonathan Cobb describe an analogous experience as 'social failure'; the combined realisation of failed social growth and social contribution, which leads to humiliation and a strong sense of personal inferiority. Sennett and Cobb conclude that as long as workers are valued for what they can do, rather than what they are, class distinctions will persist. This will only be intensified by an increased dependency and focus on the intellectual and technical abilities of workers rather than their worth as individuals.
19. 'The Student's Wife' is not the only story that exemplifies this point. 'Gazebo', 'Night School' and 'What Is It?' are three other well-known stories that hold similar parallels to Carver's experience. As if to reinforce this connection, The Library of America *Collected Stories* edition of Carver's fiction even devotes a section to his selected essays, a rather curious addition which appears to denote the intricate relationship between fiction and non-fiction in Carver's *oeuvre*.

20. Harker, 'Raymond Carver and Class', p. 715.
21. Robinson, 'Marriage and Other Astonishing Bonds', p. 41.
22. Helprin, 'Small Expectations', p. 41.
23. Foley, 'Dirty Realist', p. 12.
24. Weber, 'Raymond Carver: A Chronicler of Blue-Collar Despair', p. 8.
25. For more on Carver's working-poor claims near the end of his life see Kellerman, 'Raymond Carver, Writer and Poet Of the Working Poor, Dies at 50', 3 August 1988. At the time of his death Carver owned three homes, two cars, a boat and had nearly $215,000 in savings. For a list of Carver's assets when he died see Sklenicka, *Raymond Carver*, pp. 482-3.
26. As I have already suggested, Sennett and Cobb begin to deal with this sense of inferiority in *The Hidden Injuries of Class*, and Sennett continues to assess its significance in later publications like *The Corrosion of Character, Respect in a World of Inequality* and particularly in *The Culture of New Capitalism*. Chapter 2 of this final book deals with what Sennett calls 'the specter of uselessness', a state of alienation particularly prevalent amongst Middle Americans in the neoliberal era.
27. Williams, *Culture and Materialism*, p. 40.
28. Harvey refers to a number of movements to illustrate his point, such as the Zapatista revolution in Mexico, the '50 Years Is Enough' campaign, and Greenpeace. Harvey, *A Brief History of Neoliberalism*, pp. 200-1.
29. Carver, *Collected Stories*, p. 665.
30. Sennett, *The Craftsman*, p. 9.
31. Sennett, *The Culture of New Capitalism*, p. 4.
32. T. J. Jackson Lears, *No Place of Grace*, p. 60.
33. Carver, *Collected Stories*, p. 581.
34. Wright Mills, *White Collar: The American Middle Classes*, p. 222.
35. Carver, *Collected Stories*, p. 582.
36. Sennett, *The Craftsman*, p. 9.
37. Carver, *Collected Stories*, p. 731.
38. Carver, *All Of Us*, p. 175.
39. Carver, *All Of Us*, p. 84.
40. Harker, 'Raymond Carver and Class', p. 728.
41. Durante, 'De Minimis: Raymond Carver and His World', p. 125.
42. McGurl, *The Program Era*, pp. 321-2.
43. Bloom, *The Anxiety of Influence*, p. 5.
44. Bloom, *Raymond Carver*, p. 10.
45. Bloom, *The Anxiety of Influence*, p. 15.
46. Bloom, *The Anxiety of Influence*, p. 121.
47. Bloom, *Raymond Carver*, p. 11. Campbell aligns each of Carver's major story collections with a developmental period. Apprenticeship: *Will You Please Be Quiet, Please?*; breakthrough: *What We Talk About When We Talk About Love*; maturity: *Cathedral*; mastery and continued growth: *Where I'm Calling From*.
48. Bloom, *Raymond Carver*, p. 11. For more on the connection between Lawrence's story and 'Cathedral' see Cushman, 'Blind, Intertextual Love', in Cushman and Jackson (eds), *D. H. Lawrence's Literary Inheritors*, pp. 155-66.

49. It is worth saying at this point that because of Gordon Lish's editorial role in Carver's seminal collection *What We Talk About When We Talk About Love* there is a critical minority that argue that Carver's work ought to be seen as a composite production, and that any discussion of Carver's influence is negated because of this fact. But this argument can be countered in the following way: even if some of Carver's work involved an element of collaboration with Lish, that does not discount a discussion based on the pragmatic premise that there is a certain Carveresque aesthetic that exists and has been circulated that proves resonant and influential to other writers and artists. This is especially true since that is how, until more recently, Carver's writing has been understood, and, more importantly, it is how the artists that I analyse later understood it.

    For what I consider to be the most balanced and detailed account of the furore surrounding Lish's involvement see Sklenicka, *Raymond Carver*, pp. 352–75. For a more Carver-oriented account see Stull and Carroll, 'The Critical Reception of the Works of Raymond Carver', in Plath (ed.), *Critical Insights: Raymond Carver*, pp. 39–55. For a comparative analysis between Carver's original manuscripts and published stories see Runyon, 'Beginners' Luck', in Fachard and Miltner (eds), *Not Far From Here*, pp. 25–35; and Monti, 'From "Beginners" to "What We Talk ..."', in Fachard and Miltner (eds), *Not Far From Here*, pp. 37–49. For the original manuscript of *What We Talk About When We Talk About Love* that was delivered by Carver to Lish in 1980 see Carver's *Beginners*. Finally, for a report on the publication of *Beginners* see Rich, 'The Real Carver', 17 October 2007.
50. Adelman, *Carver Country*, pp. 104–7.
51. Sinfield, *Literature, Politics and Culture in Postwar Britain*, p. 31.
52. Williams, *Problems in Materialism and Culture*, p. 44. Writing more recently, Terry Eagleton echoes Williams's idea when he writes that 'we may see literature as a *text*, but we may also see it as a social activity, a form of social and economic production which exists alongside, and interrelates with, other such forms'. Eagleton, *Marxism and Literary Criticism*, p. 6.
53. Sinfield, *Literature, Politics and Culture in Postwar Britain*, p. 41.
54. Aside from those mentioned at the beginning of my introduction, the list included, among others: Richard Ford, Tobias Wolff, Jayne Anne Philips, A. L. Kennedy, Ann Beattie, Thom Jones, Bobbie Ann Mason, John Cheever, Richard Bausch, Elizabeth Tallent, Denis Johnson, David Vann, James Lasdun and David Means.

CHAPTER 1

'Bad Raymond':
Alcoholism, Education and Masculinity in Chuck Kinder's *Honeymooners*

In the autumn of 1973, having just completed the year-long Stegner Fellowship at Stanford University, Raymond Carver took it upon himself to hold two teaching positions at two separate universities at the same time. For readers familiar with the infrequency and transitory nature of early-career university contracts, Carver's decision will hardly seem noteworthy. However, given the location of each post, Carver's choice is more roguish than it initially appears. For one was a full-time position at the prestigious University of Iowa Writers' Workshop (the same institution, incidentally, at which, a decade earlier he had failed to complete a two-year MFA), and the other was nearly 2,000 miles west, at the University of California in Santa Cruz. Carver's plan, which could only seem feasible to an individual increasingly under the burden and influence of alcohol addiction, was to convince a sales rep at United Airlines to give him free flight vouchers on the promise to include their in-flight magazine in one of his stories, and to fly from Iowa City to San Francisco each Thursday night so he could teach his weekly poetry class in Santa Cruz on the Friday. Predictably, Carver only managed to keep the act together for a few weeks before he caved. Waking up in the San Francisco Bay Area after one particularly damaging binge, Carver petitioned his friends, the novelists Chuck Kinder and William Kittredge, to drive the fifty miles south to Santa Cruz and pin a notice to his classroom door: *Can't Teach. Sick.* The trio, known amongst their circle as the Beef Trust, then reconvened at Carver's house in Cupertino for a day of drinking. It wasn't long before many of his Santa Cruz students started to complain that they were yet to meet their enigmatic tutor. Taken aside by Provost James Hall, Carver was asked to tender his resignation and focus on the opportunity at Iowa.[1]

While the salacious details of Carver's early adult life might prove to be themselves a kind of intoxication for the well-meaning academic, what this opening anecdote serves to illustrate more than anything is the chaotic struggle that Carver faced as he tried to make a name for himself in the American literary scene in the 1970s. Not only was he faced with the task of breaking into the literary world in the conventional sense (that is, through the publication of his work by reputable publishers) but he was also trying to do so during a particularly intense period of institutional upheaval; when publishing houses were downsizing, creative writing programmes were increasing, and the pool of young, educated and ambitious writers was fast expanding. On top of this complex mini-economy of literature was Carver's own personal background as a working-class man struggling to make the transition from the world of blue-collar labour to white-collar work. In an attempt to assess the importance of this period, and its associated impact on his literary legacy, this chapter records Carver's early adult life and his peripatetic search for literary education, literary institutionalisation and literary success. Summarised by Carver as his Bad Raymond years, this chapter focuses on the period of Carver's life when his alcohol addiction was most affecting; a time when, in response to the tensions and pressures of a literary scene at home in the Academy, Carver made use of the defensive codes of working-class masculinity to retreat from the threat of educational shame and failure.

For Carver, the 1970s was a time defined by alcoholic absurdity, and yet, despite this, the first year of the decade was a period of relative creative and pedagogic prolificacy. Terminated from his first white-collar job working as public relations director for the education publisher SRA, he used his three-month severance package and subsequent unemployment benefits to supplement Maryann's teaching salary to work full-time on his writing. In constant correspondence with Lish, who had moved from San Francisco to New York to work as the fiction editor for *Esquire*, Carver had clear critical input on his writing in a way that many aspiring, non-institutionalised writers could only dream of. In 1971, after multiple revisions, Lish agreed to publish 'Neighbours'; later that summer, *Harper's Bazaar* published 'Fat'. Not long later, James Hall agreed to hire Carver one day a week as a visiting lecturer to teach poetry at Santa Cruz. Hall had met Carver when Maryann – who operated as a kind of local literary networker – threw a dinner party for the Kittredges at their rented house in Sunnyvale. Hall was just starting College V, an arts programme at Santa Cruz, and was looking for what he deemed as authentic artists to work and live in and around the university campus. He had already approached the poet William Everson and the author Annie Steinhardt and, having spent some time at their low rent, squat residence in Sunnyvale, he perceived in Carver a similar kind of artistic legitimacy. Reflecting on this time, Hall described the house as a 'mattress-on-the-floor kind of place' – the landline had also been disconnected after Carver's unemployment benefits ran out – and sympathetic towards Carver's financial situation, Hall offered Carver $115 a day to teach, subject, of course, to references. Carver, making use of an old SRA phone card, got in touch with Lish, who wrote to Hall from New York to confirm his initial perception. Carver, he wrote, 'values the well-made thing, the ellipsis, and a shape of decisive beginning and end. He is indeed a carver, onomatologic notion intended.'[2]

Still, Carver's Santa Cruz wage was hardly enough to live on, and only six weeks into the term, on the back of his new teaching experience, he began to seek employment elsewhere. Soon, he was offered a teaching post for the following year at the University of Montana in Missoula, where William Kittredge worked. When he heard about Carver's plan to move to Missoula, Hall, keen to keep Carver at Santa Cruz, but unable to offer him any more money, persuaded Lenny Michaels at the University of California, Berkeley to hire Carver to teach two fiction seminars a week. Later that academic year Carver found out that he'd also won the Stegner Fellowship at Stanford. While the legitimacy of holding all three west-coast positions at once was questionable – the Stegner did not allow for other teaching jobs at the same time, for instance – Carver figured he could manage the workload and the accumulative salaries would allow them to stay in California. The Carvers used the $4,000 from the Stegner as a deposit on a mortgage for a house in Cupertino and moved in July 1972. It was hoped that the house, which was in the same school district for their children, and close enough to Maryann's job to allow her to continue teaching, would help lay the foundation for a more settled and self-sufficient period of life for the Carvers.

However, his growing academic, literary and editorial networks were only the preface to an intense period of personal chaos that surrounded Carver from this time until his sobriety in 1977. While in the two years towards the end of his time at SRA and before taking up the Stegner Fellowship, Carver entered a relatively proficient period of writing (in total he had fifteen stories out at different magazines), between 1972 and 1977 Carver appears to have conducted very little composition (possibly only finishing 'Put Yourself In My Shoes' and writing 'So Much Water So Close To Home'). Once Carver's sobriety started, he entered another period of intense composition between 1977 and 1982. For Carver the ironic thing – indeed, the tragic thing – is that the moment in which, to all and intents and purposes, he 'makes it' is the very same moment when his creative powers are at their weakest.

When Carver began teaching at Santa Cruz in 1971, he did so during a period of major change in higher education. Between 1960 and 1980, college admission rose from 3.5 million to 12 million students and with that the rise, also, in the popularity of comprehensive and community college systems. The G. I. Bill provided college funding to hundreds of thousands of military veterans, and the 1965 Higher Education Act made federal funding available for students with financial needs. The net result is that while in the 1940s only 10 per cent of college-age Americans were in higher education, by the 1980s more than half of them were attending university.[3] Working alongside the increase in student admissions was the development of non-traditional subjects including, of course, arts subjects like the creative writing programme. By 1975 fifty institutions offered degrees in creative writing; by 1984 there were approximately 150 postgraduate degree programmes; by the turn of the millennium that figure had risen to more than 350. While institutional and departmental set-ups vary, the concept of the creative writing programme is widely known, so I can be brief in its explanation. The programme is centred around the writing workshop, a discussion seminar led by a published writer, in which students critique one another's work. The opportunity to write under the tutelage of a published writer is a strong draw for aspiring authors – this was exactly the kind of appeal that James Hall employed when he hired Carver at Santa Cruz – as is the artistic community that is created by the university programme. The model, then, is broadly one in which the master teaches the apprentice, who at the end of the one, two or three year course receives a formal document that states that they have passed a series of prescribed objectives which prove that, while not yet at the level of the master – it is nominally told to students – are now writing publishable material and so, with the right kinds of connections and the right kinds of publications, are only a few lucky breaks away from being employed to teach programmes themselves. The long-term economic viability of this model is uncertain – although it is worth noting the current financial indispensability of creative programmes to English departments the world over – for it only takes a handful of authors to disregard the departmental model to sow the seeds of distrust in what is, in recent times at least, an expensive pedagogical model. None of which is to underplay the fact that for Carver, and for other young people during this time, the university was becoming the central cultural institution of American society.[4] This was particularly true for a working-class individual wanting to make a career from writing. During Carver's time, for instance, the university was a place to study, to gain knowledge and get a degree, yes, but it was also a place to grow into adulthood, to extend family tradition, to widen social circles and, for many, to find a spouse. More than anything, and summarising all of these traits, is the fact that university attendance became hegemonic for young people in the 1960s and 70s. Which is to say, also, that attendance was preceded by an expectation that the investment of time and money was worthwhile because it would lead to greater economic and social mobility. For the working class in particular, the decline of manufacturing and industry during this period – and other sites which allowed the skills of adulthood to be learnt – meant that university attendance was an increasingly valuable commodity.

These ideas feed neatly into Carver's own mindset during this period. Reflecting on their early life, Maryann told one interviewer,

'Nobody in Ray's family had ever gone to college, so there was no tradition for it.' She continues by saying that Carver realised, however, that 'it was important that he get started in school as soon as possible'.[5] As Robert Rebein has similarly pointed out, Carver was, 'perhaps the first major American writer whose entire career was informed and shaped by the world of the university', a comment that reflects Richard Ford's earlier assessment that both he and Carver – in a move typical of his generation – were products of a very particular higher education environment that 'included college, writing workshops, sending stories to quarterlies, attending graduate school, having teachers who were writers', and, ultimately, seeking 'improvement in the standard postwar American way: through some sort of pedagogy'.[6] Carver's desire for a literary education was fuelled as a teenager when his local evening paper featured a photograph of Hemingway holding a copy of another newspaper that announced his death after a plane crash in Africa. The story's narrative – that Hemingway 'lives as dangerously as his hairy chested heroes' – stoked Carver's masculine sensibilities. Reflecting on this moment in an article for *The New York Times Book Review*, he wrote that reading about Hemingway's 'exploits and accomplishments, and his recent brush with death, was heady and glamorous stuff', particularly as the places that Hemingway frequented and wrote about – from Africa to Paris and Pamplona to Key West – were 'as far away as the moon to me'.[7] Searching for some kind of purchase on this lifestyle, Carver undertook a correspondence course called the Palmer Institute of Authorship. The sixteen-instalment programme taught the basic technical elements of story writing and focused on teaching its students marketable styles for magazine submission. After finishing the course, Carver graduated high school and began working with his father at a local sawmill. Another year on he married Maryann, who began to convince Carver of the value of higher education over traditional blue-collar labour. If Carver had the desire to learn to write, then Maryann had the educational background and knowledge of how to put that desire to use. She had been privately educated on a scholarship and had been offered a place to study law at Washington State. In one interview she reveals her attitude at the time:

I knew I wouldn't be happy unless we got a very good higher education. Nobody in Ray's family had ever gone to college, so there was no tradition for it. He hoped he could just read a lot, which he always did, and that would prepare him adequately to be a writer . . . He wasn't a natural student the way I was. However, the biggest plan in our lives was for Ray to become a first-rate, world-class writer.[8]

Maryann's comparison between their two dispositions provides a subtle critique of their individual backgrounds. She knew, for example, she 'wouldn't be happy' unless they got 'a very good higher education'; given Carver's working-class family history, it is implied, Carver wouldn't have understood that a college education could be the catalyst to help fulfil his desire to be a writer (neither was he 'a natural student', whereas she was 'idealistic and studious'). Whatever Maryann's motivations, her desire appeared to convince Carver of his need to attend university. When Maryann's mother moved to northern California in 1958, the Carvers moved with her. Maryann then convinced Carver to enrol in Chico State the following year. There Carver registered for the creative writing programme with John Gardner, whose own idealist artistic pronouncements fired Carver's literary ambition. Still, the Carvers struggled to make ends meet, and so, in a move symptomatic of their peripatetic search for education and career, in his final year, Carver transferred to Humboldt State where there was work in the lumber industry. In 1963, the year Carver received his undergraduate degree, on the back of recommendations from Humboldt and his own writing samples, he was awarded a $500 scholarship to study at the Iowa Writer's Workshop.

Despite the esteemed reputation of the programme, Carver's time at Iowa failed to have the effect that the 25-year-old hoped it would. Workshops varied dramatically depending on their tutor and, while Carver wanted to be taught by Vance Boujaily, he ended up in R. V. Cassill's class, which had a more academic bent. While Gardner's grand idealistic pronouncements at Chico had animated Carver's ambition, Cassill's classes had the opposite effect. The atmosphere at Iowa, likewise, was distinct; while some students were military veterans, others had come to Iowa on the back of careers; still others – perhaps more problematically for

Carver – possessed Ivy League educations. In all, the tone, manner and environment was distinctly different to what he was used to. Recollecting that time one of Carver's peers recalls that Carver was 'upset because there wasn't enough emphasis on turning writing into cash'.[9] While it is hard to exactly pinpoint Carver's disgruntlement and despondency, it is no stretch to suggest that the tension between his background and education and the more academically rigorous programme at Iowa led towards an affective feeling of educational shame. By October, Carver had decided that he would only stay for the minimum first year requirement to complete his master's (rather than the two years it would take to complete the MFA) – although by the end of the academic year he didn't even have enough credits to graduate.

The Carvers' move back to California in 1964 marked a break in Carver's education. In an attempt to fund his writing career, he took a number of part-time jobs, including a night janitor position at a local hospital before working for SRA, and then being hired by Santa Cruz, accepting the Stegner and teaching at Berkeley.[10] Then, in a move that could hardly have been predicted, almost a decade after leaving Iowa, he returned as a visiting lecturer to teach alongside John Cheever.[11] If Carver's first stint at Iowa was marked by the fear of educational shame brought on by a diminishing and yet still noticeable class-consciousness, then his second stint was symptomatic of his increasing literary pedigree and growing alcoholism. To be sure, Carver would have likely drunk whether or not he encountered Cheever at Iowa; but his proximity to one of the country's other notorious literary alcoholics only fuelled his addiction. Cheever, sixty-one that semester, was coming to Iowa on the back of hospitalisation after the publication of his story collection *The World Of Apples*. (Unused to sobriety, he had had hallucinatory episodes in hospital. When shown a positive review of his writing, he had thought it was a Soviet conspiracy designed to get a confession.) Now drinking again at Iowa, the pair, who were both teaching workshops alongside John Irving, William Price Fox and John Leggett, lived a floor apart in the same building. It is tempting to view the relationship between Carver – who was yet to publish a collection of fiction – and Cheever as apprentice and master, but the reality was probably less glamorous. Both men were thousands of miles from their respective families (Maryann had stayed back in California) and both were on the verge of – if not entirely subsumed by – alcohol addiction. In the interview that Carver conducted with *The Paris Review*, Carver admits that neither of them 'ever took the covers off our typewriters', which is to say, in short, that their acquaintance was not one of literary dependency.[12] The pair drank at a bar called The Mill or in Cheever's room and Carver was tasked with driving Cheever, who didn't have a car, to the state-run liquor store twice a week. In the end, Carver admits that his time spent with Cheever was not so much about learning about literature, but learning about alcohol.[13] In 1974, after finishing his year teaching at Iowa, Carver moved back to California and was appointed as visiting lecturer at University of California, Santa Barbara for a year, after which he became unemployed until 1977 when he became sober. His next appointment didn't come until January 1978 when he taught a two-week MFA course at Goddard College, Vermont, before later that year being appointed as a writer-in-residence at the University of Texas, El Paso, an appointment that turned out to be a decisive move away from his west-coast life. The following autumn he took a position at Syracuse University, which he held until 1983 when he won the Harold Strauss Living Award, an award that allowed him to write full-time without a university salary. He died from lung cancer only five years later in August 1988.

While the description of Carver's life from this point of view is useful in that it details his peripatetic existence in the 1970s, it also illustrates the difficulties that Carver faced in trying to find a long-term position in higher education: if not for his personal battles with alcoholism, or his disruptive home life, then for the fact that, as I have already indicated, he was learning to negotiate a world in which he had little bearing. In an essay written in honour of John Gardner, Carver reveals his motivation during that time:

> I felt in my bones that I had to get some education in order to go along with being a writer. I put a very high premium on education then – much higher in those days than now, I'm sure, but that's because I'm older and have an education. Understand that nobody in my family had ever gone to college or for that matter had got beyond the mandatory eighth grade in high school. I didn't *know anything*, but I knew I didn't know anything.[14]

Carver's confession to educational ignorance is, notice, firmly placed in his working-class past. Higher education was all the more valuable to him because, in his experience, it was a rare entity. While not explicit in Carver's statement, one infers that this realisation is underlined by a desire to not only escape his working-class family heritage, a place where education stopped at the 'mandatory eighth grade' and resulted in not 'know[ing] anything', but Carver also, note, tries to make a natural distinction that reinforces his desire for self-improvement; unlike other members of his family, it is inferred, he felt the need for education 'in my bones' and even had the conceptual self-awareness to realise his ignorance. Associated with these pronouncements, then, is the notion of shame, which occurs in the realisation of his lack of education and, with this, the more pertinent recognition that if he is to become a writer – a job that, by its very nature, exposes one to public judgements – it is in his interest to make sure his work is reinforced by the right kind of authoritative knowledge in order to avoid shame. Bundled with these desires is the equally strong inclination, of both Carver and Maryann, that Carver's projected writing career would help them achieve social mobility. The combination of all these aspects created a particularly potent negative affect when faced with failure. For, as Helen Merrell Lynd argues, shame is a simultaneous external and internal phenomenon. It is brought on by negative judgements in the public sphere – say, when a writer claims to be an expert in a particular field but is found to be a fraud (this was Carver's initial fear) – but it is also brought on by the prospect of exposure. It is this second internal aspect of shame that is particularly applicable to Carver because as Rita Felski argues, 'The opportunities for experiencing shame increase dramatically with geographic and other forms of social mobility, which provide an infinite array of chances for failure, for betraying by word or gesture that one does not belong to one's environment.'[15] So, when Carver travels cross-country in 1963 to study at the University of Iowa Writers' Workshop, in turn, leaving behind his native Northwest working-class heritage, he faces these kinds of geographic and socially dislocating and potentially shame-inducing affects. Which is to say, in short, that Carver faced more obstacles than most when he embarked on his quest for education in the early 1960s. For those who have studied, taught or spent any amount of time in higher education will attest that if you want to avoid a place of shame, then the university – a place full of unknown and potentially shame-inducing situations – is hardly the place to reside.

Carver's five-page, first-person narrative 'Night School' reflects something of this tension. Centred around an unemployed single man who finds himself at a bar one night, the protagonist's lack of employment becomes a critical crisis point when he meets two women at the bar who ask him what he does. The man responds, 'Right now, nothing', before adding, 'Sometimes, when I can, I go to school.' One of the women responds – presumably thinking that this man's education must be leading somewhere – by saying, 'What's your big goal in life? Everybody has a big goal in life.' Not this story's protagonist, it seems, who mumbles a consolatory and ambiguous, 'Teach. Teach school', before returning to his beer.[16] As if to emphasise the ubiquity of education during this period, as well as its role in training and retraining those who are unemployed, it turns out the women are also students at a night school. As the conversation progresses it becomes clear that the women are interested in using the man to get a lift to their tutor's house. Without a car – the protagonist is living on a cot in his parents' hallway – he suggests they walk to his parents' house and borrow theirs. But when he gets to the house, his father tells him to let the women wait outside, warning him 'you don't want to get mixed up in that'.[17]

'Everyone is getting some education', Mark McGurl writes in his analysis of Carver's text, 'if not as much as they could use.' In a moment of particularly decisive literary dissection, he goes on, 'an air of evasion and vagueness attaches to the narrator's identity as a sometime student and would-be teacher ... and his distance from the classroom, as he sits in this bar, is very much to the point'. While some critics would condemn this apparently dead-end story for its lack of narrative ambition, what this type of story illustrates more than anything is a distinct lack of self-assertion on behalf of the main character, or, to put it another way – and to borrow from McGurl once more – a resistance to look forward with 'affirmative language in which "big goals" are made visible and exposed to public judgments of failure or success'.[18] In other words, 'Night

School' illustrates that the usual disposition of Carver's characters – and, it might be added, one deduces from McGurl's discussion, of Carver himself – is not the failure to imagine, or even the failure to render dramatic narrative devices, but rather a 'wariness and waiting and protective self-concealment' based on the fact that given the characters' desire to avoid moments of educational shame any future imagining of 'big goals' risk the failure of achievement or, even in the rare instance that they are achieved, are concomitant with the nauseating feeling that at any moment they might be lost. This notion of shame stemming from failed achievement is illustrated by the protagonist's father who warns his son to stay away from the women at the bar and who, earlier in the narrative, is described as having 'tears in his eyes' when he has to refuse his son a $200 loan after his wife leaves him. In a link that suggests a connection between life and art, this idea is reflected in Carver's form, which is – for most of his early-life – static, stationary and staccato; that in moving with prosaic caution, Carver – as author – is able to retain control and avoid shameful situations himself. For McGurl, at least, this is, as much as anything, the ultimate truth that lies at the heart of Carver's fiction: 'the situation might be bad, but if it is going slowly then it is under control and unlikely to produce nasty, shame-inducing surprises'.[19] It is, then, through careful and skilful composition, through the process of craftsmanship, with its residual notion of unalienated labour, that, for Carver, the negative affects of shame are thwarted and restrained.

The relationship between shame and education is developed in another story written around the same time. 'Put Yourself In My Shoes', first published in an eponymous chapbook by Capra Press in 1974, tells the story of Myers (the only serial character in Carver's fiction) who, in a move reminiscent of Carver's own decision to leave SRA in 1970, has recently left his job as a textbook editor in order to pursue a writing career. The move draws admiration from his colleagues. When his wife, Paula, who still works at the firm phones one day to invite him to a work party, she says, 'Carl admires you, you know. He does. He's told me so. He admires your nerve. He said if he had your nerve he would have quit years ago. Carl said it takes nerve to do what you did.'[20] In a story that is full of multiple tensions, perhaps the most intriguing is this: that all the characters that Myers comes into contact with put his creative ambitions on a pedestal, but for Myers the banality of the writer's life and, in particular, the struggle (indeed the failure) to produce something successful (which is broadly defined in the story as writing that is economically productive) mutates into a shameful depression.[21] At the very opening of the story, Carver reveals that Myers is 'between stories, and he felt despicable'.[22] On top of this tension is the added layer – and here is the potent connection to 'Night School' – in which not only is Myers in a struggle against the hegemonic expectations of economic success, but the creative act is also in opposition with the values of orthodox education. If Myers feels a sense of shame because of his inability to produce something of economic value, then his shame is compounded by the fact that all the other characters in the story are, in one form or another, involved in work of broad educational value: whether Carl and Paula who are both textbook editors, or Edgar Morgan, the travelling university professor, or perhaps more ominously, Larry Gudinas, who 'helped out on science books for a while' before being fired and, in what amounts to a kind of prophetic vision of Myers's own creative impotence (and in a moment reminiscent of Hemingway's death) committed suicide by shooting himself in the mouth. Unlike 'Night School', however, there is a note of positivity in the conclusion to this story. The Myers' visit to the Morgans, a couple for whom they house-sat once, leads to an argument that provides the raw material for a new story for Myers. This new story, and even the potential of writing the story, wards off the negative affect associated with educational failure. Driving away from the Morgans' house in the snow, Myers drifts into his own mind, 'He was at the very end of the story', Carver concludes.[23]

While the experience between those in Carver's fiction who are struggling to get an education, or struggling to ward off the shameful factors of educational failure, and Carver's own experience as a working-class man trying to write productively in a higher education context aren't precisely analogous, there are, nonetheless, some interesting parallels between the two. It was while he was studying at Stanford that Carver employed his working-class sensibilities in a defensive retreat away from the perils of educational shame. And so, ironically enough, Carver's retreat into the world of working-class masculinity was strongest the year he undertook the Stegner Fellowship at Stanford in 1972. This was the year in which his relationship with higher education changed, not so much because it gave him access to one of the country's most prestigious academic institutions (and all its attendant privileges), but because while he was there he met Chuck Kinder, another writer with similar working-class sensibilities and background. The pair became acquainted after a writing workshop in 1972. Kinder had recently published his first novel *Snakehunter* and was beginning the second year of an Edith Mirrelees Fellowship. In a fast-changing cultural landscape, both men found solidarity in their working-class backgrounds. Stanford, located in what was, in the early 1970s, fast becoming the hub of Silicon Valley, was drawing huge numbers of scientific research students. Concomitant with this student migration was the kind of technological innovation that is now synonymous with California, and alongside this vast amount of creative energy was a 1960s inspired countercultural movement. Kinder, having moved to California from West Virginia, where he had grown up and worked (in a not dissimilar vain to Carver's own lumber industry experience) as a coal miner, held a certain amount of resentment towards the movement. In one interview he recalls, 'It was hip to be close to the earth and all that. Everyone was walking around wearing work books and work clothes, and since I came from West Virginia and I'd worked in a coal mine, I could affect that look with a little more authority.'[24]

This background is worth bearing in mind because it provides a useful context to Kinder's attitude to his writing peers at Stanford in the early 1970s. Carver, who Kinder recalls hardly cared for fashion – he was a 'big shambling fellow, always wore shades. I thought he dressed goofy' – stood out from the rest of the cohort. Not that this endeared him to Kinder. After one class, Kinder asked around for a lift home. Mortified when it was only Carver who offered, he felt he had no choice and went along with him and followed Carver to his old, battered convertible. (Kinder recalls the car as being 'full of crap – manuscripts, paper cups, cigarette butts everywhere'.)[25] After Carver eventually started the car and drove out of the car park a bottle of whisky rolled out from under the seat. Carver picked it up and offered a drink to Kinder. By the end of the three-mile drive the pair had nearly finished the bottle. 'I thought the guy was a nut', Kinder tells Halpert, 'I didn't want him to know where I lived on Matadora Road, so I told him to let me off at the corner at the Taco Bell.'[26] Kinder was happy to be out of the car. He figured that was the last time he'd spend any meaningful time with Carver; it wasn't, he claimed, that he didn't like him, but that he couldn't figure him out; he seemed to be an anomaly. The next day, however, Kinder heard a knock on his door. It was Carver, who had found his house – which was, parenthetically, set back from the main road, behind a stream and amongst the redwoods – and was standing at the door with two paper bags; one filled with literary magazines which featured his work and the other with booze. The pair, Kinder recalls, bonded by spending the rest of the day drinking and reading together.

The episode is important because it denotes both men's working-class defensiveness towards the world of white-collar higher education. It also speaks to the importance of that very same working-class masculinity in their relationship. Stephen Meyer, in his account of working-class masculinity in the Detroit automobile industry in the twentieth century, describes the early-life leisure time of Frank Marquart, an autoworker who later became a well-known labour radical and activist. At the end of each day shift, Marquart and his colleagues would go home to eat before later meeting in Detroit bars to discuss the day's work. Their conversation quickly turned to individual boasting, as each worker tried to 'impress the others with how important his particular job was, how much skill it required'. Meyer concludes that for Marquart and his colleagues 'manhood meant work, especially skilled work, daily drinking, and the weekend foray to what they nicknamed "Joy Street"'.[27] The parallels between the kind of behaviour undertaken by the working-class male worker in more conventional industrial enterprise and that undertaken by Carver and Kinder is remarkably uncanny. Both worlds are centred around talking shop and male bravado based on physical dominance and craftsmanship, and both worlds, notably, are not only sites of resistance to the increasing incursion of femininity on conventional masculine behaviour, but they are also sites of consolatory retreat in which they could form, nurture and deepen masculine culture.

A year later Carver and Kinder were joined at Stanford by William Kittredge, who also won the Stegner Fellowship, partly, Kittredge believes, because Carver had petitioned the selection committee. Previously acquainted at a regional MLA conference, when the semester commenced at Stanford in 1973, the trio self-titled themselves the Beef Trust.[28] The trio found solidarity in their older age (at this point all were in their thirties, many of the other students at Stanford were a decade younger) and working-class backgrounds. Scott Trurow, who was a student on the Stanford writing programme at the time, described them as 'an imposing looking group'. He continued, 'They didn't look a bit like writers – more like truck drivers.'[29] Given Trurow's vivid description it is not hard to imagine the intimidation that a group of Silicon Valley twenty-somethings might feel when three men, a decade older, and heavyset from years of blue-collar labour (sawmilling, coal mining and the like), who had bonded over drinking and writing sat down with them around the workshop table. Whether or not there was any real menace in their physical appearance is hard to say, but the group did come with a particular reputation. The trio even had truck driver call signs: Carver was Running Dog, because of his promiscuity; Kinder was Trout, named after Brautigan's *Trout Fishing in America*; and Kittredge was Buffalo, because of his large physical appearance. Writing about the group, Sklenicka observes that 'with a few exceptions, the men who populated this bad-old-days scene were provincials – small-town westerners or Southerners and country boys who brought their working-class backgrounds and literary aspirations to Silicon Valley'.[30] And it was the combination of writing and drinking – of craft and booze – and, as much as anything, the freedom that studying at Stanford allowed the trio to invest in both that formed the important context for these men to revel in their working-class masculine identities. The male-dominated world of the university workshop was a world away from the arena of women and the responsibility of children and other cultural restraints. Together, they could amuse themselves in the rough and tumble of a masculine world of fighting, rivalry and competition. In those days, the Beef Trust, as Sklenicka usefully records, 'were gaining perspective on the places they'd come from and, in most cases, readying for a move to somewhere else. If they had fellowships at Stanford and working wives . . . they could devote their days to reading and writing, liquor, and hangovers.'[31]

During their time together in the early 1970s, rumours abounded as to the behaviour of the Beef Trust. Whether it was evading bar tabs and restaurant bills – as the Carvers and Kinders did for the Carvers' sixteenth wedding anniversary – or sending the same story to multiple publications at the same time – Carver's 'So Much Water So Close To Home' was published twice in smaller magazines before *Playgirl* bought it, or even the more serious and morally troubling abusive and violent nature of their marriages, the trio fulfilled the stereotypes of rough working-class masculinity. Carver, particularly, was notorious for pushing the boundaries of institutional rules. His plan to hold the Stegner Fellowship while teaching at Santa Cruz and Berkeley was a good example of this, as was his decision to take the full-time job at Iowa while flying cross-country to teach at Santa Cruz once a week, and, even later, his decision to keep collecting unemployment benefits while he worked at Santa Barbara; a decision that ended in a State prosecution. When Carver was too hung-over to teach his class at Berkeley he would tell his students that his mother had died. When one of the students complained that Carver had used that excuse more than once, Carver reportedly said, 'Well, my mother died some time ago, but I still miss her.' At Berkeley, in particular, Carver's working-class background and behaviour seems to have been especially grating. Recalling Carver and Maryann's appearance, one student said they were 'not exactly what the UC faculty had in mind. I heard she showed up at a faculty get-together in white go-go boots, which *they* considered rather lowbrow.' When it was time for Carver to turn in his marked examinations, he travelled up to Berkeley with the Beef Trust, stopping off at liquor stores on the way. By the time they reached the university post office, Carver was so drunk that he was unable to work out how to put the envelope into the post slot.[32]

Along with the excessive drinking and associated buffoonery, Carver's marriage was beginning to unravel. Both Carver and Maryann were involved, to some extent, with other people. Kinder recalls, for instance, when Carver introduced him to a student in his Berkeley class who Carver thought had a crush on him. The trio drove up to visit another friend at the University of California,

Davis and stopped off at bars on the way. 'Nothing really happened with the girl', Kinder recalls rather vaguely, before qualifying, 'Well, not much.'[33] It was around this time that Carver initiated an affair with Diane Cecily, a woman from Missoula that he met while visiting Kittredge. The relationship came to an abrupt end when Maryann found a stack of Carver's love letters and, worried that she would destroy them, he passed them on to Kinder to take back to Diane. Kinder met Diane and, after a few weeks lodging with Kittredge, moved into an empty basement below Diane's house. It wasn't long before they were together. When Carver found out, he phoned Kittredge from California and told him to tell Kinder that he was the real Running Dog now.

As I have already indicated the Beef Trust's behaviour reflects what many scholars of masculinity argue is typical of the experience of young working-class men in the twentieth century. The critic Peter Stearns cites an anonymous young worker who stated that 'When I was eighteen I knew it took four things to be a man: fight, work, screw, and booze.'[34] Stephen Meyer similarly describes this approach to life as being symptomatic of rough working-class masculinity, a masculinity defined in association with, or in opposition to, respectable masculine culture. In the standard understanding of these two concepts, rough culture is nominally associated with younger men and the aforementioned fighting, screwing and boozing, whereas a more respectable form of working-class masculinity is nominally associated with older men, and combines familial responsibility, marriage and social respectability. While, for Carver, his time spent as a rough working-class man was a moment when he was largely creatively unproductive, it is interesting to note that through the process of moving from rough to respectable masculinity later in his life (or, at least, the perception that he had reformed his life), Carver's early roughness – despite its negative social connotations – cemented his respectable working-class image with the valuable stamp of authenticity. In other words, while the rough masculinity of Carver's life in the 1970s was a useful defensive mechanism against the tension produced by the expectations of middle-class hegemonic values in twentieth-century America, Carver's ability to graduate towards a life more associated with respectable working-class values garnered a particular kind of authentic reputation that, had he not lived the early rough masculine life, he would have not been able to attain.

Perhaps one of the most overt examples of the tension between rough and respectable masculinity in Carver's fiction occurs in the story 'Bicycles, Muscles, Cigarettes'. Evan Hamilton is trying to stop smoking. It has been two days since he smoked a cigarette and he feels like he can smell it everywhere. Despite the frantic nature of Evan's cravings – 'He looked at his hands under the kitchen light. He sniffed his knuckles and fingers' – his actions in the story, in typical Carver fashion, are for the most part measured, slow and intentional.[35] When Evan goes looking for his son at teatime, he finds another boy from the neighbourhood on his drive who informs him that his son is at the boy's house being questioned by his mother about a missing bike. Following the boy to the house, Evan comes to a part of his neighbourhood that he is not familiar with. 'He hadn't known the existence of this street and was sure he would not recognize any of the people who lived here. He looked around him at the unfamiliar houses and was struck with the range of his son's personal life.'[36] As he moves into unfamiliar geographic territory, for a character like Hamilton, on the edge of breaking an addiction, this new, unknown situation not only has the potential to unravel his will power, but also presents the opportunity for shame. Hamilton enters the house to find his son, Roger, sat round a table with one of his friends, Kip and another boy, Gary Berman. Evan knows Kip – although neither of his parents turn up to help – but doesn't know the Bermans. After discussing the missing bike around the table, Gary Berman's father shows up. Described as a 'stiff-shouldered man with a crew haircut and sharp gray eyes', Berman comes across as a kind of military man; an outsider to Evan's community.[37] When Berman and his son leave the room to discuss the matter privately, Berman comes back in and accuses Roger of breaking the bike. When Roger counters by accusing Gary, Berman shouts at the boy, 'You shut up! . . . You can speak when spoken to, young man, not before, Gary, I'll handle this – dragged out at night because of a couple of roughnecks!'[38] The slur – which indicates that Evan's background is rural white working class – is not enough to get a raise out of Hamilton who is frustrated but tries his best to fulfil his responsibility and suggests they leave and split the bill for the missing bike between the boys. Berman meets this suggestion by calling Hamilton a jerk, to which Hamilton, in a warning against rough masculinity and still able to maintain self-control, tells Berman to 'get control of yourself', before Berman engages Hamilton in physical confrontation:

> Berman brushed Hamilton's shoulder and Hamilton stepped off the porch into some prickly cracking bushes. He couldn't believe it was happening. He moved out of the bushes and lunged at the man where he stood on the porch. They fell heavily onto the lawn. They rolled on the lawn, Hamilton wrestling Berman onto his back and coming down hard with his knees on the man's biceps. He had Berman by the collar now and began to pound his head against the lawn.[39]

Unable to control himself anymore, and buoyed on by Berman, Hamilton enters into the world of the rough working-class man; it is a moment the story has been building to, but a moment that Hamilton has equally been trying to avoid. Despite his intentional and measured actions, when the moment comes, Hamilton becomes distant and detached from his own will ('He couldn't believe it was happening.'). As the fight continues, the pattern of rough masculinity is copied by the surrounding children, 'The older boys had crowded onto the porch to watch; now that it was over, they waited, watching the men, and then they began feinting and punching each other on the arms and ribs.'[40] Sweating and finding it hard to breathe (Carver writes that after the fight 'There was a ball of something in his throat so that he couldn't swallow for a minute', yes, a ball of phlegm, probably the result of smoking, but also, surely, it is his rough working-class masculine pride that Hamilton is struggling to swallow), Hamilton turns to leave with Roger who, when they get home, in a moment of admiration, wants to feel his father's muscles.[41] Sitting on his porch recovering from the encounter, Hamilton recalls a memory of his own father, when he was his son's age, getting into a fight with another man at a café. The moment comes to define (in what is surely an ominous prediction for his own relationship with his son) his memory of his father, 'But now he recalled his father's one fistfight as if it were all there was to the man.'[42]

The story, however, is particularly interesting because Hamilton moves beyond his rough encounter back into the world of respectable masculinity when he later puts his son to bed and, in a scene that leans towards the sentimental, has a moment of familial love with his son. At the very end of the story, Hamilton lets his son sniff his fingers, expecting him to smell the stale stench of cigarettes, but the boy can't smell anything. 'Now I can't smell anything, either', Hamilton says. 'It was there before, but now it's gone.'[43] This, of course, is indicative of the personal development that Hamilton has made in life – and particularly in the story – from rough to respectability; the stench of cigarette addiction being a past world of uncontrollable rough masculinity and the bedtime ending being indicative of a new life of respectability and familial responsibility. As he shuts his son's bedroom door, Roger calls out to his father and says, 'It's like – it's like I miss you already if I think about it now. That's pretty crazy, isn't it?'[44] The ending of the story, with its emphasis on respectability, responsibility, family and, more than anything, the sense that Hamilton has begun to move on from his cigarette addiction, clearly juxtaposes (and, in turn, perhaps even suggests the possibility of escape from) the rough masculinity of the earlier fight.

In 2001 Farrar, Straus & Giroux published Kinder's third novel *Honeymooners*. Thirty-five years in production, the novel, which featured a cover reminiscent of Carver's own iconic covers for the Vintage Contemporaries series, was billed by its publishers as Kinder's magnum opus; a piece of fiction so accomplished that it was worthy of fulfilling Carver's legacy. Of course, despite its advertisers' best intentions, literary merit is somewhat more objective, and the novel was released to mixed reviews.[45] The history of the book's production is as complicated as its three-decade construction might suggest. Kinder thought of the idea of basing a novel on the details of his friendship with Carver in 1982, not long after Carver's rise to national notoriety with the publication of *What We Talk About When We Talk About Love*. Kinder even showed Carver what he calls the 'kernel' of the narrative – the notorious sixteenth wedding anniversary dinner – to which Carver reportedly shook his head and called Kinder a thief and outlaw.[46] After Carver's death the manuscript's length began to spiral. At one point it was reported that the manuscript ran to 3,000 pages; an unpublishable tome befitting the kind of mythic reputation of the novel's protagonist.

True to concept, the novel's narrative focuses on Ralph Crawford and Jim Stark and their spouses, Alice Ann and Lindsay. Set in the San Francisco Bay Area around Stanford (where Jim is teaching on the creative writing programme) the narrative forms a fictional biography of Carver's life in the 1970s, including recollections of studying with John Cheever at Iowa, dinner dashes, court appearances and a foray to Montana where Lindsay, Ralph's one-time girlfriend, lives – a women, incidentally, who marries Jim later in the novel after he delivers a bundle of Ralph's love letters to her. Set on the premise that Ralph and Alice Ann are constantly trying to start a second honeymoon in a last-gasp attempt to save their failing marriage, the narrative takes its cue from the 1950s sitcom of the same name, in which two working-class men (played by Jackie Gleeson and Art Carney) act out comedy set-pieces as their wives (played by Audrey Meadows and Joyce Randolph) tiptoe the fragile line between guiding their husbands without damaging their egos. Ultimately, the layered combination of fiction and biography not only leads the novel to skirt metafictional territory but also the genre of memoir; confusion is compounded by Kinder as author, himself the basis for Michael Chabon's protagonist in his 1995 novel, *Wonder Boys*.

The biographical nature of the novel might lead some to meticulously track the real-life experience of Carver alongside Kinder's narrative. For many Carver admirers and enthusiasts this would be a worthwhile task, but for the purposes of this book the novel serves to illustrate something much richer and, I hope, more interesting; for the novel, which recasts Carver's life through the lens of American working-class masculinity, serves to solidify a powerful authenticity that holds value and purchase for other writers and artists featured later in this study. If, as Peter Stearns suggest, there are four tropes to rough working-class masculinity – fighting, boozing, screwing and working – the male characters in *Honeymooners* fulfil these leitmotifs appropriately, and while there are moments of physical violence in the novel, much of the fighting takes the form of marital bickering and masculine one-upmanship. Ralph and Jim, in particular, enter into a sibling rivalry over their ability to drink, screw and work. Their competition opens near the beginning of the novel when the narrator declares that what binds their friendship together is their joint ambition, 'the stupendous dream Ralph and Jim shared was for fame'; an ambition, incidentally, linked to their male fantasies, for neither of them are 'above taking shortcuts to the rewards of fame, such as enjoying sexual congress with comely strangers'.[47] If only writing was a famous cultural enterprise in California in the 1970s, then both men might stand a chance. For Ralph, who at one point tries to impress a barmaid by telling her that 'he was none other than Philip Roth, the professor of passion, the doctor of desire', soon discovers that the barmaid has 'never heard of Philip Roth', and, in a similar moment of identity theft, Jim tries to tell 'a beer-joint beauty at a crucial moment that he was Norman Mailer, that lionized lover and mayor of American letters', and is told – above the cacophony of bar music and chatter, no doubt – 'Norman who?'[48] As if this doesn't suggest the underlying illusion of their ambition, later in the novel, as Ralph recalls the year he spent at Iowa as Cheever's student to Jim and his first wife, Judy – a tale aimed to cement his literary ambitions in the tradition of the American short story canon, thus granting his talent and projected future the relevant amount of posterity – a 'very pretty, perfectly nice, sensible young woman', asks, 'Who is this John Cheever guy, anyhow?', to which Alice Ann replies, 'He's a pretty famous writer.' Not famous enough, it seems.[49]

Despite Ralph's claimed literary lineage, given both his and Jim's propensity to the other three qualities of rough working-class masculinity, the pair do not conduct much constructive creative work in the novel. While Jim holds a three-year lectureship at Stanford while finishing a novel and Ralph teaches at Berkeley, the actual act of writing is conspicuous by its absence. And yet, if the novel – which is ostensibly about writers – is notable for its lack of writing then it is just as notable for its characters' penchant for talking about writing. The blurb that Lenny Michaels (another real-life figure that features in the narrative) writes for Ralph's first collection of stories says, for instance, 'Ralph Crawford's stories are extraordinary in their language, their music, and their huge terrifying vision of ordinary human life.'[50] Alice Ann reiterates the pseudo-biographic nature of Ralph's stories when she says, 'I remember every single draft of every single story in this book ... I know these stories by heart. And I know the stories behind the stories by heart, too.'[51] Earlier, though, her tone is more critical, when during an argument she condemns Ralph's writing, 'The thing about you', she says in the motel suite they book the night before they are due to declare bankruptcy, 'is you don't want to probe new possibilities. You don't have the imagination for it. And your stories suffer.'[52] Then, in a critique reminiscent of those who view Carver's fiction as being, in the words of John Aldridge, 'wholly without talents, ambitions, or prospects', says, 'You won't let your imagination seek the deeper mysteries of this world of veils. That's why your stories are about colourless people going about the business of their mundane, colourless lives.'[53]

This kind of critical angle is important because, as Meyer distils from his analysis of automobile workers in Detroit, a large part of rough masculinity is the ability to boast about the craftsmanship of work. And while Ralph appears to have the upper hand over Jim when he receives a box of complimentary copies of his published short story collection – in the novel Ralph shows them off in the kitchen by piling them edge on edge in a pyramid on the dining room table as he imagines they would be in a bookshop (thus, confirming his emphasis on the economic value of his work) – Ralph's publication (initially at least) is unable to keep him from declaring bankruptcy or protect him from the California State who are prosecuting him for fraud. Ralph's humiliation appears to be completed, then, when Jim, who, at his birthday party, and in front of a room full of San Francisco Bay Area authors (the equivalent of a Detroit bar filled with off-shift automobile workers) brings in a home-made birthday cake topped with trick candles. Before handing Ralph a cake knife, Jim stands up to address the crowd and in stark contrast to Ralph's dire legal and artistic situation thanks 'old Running Dog Ralph Crawford for all the little words of encouragement' he had given him during those 'dark, discouraging days' he was 'struggling to complete his new novel', which, he adds, is 'soon to be published by Harcourt Brace Jovanovich'. Elaborating further, and in a move that seeks to demote the quality of Ralph's craft, Jim declares that Ralph's help came through the form of hopeful platitudes like 'stay the course', 'never say die', 'all's well that ends well' and, most clichéd of all, 'it's not over until the fat lady sings'. He then hands Ralph the knife which, when he cuts the cake, gets stuck on a metal file that Jim has hidden inside. 'You'll want to employ this little item as soon as possible to break out', he announces.[54]

In general, male shenanigans and bravado prevail throughout the novel. Both men constantly try to sneak up on each other while they undertake illicit acts. One time, Jim successfully catches Ralph writing a love letter to Lindsay; Jim also discovers that Ralph has drilled a peephole in his office to spy on a 'gorgeous blond coed' who rents next door – a peephole hidden, not entirely accidentally, one imagines, behind a framed *Life* magazine cover photograph of Hemingway (and therefore recalls Carver's own teenage desire to write fiction reminiscent of Hemingway's masculine idealism). The pair also undertake a competition as to who can hide their booze most successfully from prying hands – Ralph's favourite places are his father's old trunk and a coffee pot which he fills with whisky and drinks straight from the spout. Physical dominance is also important (although Jim regularly beats Ralph in this area) and includes verbal threats, such as the time that Jim warns Ralph that his antics will result in him 'deservedly eating hot lead'. Later, after Ralph is prosecuted for fraud, Jim tells him that if he spends 'any time in county lockup you might even get buggered' (this complete reversal of orthodox masculine sexuality is, it seems the worst form of punishment for Ralph), and Jim would know, he tells Ralph, because when he spent some time in country (for an unspecified crime) 'I found out who was supposed to be the meanest motherfucker in the joint. I took the cat on. I'm not claiming I won, but I fought him good enough that nobody ever wanted a piece of my ass', to which Ralph, in a moment of humiliation reminiscent of Leo in Carver's 'What Is It?' tells Jim, 'I think I'll just go hang myself right now . . . while I still have my belt.'[55]

While Ralph conducts a string of smaller indiscretions, ultimately, they all culminate in his affair with Lindsay, a woman from Montana that he met through his friend Buffalo Bill. The affair comes to an abrupt end when Alice Ann finds the stack of letters and Ralph is forced to give them to Jim to take back to Lindsay for safekeeping. And so, and as I have already suggested, in the novel, if Ralph and Jim aren't screwing other women, then they are forever screwing over each other. In a moment in which Jim tries to assert physical dominance over Ralph, he slaps Lindsay's ex-husband at a party and then takes Lindsay to a viewpoint at the edge of town and reveals that when Alice Ann found Lindsay's letters, Ralph denied their existence and went into one of his 'weasel who-me routines'.[56] Jim elaborates further and tells Lindsay that Alice Anne does not really have cancer – Ralph's excuse for not being able to leave her – and, to cap it off, Ralph has a student girlfriend at Berkeley and also writes to another lady in Iowa City. 'It is not like Jim is ratting Ralph', the narrator declares with tongue-firmly-in-cheek, 'Lindsay has to pull this information painfully from him. Jim clearly loves Ralph and is really very loyal.'[57] To which end, he continues to spin a tale about his own desire for a family, his creative ambitions – he is on 'leave from Stanford until the next winter's term and hopes to have his new novel completed by then'; a creative aim that appears to exceed Ralph's own collection of short stories – and then seeks to solidify his masculine dominance by combining these declarations with his superior physicality. 'Lindsay asks Jim why he slapped Milo, and he just smiles and shrugs . . . he wasn't really being brave, for even with all Milo's leathers and tattoos and his big Harley, Milo was still basically just a fruity poet type.'[58] When Ralph phones later that evening to try and rectify the situation, he ends the call by reminding Lindsay that 'Jim Stark is a legendary liar' and implores her not to believe 'a single word about anything coming from the lying motormouth of that hypocrite deceitful running dog Jim Stark'.[59]

The bulk of the novel, which is given over to scene after scene of alcohol-fuelled masculine buffoonery, operates as a prelude to a court scene near the novel's conclusion in which Ralph is accused of perjury and fraud. The ending reveals that the real casualty of his rough masculinity is his wife, Alice Ann. The court proceeding comes not long after the publication of Ralph's story collection which, despite his apparent inability to write constructively throughout the course of the novel, denotes graduation to the world of literary white-collar respectability. For Ralph, then, the underlying fear about the upcoming court appearance is not so much a fear of being found guilty, not even the fear of incarceration itself, but it is the fear of losing his white-collar privileges and having to return to the world of blue-collar labour. When Alice Ann reveals that she has arranged to sell their house in order to pay back the money that Ralph stole, she reveals that Ralph's attorney has told her that 'if you throw yourself upon the mercy of the court, you'll get off with a white-collar criminal slap on the wrist. Probation and maybe some community service'.[60] Which might be good news to most, but Ralph is more concerned about what 'community service' might be a euphemism for, 'You mean things like road work?', he says. Ralph's published book, then, has a double value. Not only does it mark Ralph's attainment – through public recognition of his craftsmanship – to the middle class, but it also becomes his saving grace in the courthouse. When it becomes apparent to Alice Ann that the 'avenger-asshole of an assistant district attorney had his flinty heart set upon making a white-collar-criminal example out of Ralph', she takes the stand and, holding up a copy of Ralph's book, says, 'What happened to him . . . no, what has happened to us both, is that we reached that point where the fiction of our lives began to feed on itself. Sir, I would like to offer the fiction of our lives into evidence as exhibit A for the defense', before swearing an oath that 'Mr. Crawford has been rehabilitated by this book and he is full of remorse for the horrific events of his life that he drew upon in order to write this book.'[61]

Yet, while in the narrative, Alice Ann's plea is enough to get Ralph off jail time, it is not a true representation of Ralph's attitude. For Ralph does not repent of the 'horrific events of his life' – that is, of course, the world of rough masculinity that he is purported to have drawn upon for his fiction – but instead continues, in the closing chapters of the novel, to revel in them. And it is the realisation of this that finally breaks up their marriage and causes Alice Ann to leave. In celebratory mood and in one final attempt to reinvigorate their marriage, Alice Ann suggests a second honeymoon trip to Seattle. She buys an expensive white dress to wear and shows it off one night. But Ralph is more concerned by how much the dress costs. In an attempt to placate him, Alice Ann tries to get him to dance, which starts an argument that quickly escalates when Alice Ann alludes to Ralph's indiscretions:

What I need to figure out, Alice Ann said, is exactly when my husband decided to hate me. I need to know when he decided to turn on me and cause me anguish and humiliation and to expose my pain to the world and then abandon me forever. And all the bitter, hard, sad things about my only marriage, which is the single greatest failure of my lifetime, have been laid bare for the world's amusement. That tragic rock has been rolled over again and again, and finally anyone I once thought I was or could again become is dead and buried. All my life's blood has been slowly drained from my body over the long reincarnations of my failed marriage.[62]

After another tirade Alice Ann flings a glass at him and then grabs a cheese knife and starts at Ralph, before Ralph grabs an empty wine bottle and hits her on the side of the head. Jim, who has been watching from the other side of the room, jumps on Ralph and Alice Ann runs from the room as the men 'wrestle around on the floor, cursing, grunting, flailing arms and legs'.[63] Unable to overpower each other – perhaps a sign of their diminishing powers of masculinity – the men come to a grinding halt. The fallout from the incident is suitably dramatic. Once Lindsay and Jim find Alice Ann she tells them 'I wonder how even Ralph will make something timeless out of this tawdry business, Alice Ann said. – I wonder if he can make even this shit sublime. Oh well, my work is done now. I give up. I've lost. I'm throwing in the towel.'[64]

It would make a neat summary to suggest that the result of going through a decade of rough working-class masculinity is that Ralph graduates – through a process of reflection and pseudo-religious moral reformation – to faith in a new kind of respectable working-class masculinity; one not defined by fighting, screwing and boozing, but rather by social pride, skilled craftsmanship and economic security. Indeed, if life and novels were fairly judged then Ralph would not have ended up as the nationally famed author that he does at the end of the novel. Instead, like Alice Ann, he would have drifted into obscurity and viewed the chaos of his early life in a repentant manner. As it is, the novel closes as Ralph, on the back of his second story collection, becomes the nationally famed author that he always dreamed of and embarks on a countrywide road trip with Jim to tour the book. Landing in Iowa City he recalls the very early days, when he and Alice Ann moved there for his studies.

'Sure, the facts of their lives didn't match the myth they had begun to make of their marriage, but those two weeks of pure, wondrous, abandoned, six-and-seven-course sex in that shabby cabin fed the fantasy of their lives for years to come.'[65] The projection of what their life would be like (at another point Alice Ann reveals that she views them as the fulfilment of prophetic literary history when she ominously declares, 'We'll be the Scott and Zelda of our day') is summed up by the narrator, 'Iowa City felt like a hometown to Ralph, a sort of hometown of spirit, for it was there that he felt as though his life had been released into significance as a writer, and where, for better or worse, he and Alice Ann had drifted firmly into that mythology that had carried their marriage forth so many more years.'[66]

If the character in *Honeymooners* is unrepentant, then the real Carver – famously, even mythically – appeared to show signs of moral reformation in his later life. Questioned by multiple interviewers about his alcoholism, Carver was characteristically repentant and regretful (although he typically stopped short of apology). Looking back, Carver said, 'I don't see anything coming out my drinking experiences except waste and pain and misery.' Comparing his ten-year alcoholic binge to a prison sentence he concludes, 'you have to take it on faith that prison life is not the best for a writer'.[67] Elsewhere, he reflected, 'It's very painful to think about some of the things that happened back then. I made a wasteland out of everything I touched.'[68] Or again, elaborating on his alcohol dependency, he said, 'purely and simply, drinking is *not* conducive to artistic production. Quite the contrary, I think it's a disaster and a terrible hindrance.'[69] Carver's tone in these interviews is picked up in 'Intimacy', a story he wrote near the end of his life. The narrative takes the form of a monologue delivered by the estranged wife of a nationally famous writer. When the writer takes an unscheduled visit to her home she welcomes him in and makes some coffee before launching into a near-fifty-paragraph tirade. The major point of her complaint – besides the fact that she wishes she had, during one drunken argument, actually used a knife she had picked up to cut him – is the way her ex-husband has achieved literary fame and notoriety by mining their dysfunctional marriage for material. 'I was there. I served, buddy boy', she reminds him.

'Then', as if that wasn't punishment enough, 'you held me up for display and ridicule in your so-called work. For any Tom or Harry to pity or pass judgment on.'[70] When the husband, in an attempt to be endearing and offer some kind of apology, tells her that he remembers the years they spent together, she takes it the opposite way and scolds, 'That's the bone of contention here, if you hadn't noticed.'[71] The story, perhaps more than anything, suggests that the only way to gain purchase on the past is to engage with it, but, given the ambiguity of memory, and the means by which recollections are subject to misinterpretation, this is more complex and slippery for the characters than it might initially seem. The climax to this episode comes when the husband, apparently not entirely in control of his actions, and overcome with contrition – or, at least, the need for some kind of reconciliation – gets on his knees in the living room and holds on to his former wife's dress:

> Then here's the thing I do next. I get down on my knees, a big guy like me, and I take the hem of her dress. What am I doing on the floor? I wish I could say. But I know it's where I ought to be, and I'm there on my knees holding on to the hem of her dress.[72]

In his earlier work, such an impulsive move might have risked the shame of public exposure, but in this later-life story, the move seems more associated with moral restoration or even, to draw a muted comparison with the ending of stories like 'Boxes' and 'Menudo', and despite the tendency towards a type of flawed self-interest, a kind of healing associated with social craftsmanship. This story ends, finally, in what amounts, in Carver's work at least, to an ironic twist, as the former wife announces her forgiveness for his writing – and perhaps even other personal sins committed against her – and does so in the anticipation that he will use this very episode for a future story. As they say goodbye, she moves close to him, three inches away – 'We haven't been this close in a long time', the husband notes – and she says, 'You just tell it like you have to, I guess, and forget the rest. Like always. You been doing that for so long now anyway it shouldn't be hard for you.'[73] In another context, it might be tempting to read this ending as playfully postmodern, a guileful reminder that this story might itself be the very product of a real-life encounter between Carver and Maryann, but that, surely, is not Carver's point. Instead, given the incongruous fact that the very same dysfunctional behaviour that kept Carver from writing, ruined his health and fractured his marriage was the very thing that made him the distinctive – if opportunistic – writer that he was, the prevailing notion at the end of the story is the importance of telling it like you have to, and the concomitant perception that that is exactly what Carver's fiction does, an approach that the writer in 'Intimacy' appears to have built a career out of, and that Carver, ultimately, suggests is the only way to write, no matter what the consequences might be.

Notes

1. The most cohesive account of Carver's life during this time is found in Sklenicka's chapters 'Astounding and Amazing Times', pp. 233–49 and 'Drowning', *Raymond Carver: A Writer's Life*, pp. 250–67. The report of Carver's free flights is verified by novelist Jon Jackson, who claims, in an interview with Sklenicka, to have received one of Carver's free tickets.
2. Sklenicka, *Raymond Carver*, p. 203.
3. For increased access to higher education between 1940 and 1970 see Table 5.1 in Davis, *Prisoners of the American Dream*, p. 191.
4. In his analysis, McGurl, borrowing from Daniel Bell's assessment of higher education during this period, calls it the 'axial institution of postindustrial society'. McGurl, *The Program Era*, p. 283.
5. Halpert, *Raymond Carver: An Oral Biography*, p. 58.
6. Rebein, *Hicks, Tribes, and Dirty Realists*, p. 24. Available at <https://www.newyorker.com/magazine/1998/10/05/good-raymond> (last accessed 11 April 2019).
7. Carver, *Call If You Need Me*, p. 276.
8. Halpert, *Raymond Carver: An Oral Biography*, pp. 58–9.
9. Sklenicka, *Raymond Carver*, p. 90.
10. It would be remiss not to point out that the chronology of Carver's life is a little more complicated than this truncated description suggests. After working at the hospital for two years, the Carvers filed for their first bankruptcy in 1967. Later that year Carver was hired by SRA; the following year he took a career break to travel with Maryann to Tel Aviv University, where she had been awarded a scholarship; they returned to Hollywood later that year and Carver sold cinema programmes, before being rehired by SRA again.
11. Carver was given the position by John Leggett, who had read Carver's submissions for the Iowa Writers' Prize that year. While Carver did not win the award, Leggett was so impressed by Carver's work that he phoned him to offer him a job.

12. Simpson and Buzbee, 'Raymond Carver, Art of Fiction No. 76'.
13. Sklenicka records that Carver told one his students at Iowa, Dan Domench, that what he'd learned from Cheever was 'what alcohol was really all about'. Sklenicka, *Raymond Carver*, p. 258.
14. Carver, *Fires*, p. 40.
15. Felski, 'Nothing to Declare: Identity, Shame and the Lower Middle Class', p. 39.
16. Carver, *Collected Stories*, p. 72.
17. Carver, *Collected Stories*, p. 76.
18. McGurl, *The Program Era*, p. 275.
19. McGurl, *The Program Era*, p. 295.
20. Carver, *Collected Stories*, p. 102.
21. Carver, *Collected Stories*, p. 106.
22. Carver, *Collected Stories*, p. 102.
23. Carver, *Collected Stories*, p. 115.
24. Halpert, *Raymond Carver*, p. 35.
25. Halpert, *Raymond Carver*, p. 36.
26. Halpert, *Raymond Carver*, p. 36.
27. Meyer, *Manhood on the Line*, p. 2.
28. Carver first met Kittredge at a literary convention in Seattle. Browsing the convention bookstall one night, Kittredge was looking at an anthology edited by Curt Johnson when Carver came up behind him and claimed he had a story in the book. Kittredge, thinking this was male bluster, laughed Carver's claim off, until Carver made a vociferous argument to the contrary and pointed to his name on the cover and Kittredge, conceding that it was unlikely that anyone would go to such lengths to trick him, suggested they continue their conversation at the bar. Later that year, Carver wrote to Kittredge to tell him that he was planning on visiting him in Missoula, Montana. Having only met once, Kittredge thought this to be an unusual request at the time, but Carver visited and the pair became friends.
29. Halpert, *Raymond Carver*, p. 48.
30. Sklenicka, *Raymond Carver*, p. 236.
31. Sklenicka, *Raymond Carver*, p. 237.
32. For more on the State of California's charge against Carver see Sklenicka, pp. 281–2; for Carver's excuses and working-class behaviour see Sklenicka, pp. 246–7.
33. Halpert, *Raymond Carver*, p. 41.
34. Stearns, *Be A Man! Males in Modern Society*, p. 86.
35. Carver, *Collected Stories*, p. 147.
36. Carver, *Collected Stories*, p. 148.
37. Carver, *Collected Stories*, p. 150.
38. Carver, *Collected Stories*, p. 152.
39. Carver, *Collected Stories*, p. 153.
40. Carver, *Collected Stories*, p. 153.
41. Carver, *Collected Stories*, p. 153.
42. Carver, *Collected Stories*, p. 154.
43. Carver, *Collected Stories*, p. 155.

44. Carver, *Collected Stories*, p. 156.
45. *Publishers Weekly* perhaps summarised it best when they forecasted that 'if the media pick up on this book's unusual history ... it might garner feature as well as review coverage'. See <https://www.publishersweekly.com/978-0-374-17258-9> (last accessed 11 April 2019).
46. Sklenicka, *Raymond Carver*, p. 382.
47. Kinder, *Honeymooners*, p. 17.
48. Kinder, *Honeymooners*, pp. 17–18.
49. Kinder, *Honeymooners*, pp. 9, 56. In the anecdote, Ralph sets himself up as Cheever's apprentice by declaring, 'the first thing I remember Cheever saying to me about writing was that you aren't your characters but your characters are you. The man took me seriously enough to sit down with me and go over a story and move words around until they fit properly.' Kinder, *Honeymooners*, p. 56.
50. Kinder, *Honeymooners*, p. 154.
51. Kinder, *Honeymooners*, p. 156.
52. Kinder, *Honeymooners*, p. 129.
53. Aldridge, *Talents and Technicians*, p. 48; Kinder, *Honeymooners*, p. 130.
54. Kinder, *Honeymooners*, p. 277.
55. Kinder, *Honeymooners*, pp. 20, 19, 194–5.
56. Kinder, *Honeymooners*, p. 95.
57. Kinder, *Honeymooners*, p. 96.
58. Kinder, *Honeymooners*, p. 96.
59. Kinder, *Honeymooners*, p. 99.
60. Kinder, *Honeymooners*, p. 280.
61. Kinder, *Honeymooners*, pp. 282–3.
62. Kinder, *Honeymooners*, p. 332.
63. Kinder, *Honeymooners*, p. 334.
64. Kinder, *Honeymooners*, p. 336.
65. Kinder, *Honeymooners*, p. 335.
66. Kinder, *Honeymooners*, pp. 157, 354.
67. McCaffery and Gregory, 'An Interview with Raymond Carver', in Gentry and Stull (eds), *Conversations with Raymond Carver*, p. 115.
68. Simpson and Buzbee, 'Raymond Carver', p. 38.
69. Bonetti, 'Ray Carver', in Gentry and Stull (eds), *Conversations with Raymond Carver*, p. 55.
70. Carver, *Collected Stories*, p. 565.
71. Carver, *Collected Stories*, p. 563.
72. Carver, *Collected Stories*, p. 566.
73. Carver, *Collected Stories*, p. 567.

CHAPTER 2

'Carveresque Realism':
Raymond Carver and Jay McInerney

The traditional account of the first meeting between Jay McInerney and Raymond Carver goes something like this: on the afternoon of 9 December 1980 McInerney was in his Greenwich Village apartment in New Yo1rk City when he received an unexpected phone call from his best friend Gary Fisketjon. Fisketjon, an assistant editor at Random House, had just finished a lunch meeting with Carver and Gordon Lish. In lieu of a tour guide, he told McInerney that he was sending Carver to his home for the afternoon before a scheduled reading at Columbia University later that evening. McInerney, at the time an aspiring writer and Carver admirer, thinking this was some kind of practical joke, immediately hung up the phone. Fisketjon had to re-dial and insist that Carver really was on his way. Moments later, it seemed, there was a knock on his door and Carver's lumbering frame shadowed the threshold. The two men spent the afternoon taking cocaine together and talking about writing. Later Fisketjon turned up and sped Carver uptown via the subway just in time for the reading. Carver and McInerney parted that evening, so the story goes, with Carver entreating McInerney to leave the financial and creative drain of New York City and move to Syracuse to study on the creative writing programme with him.[1]

To fully understand the significance of this event for McInerney it is worth revisiting, for a moment, his undergraduate years at Williams College. Five years earlier McInerney was studying for a philosophy major (hoping to become a writer after he graduated) and came across Carver's collection *Will You Please Be Quiet, Please?*

He describes the initial experience of reading Carver as 'a bolt out of the blue' that illuminated the reality he saw around him. 'Suddenly this very new language, this wonderful new idiom. It's the world as you always suspected, but you never realised it was until you read the book', he told Sam Halpert in an interview.² McInerney's reaction was, as I'll argue later, remarkably similar to both Murakami and Vlautin's initial experience of reading Carver, and adds weight to the idea that Carver's fiction reveals or sheds light on a particular type of reality that, up to that point, exceeds conceptual mapping. Richard Ford echoed this notion when, describing hearing Carver read 'What Is It?' for the first time, he wrote in *The New Yorker* that 'One learned from the story, many things ... Life was this way – yes, we already know that. But *this* life, *these* otherwise unnoticeable people's suitability for literary expression seemed new.' He concluded, 'One also felt that a consequence for the story was seemingly to intensify life, even dignify it, and to locate in it shadowed corners and niches that needed revealing.'³ For McInerney, reading Carver's collection cemented his authorial ambitions and, in an experience that he fictionalises in his recent novel *Bright, Precious Days*, he passed Carver's collection on to his roommate, Gary Fisketjon. It was perhaps only appropriate, then, that Fisketjon return the favour and introduce Carver that December afternoon five years later. While it appears that Carver's literary text initially had a profound impact on McInerney, after their initial meeting in 1980 the two also developed a correspondence, and Carver began to exert a significant pedagogical influence. The mentorship soon developed into a friendship that ran throughout most of the 1980s. Writing after Carver's death in *The New York Times Book Review*, McInerney recalls that in those early years Carver changed his life in an irrevocable way.⁴

When they first met in 1980, McInerney had been living in New York City for just over a year. He moved there from Japan, where he had been studying on the Princeton-in-Asia Fellowship, and arrived in New York just as the city was coming out of its own fiscal crisis and implementing a new pro-business era.⁵ At the time, McInerney had yet to publish anything of repute. He had a draft of a novel, but was making a living writing book reviews and doing research. Carver, meanwhile, was coming out of the despair of his alcoholic years. While his literary stock was continuing to rise (he published 'Where Is Everyone' in *TriQuarterly*, and 'A Serious Talk', 'Want To See Something?' and 'Gazebo' in *The Missouri Review* that year) it wasn't until the following spring that he rose to national fame and notoriety with the publication of *What We Talk About When We Talk About Love*.

This biographical background is worth bearing in mind because popular folklore suggests that the first step on the Carver mentorship programme was to convince McInerney that New York City was a financial and creative drain on the young, aspiring writer. This, for instance, is Sklenicka's opinion. She writes, 'Ray saw that McInerney was dissipating his energy in New York. He urged him to study fiction writing at Syracuse.'[6] The benefit of this narrative for both writers is clear. On that December afternoon, it is intimated, Carver must have spotted the talent and promise of the young McInerney, while McInerney, for his part, realised that studying with a great American writer like Carver would propel his career. The truth, however, is probably far less glamorous – and the narrative certainly problematised by McInerney's lack of publications and Carver's rather modest career at the time. Of course, this does not discount the fact that Carver may well have tried to convince McInerney that New York City was not necessarily conducive to literary development, and it is worth conceding the obvious, that the financial drain of city life stifled creativity – a truth the twice-bankrupt Carver knew only too well – but it does highlight the necessity of exercising caution when collating these biographical accounts. Memories fade; stories change. Not to mention, if Carver and McInerney did spend the afternoon inhaling cocaine their senses would have been, at the very least, inhibited. Even so, it seems reasonable to suggest that the developing friendship between the two men, along with McInerney's migration upstate to study under Carver, formed the start of a period of mentorship for the young writer, and that by being in close proximity, Carver was able to not only help in the artistic aspect of writing but also offer a model of how to negotiate the practicalities of becoming a writer.

In the fall of 1981 McInerney moved to Syracuse and began the creative writing programme. He received a fellowship that he suspected Carver was behind which afforded him financial stability and he moved into an apartment half a block from Carver's house.[7] This was the end of a defining year for the young writer – fired from the fact-checking department of *The New Yorker* for incompetence, separated from his first wife, and moving away from the drug-fuelled nightlife of Manhattan Island – this must have seemed like a chance for reinvention. Thus, his close proximity to working writers was important in establishing a new routine. He took classes with Carver and often brought stories to him on a one-to-one basis. All the while McInerney was a keen sender of stories to magazines and small publications in an attempt to make some kind of breakthrough. Unusually, perhaps, McInerney published a story in a national magazine early on at his time in Syracuse. After submitting a story to *The Paris Review* in the winter of 1981, he received a phone call from the editor George Plimpton asking for more writing. Taking a look at what he might be able to send Plimpton that night, McInerney found nothing satisfactory, but instead 'chanced' upon a fragment he had written after a party at Fisketjon's apartment and was 'inspired' to write a new story.[8] The fragment, which ran, 'You're not the kind of guy who would be at a place like this at this time of the morning, but here you are', became the story 'It's Six A.M. Do You Know Where You Are?', and famously, the opening of his bestselling debut novel *Bright Lights, Big City*. He sent the short story to Plimpton and received another phone call from assistant editor Mona Simpson letting him know that the story had been accepted. It was published the following January.[9]

Despite his publication in *The Paris Review*, McInerney struggled to secure a second publication. Carver, of course, could empathise with McInerney's position. He had spent much of the 1960s attempting, often unsuccessfully, to publish in magazines and small quarterlies, too. And like McInerney's prominent publication in *The Paris Review*, when Carver eventually managed to get his story 'Neighbours' published by Lish in *Esquire* in 1971, such a prominent publication did not lead to instant acceptance at other magazines in later years. Still, Carver's personal essays reveal a belief in the power of these magazines as a route to literary success and posterity. In 'John Gardner: The Writer as Teacher', Carver reveals that it was his own tutor, John Gardner, who convinced him that literary periodicals were the place where 'most of the best fiction in the country and just about all the poetry was appearing'.[10] It is fitting, then, that McInerney's second publication came in one of these small quarterlies when, a year and a half later in July 1983, a guest editor at *Ploughshares* accepted his story. The editor was Raymond Carver. This acceptance placed McInerney's story alongside writing by Joyce Carol Oates, Tim O'Brien, Mona Simpson, Tobias Wolff, William Kittredge and Tess Gallagher. Accepted the summer he graduated from Syracuse, the story can be seen as the completion of his formal education. 'Amanda', the short story that Carver chose for *Ploughshares*, was another section from the draft of his novel *Bright Lights, Big City*. McInerney had recently finished the draft, which he started after sending Plimpton the opening for *The Paris Review*, and that Fisketjon would soon publish at Random House as a headliner for his new Vintage Contemporaries Series in September 1984. It is, perhaps, hard to quantify exactly how important Carver's selection of 'Amanda' was in McInerney securing the publication of *Bright Lights, Big City* given his close acquaintance with Fisketjon at Random House, but Carver's selection of 'Amanda', at a time when he was fast becoming one of the country's most recognisable short story writers could only have amplified McInerney's literary credentials.

When McInerney graduated from Syracuse University in 1983 and secured the publication of his debut novel only a few months later it was not hard to understand the commercial appeal of the young writer. By the time *Bright Lights, Big City* was published in September 1984 the 29-year-old had accumulated an extensive catalogue of experiences: the son of a sales executive, he spent his childhood sojourning in a number of countries and states. Later to become best friends with one of the brightest young editors in New York, he spent his early twenties sampling both the spiritual mysticism of the Far East and the consumerist excess of the West; he settled for the hedonism of the latter, and became familiar with parties and substance use – the benchmark of all mythic urban writers – all before he was fired from a job as a fact-checker at *The New Yorker* in order to commence the pursuit of his craft under the instruction of some of America's principal living writers. In all, his early life epitomised the high-speed ephemerality of many young urban Americans living in the 1980s. *Bright Lights, Big City*, which takes its realism – and comic tone – from McInerney's experience, presented Fisketjon with the perfect combination of in-vogue literary and cultural fashions. All Fisketjon required, it seemed, was a matching format to partner the text.

The idea behind the Vintage Contemporary Series, the publication banner under which McInerney was first published, came a number of years earlier while Fisketjon was writing a review of Carver's small press publication *Furious Seasons* for the *Village Voice*.[11] E. Graydon Carter suggests that Fisketjon was frustrated that Carver, who had been nominated for a National Book Award for his first work, in lieu of a novel, was forced to release his second collection with the small press publisher Capra Press.[12] Believing that current practices were therefore not serving writers well, Fisketjon began to formulate a plan that would increase a smaller writer's commercial viability. Fisketjon's solution was to produce a uniform trade paperback series that combined well-known and newer writers behind a series of distinctive covers. This overcame the problem of market saturation as Stephanie Girard explains:

> By the early 1980s bookstore resistance to the mass-market paperbacks had been overcome; hardcovers, quality paperbacks, and mass-market paperbacks were all competing for shelf space. In general, the kind of name-brand associations that sold other products were not operative in the book marketplace; each book fended for itself. Without help from the publisher, a title could easily get lost; in 1984 alone, 51,058 titles competed for sales.[13]

Fisketjon's plan, however, took a number of years to come together. It began in 1978 when he phoned Carver from New York and enquired if he would be interested in publishing an expanded edition of *Furious Seasons* for Random House. Carver, it seems, was willing, but poor paperback sales on *Will You Please Be Quiet, Please?* discouraged the executives at Random House from committing to the project and Carver's contract with McGraw-Hill complicated the republication of the stories.[14] Forced to set aside the Carver project temporarily, Fisketjon moved to trial his marketing idea with Don DeLillo, and after succeeding commercially with the series, convinced Random House to purchase Carver's reprint rights for *Will You Please Be Quiet, Please?* and *What We Talk About When We Talk About Love* and then began publishing paperbacks of Carver's collections in a uniform edition. After the success of both trials, Fisketjon created a more comprehensive trade paperback series. He called it Vintage Contemporaries, immediately granting a suitable amount of literary and cultural appeal to the publications, and then convinced McInerney to bypass the usual route of a hardback first novel and to publish *Bright Lights, Big City* in paperback.

The seven titles released in the first series of Vintage Contemporaries were: *Bright Lights, Big City* by McInerney, *Cathedral* by Carver, *Dancing Bear* (1983) by James Crumley, *Dancing in the Dark* (1983) by Janet Hobhouse, *The Timeless People* (1969) by Paule Marshall, *Far Tortuga* (1975) by Peter Matthiessen and *The Bushwhacked Piano* (1971) by Thomas McGuane. For several weeks, *Cathedral* and *Bright Lights, Big City* alternated at the top of the *Village Voice's* bestseller list and by the end of its first year, McInerney's novel had sold 300,000 copies. After two years an estimated 500,000 copies had sold.[15] As well as being a commercial success the series also won Fisketjon the 1984 Carey-Thomas Award for creative publishing. And while a large part of its popularity was also down to the quality of fiction that Fisketjon selected, his marketing was an important aspect of the series' commercial success.

Perhaps then, the true brilliance of the series lay in the interrelation of new authors alongside more established names. In this sense, as Girard explains, much of the synergy of the series derives from what she calls the 'cross-fertilization' of cover blurbs.[16] In this regard Fisketjon was very deliberate in his choice of authors for the series. Prominent on *Bright Lights, Big City's* front cover was a recommendation from Carver while on the back cover was a quotation from Thomas McGuane.[17] McGuane's own novel, *The Bushwhacked Piano*, and Carver's collection, *Cathedral*, were, as I have already noted, both printed in the Vintage Contemporaries Series alongside McInerney. Fisketjon also asked Tobias Wolff to write a blurb, and in it Wolff compares *Bright Lights, Big City* with McGuane's *The Bushwhacked Piano*.[18] Not only, therefore, did the self-referential blurbs and recommendations grant kudos to less established authors – like McInerney – but the cover designs, which were more akin to album covers, appealed to a younger and, importantly for the publisher, a more consumer orientated readership in an increasingly buoyant US economy.[19] Paperback editions also had smaller overheads so Fisketjon was able to set price-points lower than traditional first edition hardbacks. He retailed the books between $4.95 and $6.95, more expensive than traditional mass-market paperbacks, thus finding a market somewhere in between the commercial market of paperbacks and critical recognition of literary hardbacks. While this kind of quality paperback was not a completely new idea – Penguin had a trade paperback series which started in 1979 – the combination of well-known and debut authors, with fresh, innovative designs and pricing created the ideal context for commercial success and critical acclaim.[20] 'Although this cross-blurbing was originally designed to help the first novel of a relatively unknown author earn respectable sales', writes Girard, 'we can assume that it also worked in reverse when that first novel became a bestseller, attracting a new audience for the other six reprinted titles.'[21] Even here, then, at McInerney's early commercial success, Carver's presence is not far away – the success of Fisketjon's experiment with his early paperback editions eventually culminated in the commercial success of McInerney's debut novel.

While Fisketjon's deliberate orchestration of Vintage Contemporaries manipulated the buyer into thinking there was a strong literary connection between the established and the new, the reality, of course, was that there was not. The contents of McGuane's novel – a satirical narrative about a nefarious *flâneur* – had very little to do with the fiction found in Carver's collection. What was associative though, was the network of friendship Fisketjon built that allowed him to take advantage of the opportunity of a publication series like Vintage Contemporaries. Whether Wolff – who was not published in the series – knew that he was partaking in such nepotism when he compared McInerney with McGuane is not entirely certain, but it seems likely he was party to the idea because he was living and working with Carver and McInerney in Syracuse in the early 1980s. While the marketing and blurb attached to a novel is now widely accepted to have a marketing bias, it is interesting to note the innovation and success of Fisketjon's campaign in the 1980s, an era when, I will argue later, McInerney explores the sharp increase in financialisation of the publishing industry.

Given his sudden rise to literary celebrity on the back of his debut publication, 1984 must be considered the seminal year for McInerney's career. Aside from Fisketjon's marketing, a large part of the success of *Bright Lights, Big City* must also be put down to McInerney's text itself. The novel, which tells the story of a young twenty-something attempting the negotiate life in a glamorous New York City in the early 1980s, appealed to an emerging market of young urban professionals. Narrated in the second person, the novel is fashioned in the kind of self-confident, exuberant style that epitomised the era. As if to reinforce this idea, soon after publication, the book was optioned by MGM and McInerney was given the task of adapting the novel for the big screen. After nearly a decade of part-time jobs and small bursaries, the success of *Bright Lights, Big City* opened the door to financial stability. This is the period in McInerney's life when it might be said that his mentorship with Carver began to come to an end. Now he and Carver became, for want of a better phrase, good friends. In 1984 Carver wrote a poem called 'My Boat' in which he imagined space for a couple dozen of his closest friends, and included McInerney on a list with others like Kinder, Kittredge, Ford and Wolff.

The association that McInerney makes between Carver and other writers amounts to one of his major victories as a young writer in the literary world. Not only was he becoming increasingly close to Carver, but he was also close friends with Fisketjon – soon to be Carver's editor – and he came to know and correspond with other writers like the aforementioned Kinder, Ford and Wolff as well as Tess Gallagher, Mona Simpson, Tom Jencks, Thomas McGuane, Haruki Murakami, Geoffrey Wolff and Gordon Lish. These friendships were noted, at times, for their excesses and hedonism as well as frequent story sharing and editing. What the period of mentorship between Carver and McInerney reveals so pertinently is that Carver offered a model to navigate such a landscape.[22] The mantra told time and again by Carver, through his work, lifestyle and letters was simple: as McInerney recalls in one interview, 'Get black on white'.[23]

It would be fair to say that getting 'black on white' became a motto for McInerney's early career. The phrase became a useful guidepost for McInerney, who, at the time, held noticeably different ideas to Carver on the nature of the writing process:

> When I met him I thought of writers as luminous madmen who drank too much and drove too fast and scattered brilliant pages along their doomed trajectories. Maybe at one time he did, too. In his essay 'Fires', he says, 'I understood writers to be people who didn't spend their Saturdays at the Laundromat' ... In the classroom and on the page, Carver somehow delivered the tonic news that there was laundry in the kingdom of letters.[24]

In other words, Carver appears to have dispelled the connection between excessive experience and artistic success – a notion closely aligned to innate, untrained talent – and replaced it with a more artisanal, and perhaps more conventionally American work ethic. This transition is important because it meant that for McInerney the writing process became more akin to a kind of labour or traditional craft than a spontaneous sensation projection. The result was that writing became a skill which could be honed and mastered. In this sense McInerney's move from New York City to Syracuse marked an important spatial transition. In interviews he admits that he was reluctant to move upstate. 'I had some resistance', he explains to Halpert. 'I still felt I was in the center of the media and publishing world.' But Carver quickly dispelled that belief by insisting that the literary world was wherever a man or woman was writing. This idea was only reinforced when McInerney eventually moved to Syracuse and he knew that 'one of the masters of American prose' was clacking his typewriter just up the street.[25] Carver's practical example, then, appears to be an important partner to his textual influence. This insistence on working and practising writing as a craft, is often repeated in McInerney's accounts of his time at Syracuse. Carver, who apparently took a very hands-on approach to his mentorship, became intricately involved in his life – more, certainly, than a tutor reasonably should:

> He used to call me up in the morning and he'd see if I was awake and he'd say, 'Are you writing?' or, 'Are you going to write?' Or he'd call me at the end of the day and say, 'Did you write?' It sounds unglamorous and I guess that's the point, for Ray it was about getting black on white. It was

plugging away every day, as he quoted, I think Chekhov, 'With hope and without despair'. It was going at it like a job.[26]

Whether McInerney saw his excessive, sensual and highly experiential life in New York City as the route to literary success is not completely clear – he may well have been drawn to those places because he was a 25-year-old with a taste for excess – but Carver's insistence that the heart of the writing process was the following trade secret appears to have had a profound impact on him: 'you had to survive, find some quiet, and work hard every day'.[27] McInerney's 'luminous madmen' were replaced at Syracuse by long (daylight) hours at the typewriter.

As I develop my discussion of Carver's influence on McInerney it is important to map the landscape and outline some boundaries. McInerney, who first read Carver in 1975, began his correspondence and mentorship in 1980 and studied with Carver at Syracuse between 1981 and 1983. It was during that time that McInerney published his first stories in *The Paris Review*, *Ploughshares* and *Granta*, all extracts from his bestselling 1984 novel *Bright Lights, Big City*. It was also during his Syracuse years that it might reasonably be argued that McInerney felt the influence of Carver's presence most keenly. The practical example and emphasis that Carver placed on routine and regularity in particular allowed McInerney the time to practise craftsmanship. In one sense it is regrettable that his early published stories are only extracts, for if they had been independent pieces Carver's influence might have been assessed on a larger plain. Although this chapter does not discuss it in detail, McInerney's second novel *Ransom*, written at the same time as *Bright Lights, Big City*, may also bear the hallmarks of Carver's influence. His third novel, *Story Of My Life*, returns to the atmosphere of hedonistic New York in the manner of his debut and has a suggestive Carveresque feel in its use of colloquial, non-literary nuances and idioms. From then on McInerney published about one story every year in national magazines: 'The Real Tad Allagash' in *MS* (1985), 'Smoke' in *Atlantic Monthly* (1986), 'Reunion' in *Esquire* (1987), 'The Business' in *Granta* (1988), 'Lost and Found' in *Esquire* (1988) and 'Jimmy' in *Granta* (1989). After Carver's death in 1988 McInerney's short story publishing become more sporadic, perhaps because his novels increased in size and scope. His fourth novel, *Brightness Falls*, appears particularly significant in this regard. Twice the length of anything he had published previously, it took him five years to write. While clearly different in size and scope, the novel is the pinnacle of Carver's influence on McInerney, in that it presents the formal distillation of many of the ideas that Carver held about writing and literature. It is with this in mind that I shall begin to chart a more specific map of Carver's influence. First, I will briefly assess Carver's own publications in the 1980s, then analyse the important principles that underpin his writing – which are sourced from his mentor John Gardner – before I finally analyse how Carver's writing and teaching are transmitted to McInerney's work. I will begin briefly with McInerney's first novel, *Bright Lights, Big City*, before focusing, in more detail, on *Brightness Falls*.

First published in *The New York Times Book Review* in 1981, 'A Storyteller's Shoptalk' is the clearest personal account of Carver's writing process. The essay, which was re-titled 'On Writing' and collected two years later in *Fires: Essays, Poems, Stories*, may in this sense be classed as Carver's very own literary manifesto. Appearing alongside three other short essays in the collection, it combines Carver's pragmatism with the kind of fundamentalism that epitomised his folklore image as the arch-minimalist.[28] His primary argument, often reduced to a few sound bites – 'Get in, get out. Don't linger'; 'No cheap tricks'; 'Fundamental accuracy of statement is the ONE sole morality of writing'; 'No iron can pierce the heart with such force as a period put just at the right place' – not only solidifies the Carver myth of ideological literary austerity but is also Carver's attempt at providing a defence for literary realism in an age when experimentalism was popular.[29]

The literary atmosphere in which Carver learnt to write was one where literary experimentalism was fast replacing realism as the dominant form. At the time, a wave of anti-realists – Thomas Pynchon, Kurt Vonnegut, William Gass, Richard Brautigan, Robert Coover, Donald Barthelme and John Barth, to name just a few – were attempting to push the boundaries of literary style, and Carver, I propose, saw this as a deliberate attempt to dismantle the foundational principles of realism. While I could give space to a lengthy assessment of realism's waning in the twentieth century, to do so would exceed the purpose of this book. Indeed, debates about the relevance of realism in the twentieth century have been argued in various forms in the past and so there is little need to address them directly here. However it is beneficial to provide a short summary of the key components so that I can better contextualise the historical circumstances in which Carver (and McInerney) learnt to write.[30]

In the first instance, it was the literary modernists – especially Virginia Woolf, T. S. Eliot and James Joyce – who resisted the orthodox narrative of realism. They particularly viewed the realism practised by nineteenth-century authors such as James, Balzac and Dostoevsky as an inadequate mode for detailing life in the new century. It was Virginia Woolf who infamously summed up the mood when she asserted that 'On or about December 1910, human character changed', before adding that 'for us those conventions are ruin, those tools are death'.[31] In light of the progression from modernism to postmodernism the emergence of the influence of the New Critics in America in the second quarter of the twentieth century was important in propelling ideas concerning aesthetic autonomy. William Faulkner's fiction was significant from this point of view. Written at the start of this period, his 1936 novel *Absalom, Absalom!*, it has been argued by Brian McHale, exemplifies a secondary step away from the principles of realism. In *Postmodernist Fiction*, McHale uses Roman Jakobson to describe the shift, claiming that the fundamental distinction between the modernist and postmodernist period is a move from an epistemological to an ontological dominant.[32] This new dominant, which is prefigured in Faulkner's novel, was clarified by his literary descendants in the second half of the twentieth century. Such a shift from questions of 'knowing' to questions of 'being' fit closely with the emergence of post-structuralism, and in particular Jean-François Lyotard's argument in *The Postmodern Condition* for the demise of meta-narratives and the emergence of micro-narratives. As one critic has recently pointed out, 'The rise of postmodernism and poststructuralism in the late seventies and eighties added powerful new philosophical and socio-historical elements to the anti-realist argument.'[33] Malcolm Bradbury and Sigmund Ro assert that in America these new ideas were established out of a rejection of pre-war modernist myths – Fitzgerald's American Dream, Faulkner's experimental rhetoric and Hemingway's economic reportage.[34] Writers appeared to be exasperated by both nineteenth-century realism and modernism and began to move away from their precursors' literary style. 'Literature was exhausted', cried John Barth in his seminal essay of the same name. Perhaps in reaction to the first global wars, the increasing rejection of meta-narratives and the significant time-space compression of late capitalism, the very idea of a controlling artist was condemned by Barth as 'politically reactionary, authoritarian, even fascist'.[35] The condition was diagnosed in fiction too. 'Everything there was to know about life was in *The Brothers Karamazov*, by Feodor Dostoevsky', Kurt Vonnegut wrote in *Slaughterhouse-Five*, 'But that isn't enough any more.'[36]

In terms of literary form, linguistic fragmentation became prominent. Central to the anti-realist's agenda was a Saussurean understanding of linguistics combined with the idea that literature had exhausted the conventions of realism. As a result Tom LeClair and Larry McCaffery grant the terms 'visible' and 'invisible' to describe the opposing sides. In their estimation the 'visible' anti-realists deliberately drew attention to their techniques and moved away from what Barth described as the exhausted conventions of 'invisible' realism. Such linguistic opacity was seen to be as much a break with, as a deliberate attack on, the foundational principles of realism. Although, of course, as much as Carver and his realist contemporaries resist their categorisation into a literary subset, so those who wrote anti-realist fiction struggled against any attempt to be coined a homogenous movement.[37] And yet, despite their distinctiveness there is enough similarity to build a binding nexus, which, to come back to the opening point, is that they challenge the psychological realism of orthodox literature.

Considering all of this, what is therefore quite remarkable is that, despite coming of age in this period, Carver fervently resists the aesthetic autonomy of the anti-realist paradigm, and attempts to write fiction that is decidedly realist. As he explains in 'On Writing':

> I overheard the writer Geoffrey Wolff say 'No cheap tricks' to a group of writing students. That should go on a three-by-five card. I'd amend it a little to 'No tricks.' Period. I hate tricks ... Writers don't need tricks or

gimmicks or even necessarily to be the smartest fellows on the block. At the risk of appearing foolish, a writer sometimes needs to be able to just stand and gape at this or that thing – a sunset or an old shoe – in absolute and simple amazement.[38]

As a response to the experimental ideology posited by anti-realists such as Barth, Carver's proposition offers a limited attempt at re-establishing the principles of realism he believed in. Its rhetoric – which he truncates, thus cementing his minimalist mythology – admits no qualification, and might equally refer to the literary style of the anti-realists as it does to the conventions of genre fiction. Likewise, when the essay is set within the context of the editorial process of *What We Talk About When We Talk About Love* (which only predates it by a matter of months) Carver's fundamentalist stance emits, as Sklenicka argues, a strong sense of ambiguity.[39] We might highlight further flaws in Carver's manifesto. Not only does his rhetoric present a weak and inconsistent defence, but it also fails to answer Barth's dismay at what he calls 'technically old-fashioned' writers, that is, novelists and writers grounded in the socio-historical context of the twentieth century and yet who deny – from Barth's point of view – the existence of 'the great writers of the last sixty years'.[40] And while Barth is markedly unspecific about who it is who is writing in this style (a denial that masks any attempt to fully engage with the debate it seems) Carver certainly fits his mould.

Carver, however, did not simply 'happen' upon a realist aesthetic. His opposition to anti-realist experimentation is anchored in the ideology of the man he called his first mentor, John Gardner. Gardner's militant stance and his instruction of Carver at a young age were instrumental in guiding Carver towards the realist mode. There is also an extraordinary correspondence between Carver's development as a young writer under Gardner and McInerney's maturation under Carver. In this regard it is notable that much of the instruction that Carver imparts to McInerney is sourced from Gardner's philosophy.[41]

As I noted in Chapter 1, Carver met Gardner in September 1959 when he moved to California to begin his first degree at Chico State University. In 'John Gardner: The Writer as Teacher' Carver recalls that he saw Gardner behind the registration desk in the woman's gym when he signed up for an elective creative writing class. At the time Gardner held the mythical mantle of being what Carver calls a 'real writer' and, having moved halfway across the country from Oberlin College, Ohio, his reputation radiated the enigma worthy of what the young Carver thought a writer ought to be.[42] In the opening of his essay, Carver writes that in those early years he wanted to write articles for '*Sports Afield, True, Argosy* and *Rogue* (some of the magazines I was then reading)', reflecting a debonair ideal – sourced most obviously from Hemingway – that the writer is at once commander of nature and seducer of women.[43] It is with some disappointment then, that Gardner, a 'real writer' – in a similar way to Carver's initial impact on McInerney – soon shattered the young Carver's rakish vision of a writer's life. Recalling his initial impression with some dissatisfaction he wrote, 'Gardner had a crewcut, dressed like a minister or an FBI man, and went to church on Sundays.'[44] As I've already alluded, in his essay 'Fires', Carver recalls that at the time he 'understood writers to be people who didn't spend their Saturdays at the Laundromat and every waking hour subject to the needs and caprices of their children'.[45] But Gardner undermined Carver's ideas and projected an image of ceaseless hard work and social responsibility as the route to literary success – an ideal, as we have already seen, that became synonymous with Carver later in life, and which he imparted to McInerney, and yet, also an ideal that Carver failed to adopt for the first part of his life. In her account, Sklenicka describes Gardner as 'indefatigable' having undertaken a translation of *Sir Gawain and the Green Knight* at the same time as planning a biography on Chaucer while also working on several novel manuscripts. Despite the model that Gardner, who was only five years older than Carver, provided, it was not until nearly twenty years after their time together, after his recovery from alcoholism, that Carver could look back with the required pragmatism and recognise that his life changed when he met Gardner at Chico State in 1959. Significantly it was Gardner's loan of his office key at weekends that Carver describes as, 'a turning point in my life', providing the typewriter, desk and isolation that he needed to make his 'first serious attempts at being a writer'.[46]

Gardner's pedagogic style was known for being abrasive and direct. His classes were often dominated by his strict opinions on the nature of what he thought good fiction was. At the start of the academic year he took his students outside, sat them down and, as Carver remembers, told them that not one of them had the necessary fire to become published writers. If these theatrics were meant to scare, they had the opposite effect on Carver who associated writing with a high calling, 'a thing to be taken very, very seriously'.[47] Much of the fundamentalism that Gardner taught at Chico State was published later in his life.[48] His most significant publication in this regard, *On Moral Fiction*, first published in 1978, is a polemic that opposes Barth's 'Literature of Exhaustion' and other anti-realists who Gardner viewed as producing superficial literature.[49] The opening of the book outlines his basic argument:

> In a world where nearly everything that passes for art is tinny and commercial and often, in addition, hollow and academic, I argue – by reason and by banging the table – for an old-fashioned view of what art is and does ... My basic message throughout this book is as old as the hills, drawn from Homer, Plato, Aristotle, Dante, and the rest, and standard in Western civilization down through the eighteenth century; one would think all critics and artists should be thoroughly familiar with it, and perhaps many are. But my experience is that in university lecture halls, or in kitchens at midnight, after parties, the traditional view of art strikes most people as strange news.[50]

Gardner's traditional view is summed up in this way, 'true art is moral: it seeks to improve life, not debase it', and is anchored in the foundationalist principles of the nineteenth-century realists, especially Tolstoy, whose small polemic *What Is Art?* is Gardner's precursor text.[51] Remarkably, however, despite spending two hundred pages denouncing 'false' art – which is interchangeable in Gardner's mind with 'immoral' art – Gardner carefully skirts any authoritative definitions – he does not pin morality to a religious origin or societal consensus – and only claims that its value comes from its ability to 'inspire and incite human beings toward virtue'.[52]

Gardner then moves on to develop his argument into a defence of realism against postmodern literary experimentation. While he admits to there being a certain kind of aesthetic beauty in experimental fiction, he argues that its emphasis on language results in a new kind of impenetrable literature. The problem with such a technique for Gardner is that it shifts the writer's priority from the orthodox realist notion that literature should be made up of a 'sequence of dramatized events tending toward understanding and assertion' to what is now best understood as a Derridean – or decentred – understanding that nothing exists outside of the text.[53] For Gardner, this new position is undermined by its inability to present a critical social or moral statement:

> Fiction as pure language (texture over structure) is *in*. It is one common manifestation of what is being called 'post-modernism'. At bottom the mistake is a matter of morality, at least in the sense that it shows, on the writer's part, a lack of concern. To people who care about events and ideas and thus, necessarily, about the clear and efficient statement of both, linguistic opacity suggests indifference to the needs and wishes of the reader and to whatever ideas may be buried under all that brush.[54]

But underlying this broader critique is a more personal aspect, for Gardner continues to argue that:

> One reason we read fiction is our hope that we will be moved by it, finding characters we can enjoy and sympathize with, an academic striving for opacity suggests, if not misanthropy, a perversity or shallowness that no reader would tolerate ... Where language is of primary concern to the writer, communication is necessarily secondary.[55]

Read with the benefit of almost half-a-century's worth of hindsight, Gardner's ideas in *On Moral Fiction* may come across to contemporary readers as rather antiquated, but the fact remains that the principles that underpin them filtered through to Gardner's classroom. The assignment for Carver in Gardner's class was to produce one story at the end of the semester. The 'kicker', as Carver described it, was the story would have to be 'revised ten times in the course of the semester for Gardner to be satisfied'.[56] This led to a series of personal conferences between Gardner and Carver, in which Gardner would go over Carver's manuscripts in painstaking detail. 'Before our conference he would have marked up my story', Carver wrote in his tribute to Gardner, 'crossing out unacceptable sentences, phrases, individual words, even some of the punctuation.' He adds, 'In other cases he would bracket sentences, phrases, or individual words ... We'd discuss commas in my story as if nothing else in the world mattered more at that moment.'[57] In these conferences Gardner placed a special importance on prosaic specificity. 'He helped me to see how important it was to say exactly what I wanted to say and nothing else', Carver writes in 'Fires'. 'The word "ground" and the word "earth," for instance. Ground is ground, he'd say. It means ground, dirt, that kind of stuff. But if you say "earth," that's something else, that word has other ramifications. He made me see that absolutely everything was important in a short story', Carver explained.[58]

The aim of Gardner's assignments and his meetings with Carver was to instil in him the idea that it was through the rewriting process and gradual revision that the story reached its most effective form. 'What the writer understands', Gardner argues in *On Moral Fiction*, 'is that the writer discovers, works out, and tests his ideas in the process of writing.'[59] At the time, Carver admits that this idea struck him with the 'force of revelation'. 'From the very beginning I loved the rewriting process as much as the initial execution', he told Larry McCaffery and Sinda Gregory in 1984:

> There I was, groping to find my own way, and here someone was telling me something that somehow conjoined with what I already wanted to do. It was the most natural thing in the world for me to go back and refine what was happening on the page.[60]

These ideas of revision, which seem to be closely related to notions of craftsmanship, or doing things well for their own sake – even, possibly, to reiterate Sennett's argument in my introduction, to focus 'on objective standards, on the thing in itself' – proved highly informative for Carver's own writing method and process. He concludes the matter in his reminiscence, 'A writer's values and craft. This is what the man taught and what he stood for, and this what I've kept by me in the years since that brief but all-important time.'[61]

These ideas also, significantly, were helpful later in life when he was teaching writing classes himself. When asked about his teaching methods, he told an interviewer, 'The real model I had, of course, was John Gardner.'[62] And while McInerney reports that Carver favoured listening to lecturing, when the opportunity arose Carver would emphasise the importance of word-economy and Gardner's idea of 'honesty in writing', often, McInerney emphasises, 'hammering away at that point'.[63] When it was possible, Carver would also arrange personal conferences much like Gardner. McInerney recounts that many students received much of the same kind of treatment his manuscripts received from Gardner:

> Fortunate students had their stories subjected to the same process he employed on his own numerous drafts. Manuscripts came back thoroughly ventilated with Carver deletions, substitutions, question marks, and chicken-scratch queries. I took one story back to him seven times; he must have spent fifteen or twenty hours on it. He was a meticulous, obsessive line editor. One on one, in his office, he almost became a tough guy, his voice gradually swelling with conviction.[64]

In what can be interpreted as either a symbolic duplication or a convenient reaffirmation, it was during one of McInerney's own personal conferences that Carver took the time to debate with him the same point as Gardner, 'Once we spent some ten or fifteen minutes debating my use of the word "earth." Carver felt it had to be "ground," and he felt it was worth the trouble of talking it through.' Like Carver's comment on Gardner, McInerney writes, 'That one exchange was invaluable; I think of it constantly when I'm working.'[65]

Given this history, it would be reasonable to expect to find in McInerney's early writing – the fiction he produced while he was still under the mentorship of Carver at Syracuse – a similar defence of realism, or even, perhaps, an extension of a conservative aesthetic that attempts to communicate some kind of Gardneresque morality. And yet, counter-intuitively, his early work became a flagship for the kind of surface and ephemerality – the 'tinny and commercial' as Gardner might put it – associated with late capitalism. His first novel, *Bright Lights, Big City*, was dubbed by *Playboy* as the 'Catcher in the Rye for the MBA set' – a comment, interestingly enough, that became a stamp of cultural approval and was subsequently printed on the inside cover of the book – and was part of a new wave of urban texts written by authors like Bret Easton Ellis, David Leavitt and Tama Janowitz.[66] This melange of twenty-somethings were soon dubbed the Literary Brat Pack – who, to adopt the tagline from David Blum, were what people wanted to see, be and read.[67] The culmination of this movement was a sensationalist, transgressive fiction: Ellis's *American Psycho*, which only appeared to confirm the groups' adherence to the grotesque void of consumerism and superficiality.

McInerney's first three novels, all published within Carver's lifetime, detailed young, peripatetic protagonists indulging in a pervasive commodity culture. Caught in the perpetual consumption of alcohol, drugs and sex, his protagonists blamed their behavioural misconduct on broken relationships and took little responsibility for their actions. His novels were epitomised by slick dialogue inflected with young urban vernacular and Valley Girl vocal nuances, branded goods were ubiquitous and characters were constantly orientated to built environments. It is perhaps understandable, then, that at the time many critics read McInerney's early work as a mere surface reflection of the excess and hedonism of New York neoliberal culture, rather than a satirical critique in line with the principles of orthodox realism.

Typical of these critics was Josephine Hendin, who called *Bright Lights, Big City* the 'first Yuppie bestseller' that was merely 'the compression of the novel of manners into an equivalent of upscale ads'. She argued that the novel confuses surface with substance, that 'the title is supreme', citing the protagonist who claims to know the high points of the English language, even knows the titles of the best works – *Anna Karenina*, *As I Lay Dying*, *Being and Time* – but has kept himself innocent of their content. In this way, Hendin presents McInerney as a key participant in postmodern culture. His art is, 'a fiction not of insurgency but of cultural collaboration'. What stands out, she observed, 'is an assimilation, to the point of wholesale adoption, of advertising culture'. Elaborating further, she offers the following provocative analysis:

> Labels, name brands, surface signs have become the sole social referents and methods of character definition. McInerney's characterization of a man of literary sensibility is effected not through a representation of consciousness but by the ownership of unread books, contempt for the underyuppie class, and the ability to give such imaginative names to cocaine as 'Bolivian Marching Powder'. What motivates the Nostril-hero is obscure; he has too little feeling for the gradual and now final withdrawal of his wife, a fashion model and perfect label-wearer. In a belated effort at explaining what drives his hero, when the book is nearly over, McInerney, introduces his mother who, near death, wishes she could have lived the way he does. Not even a dying mother runs deep.[68]

We might view Hendin's analysis – which operates, if not explicitly then implicitly, as a wider critique of neoliberal culture – as echoing Jameson's critique of 'Warhol's Diamond Dust Shoes' in *Postmodernism*, which he argues, 'turn centrally around commodification', and, do not, 'really speak'. We might push further and argue, in the words of Jameson, that McInerney's novels, 'ought to be powerful and critical political statements. If they are not that, then one would surely want to know why, and one would want to begin to wonder a little more seriously about the possibilities of political or critical art in the postmodern period of late capital.'[69] For if *Bright Lights, Big City* does not move beyond surface representation it suggests only two clear perspectives: an aspirational model for young urban professionals, or a sympathetic portrait of the dangers of youthful excess.

The issue is complicated by the fact that in much the same way as the media conflated Carver's fiction and his historical and biographical background, the same media merged the actions of the novel's protagonist with McInerney himself. If part of Carver's appeal was his authentic working-class background, then the same kind of idea about authorial authenticity is true for McInerney. Even very early reviewers made this connection. On two separate occasions in *The New York Times Book Review*, two different writers summarised the novel in this way, 'A daring fellow, this narrator, who we suspect is Mr. McInerney's himself or a close facsimile', and later, 'A young man who sure sounds like the author is hired – and fired – by a magazine that sure sounds like *The New Yorker*.'[70] These ideas were cemented by regular *People* magazine columns detailing McInerney's social life, *Newsweek* declaring 1984 as the 'Year of the Yuppie' and a review of publishing in 1984 by George Garrett that argued that in order to understand the publishing scene one must read, 'a cornucopia of slick-coated-paper magazines', which offer, 'news of the publishing world in a contextual reality of expensive cars and wristwatches, of lingerie and perfume advertisements'.[71]

Issues surrounding the commodification of literature provide a persistent problem for any literary interpretation of *Bright Lights, Big City*. Nonetheless if there is to be a defence from McInerney's perspective against Hendin's accusation of 'cultural collaboration', it is important that McInerney provide critical distance between his actions and those of his protagonist. It is significant then (and perhaps indicative of the novel's aim), that McInerney not only anticipates this perspective but also attempts to defend his intentions in writing the novel. 'Readers tend to confuse author and protagonist', he said in one interview, 'the alluring vision with its unqualified endorsement.' 'I've heard myself described as a Yuppie hero', he continued, 'I thought I was writing a book about someone coming to terms with failure.'[72] His denial would help settle the matter if it were not for one problem: his instant and unassailable rise among critics, socialites and bankers in the cultural urban sprawl epitomised the very culture he was trying to critique. This blurring of boundaries extends to the novel. The protagonist's humorous remarks, for instance, obfuscate the distinction between repulsion and attraction – a symptom, perhaps, of McInerney's own hedonistic lifestyle. Moreover, the predicate for the protagonist's behaviour – the avoidance of all collective social responsibility – is weak. It is 'only a matter of conducting an experiment in limits', he argues, and despite the apparent profundity of such Solomonic wisdom, it ultimately offers an unsatisfactory riposte for his familial failure (the avoidance of his brother and father), his occupational failure (fired from the magazine), his societal failure (soliciting drugs from a teenager) and his relational failures (negligence of his marriage and friendships).[73]

And yet despite this there are indications that McInerney was attempting, at least on some level, to do more than provide superficial entertainment. The second person perspective, for example, implies that the protagonist's problems extend to a collective or suggest a social, psychological group, and draws in any reader who recognises even a shade of shared experience. 'We have all been victimized just like the "hero"', David Kaufman exclaims, who notices, in a more affirmative critique, that the novel is, 'about the person it addresses, about the "you" who is both the reader and the narrator'.[74] In this sense, *Bright Lights, Big City* performs a kind of allegorical surgery, represented in the opening scene as the protagonist talks to the girl with a tattooed scar on her scalp. It is a startling image that elicits this foreshadowing response, 'I could use one of those over my heart', which in turn exposes the superficiality of the urban culture, her response, 'You want I can give you the name of the guy that did it.'[75]

The final chapter of this short novel goes some way to restore hope for the protagonist and his situation. Finally beginning to accept and digest both the loss of his mother and his wife, the protagonist makes his way to another party with the last of his money. The night then takes a sharp turn when his estranged wife appears, but the inevitable confrontation is anti-climatic. Shirking, for the first time, thoughts of Amanda and distancing himself from the influence of his friend Tad Allagash, he seeks out a phone and calls Vicky, a woman he has recently met (a philosophy major from Princeton) and who appears to represent a return to a state of innocence or, at least, a chance at second-life reformation. Confessing his past transgressions (and also notably telling her about the death of his mother), the protagonist leaves the party and begins to walk home. At this point the religious imagery is heightened. It is Sunday morning. Redemption is prefigured, 'After a few minutes you notice the blood on your fingers. You hold your hand up to your face. There is blood on your shirt, too' (p. 180).[76] Nearby, a homeless man offers a benediction, 'God bless you and forgive your sins' – a phrase that is amplified because the protagonist observes that it is not followed by a request for money.[77] Then, noticing a bakery up ahead he is reminded of his hunger – a physical need as much as spiritual – he has not eaten since Friday night. He trades his sunglasses – a symbol of blindness – for the bread. The novel ends with the protagonist in a position of petition, 'You get down on your knees and tear open the bag. The smell of warm dough envelops you. The first bite sticks in your throat and you almost gag. You will have to go slowly. You will have to learn everything all over again.'[78]

Girard argues that McInerney's communion ending probably has as much to do with Carver as it does with any explicit Christian experience. Carver's story 'A Small, Good Thing' – first published in a truncated form as 'The Bath' in *What We Talk About When We Talk About Love*, before its restoration in *Cathedral* – closes, for instance, on similar imagery.[79] In Carver's story the parents of the boy hit by a car on his birthday are harassed by a baker for not picking up their cake. When the trio eventually meet in the early hours of the morning the baker's repentance and the parents' forgiveness is confirmed over 'warm cinnamon rolls just out of the oven', and later, a heavy, rich bread that tastes of 'molasses and coarse grains'. Carver closes the story in an affirmative tone that suggests that the reconciliation prefigures hope for the parents' situation, 'They talked on into the early morning, the high, pale cast of light in the windows, and they did not think of leaving.'[80]

While it's worth noting these similarities, a more stimulating nexus exists around the stylistic and formal approaches of both writers. David Kaufmann, in his short comparison of the two, argues that the connection is not content but style, claiming that 'Carver and McInerney share a commitment to resolute parataxis.'[81] The emergence of paratactic fiction, which Kaufmann defines as a 'disjunctive style marked by its avoidance of grammatical subordination' is entwined, he argues, with the socio-historical context of the US in the 1980s. Leaning on a lecture by Habermas titled 'The Crisis of the Welfare State and the Exhaustion of Utopian Energies', and his terms 'system' and 'lifeworld', Kaufmann argues that economic crises in society cause broader crisis tendencies in non-economic forms, so that the changes to US capitalism in the 1970s and 80s (the move from embedded liberalism to neoliberalism and the associated trends in labour and socio-economic mobility in particular) has an important impact on the organisations of everyday life:

> Most tellingly, it has deformed the structures of representation through which we depict our lives to ourselves by undermining the very institutions of solidarity through which individual and collective identities are

interpellated and asserted. As the constellations on which the welfare compromise was based disintegrate, so the horizon of hope – that is, the collective and universalizable orientation toward an improved future we call utopia – has been undercut, if not destroyed. [82]

Kaufmann argues that the disintegration of the 'horizon of hope', and the acceptance of neoliberal common sense, leads to a new structure of feeling embodied by the paratactic fiction that was produced by both Carver and McInerney (and other writers such as Ellis, Leavitt, Janowitz and Bobbie Ann Mason). Through an analysis of Carver's language in his stories 'Fat', 'Gazebo' and 'Why Don't You Dance?' he argues that the paratactic sentence structure is not 'a stylistic quirk but is rather integral to the construction of the story: the inability to subordinate, to organise material in anything other than chronological order, gets folded back into a larger inability to conceptualise and articulate'. Kaufmann sees a similar trait in McInerney's use of the 'present tense and his wittily disjunctive prose [which] are meant to signal both a hidden trauma and the means by which that trauma is overcome'.[83] In an era, as Kaufmann writes, 'marked by the growth of service labour and deskilling, work no longer serves as the key category for sociological self-definition'. In this sense, therefore, it seems significant that he identifies the rise of parataxis, because it is a style which ultimately 'signals both the loss of complexes of meaning as well as ways of dealing with that loss'.[84] In other words, the rise of paratactic fiction suggests a retreat, a form of consolation, a way of dealing with the bewildering world of neoliberal capitalism.

While the link between McInerney's early work and Carver's short fiction might be aligned to a similarity in style or imagery, this model appears somewhat unfulfilling in light of the fiction that McInerney published after the 1980s. In fact, *Brightness Falls*, his fourth novel, published in 1992, moves beyond any kind of Carveresque form. The novel's tone, style and length appear to mark a significant break from McInerney's early work; and his lengthy cultural summaries, in particular, develop what Kaufmann perceived as his early paratactic inarticulacy into a prescient commentary on the socio-economic and cultural situation that McInerney saw around him in New York City neoliberal era:

After years of inflation someone had noticed that the equity of corporate America, as reflected in stock prices, was undervalued. A new, pro-business president said it was morning in America, inflation subsided, and smart shoppers began to wake up and call their brokers. The financial-services industry grew like an oil town in full boom. And if buying stocks on margin in a rising market could double your rate of return, buying companies outright with borrowed money and reselling the parts seemed to be the fastest way anybody had ever thought of to get fabulously rich. Interest payments were tax-deductible, so it was just dumb not to borrow as much as possible and buy everything in sight. Debt was good, equity boring.[85]

One need only consider the development of neoliberal financialisation in New York City in the 1980s to see how insightful McInerney's description is. The banks' victory over the government in the 1975 budgetary crisis and their increasing ability to bypass or find loopholes in the Glass-Steagall Act conjoined with the relatively recent liberalisation of international financial markets and recycled petrodollars from the OPEC oil crisis to create an environment of increasing legislative autonomy and free-flowing capital. The focus on financialisation was, of course, just one trait of neoliberalism's need to constantly accumulate capital, and a reflection of its unerring ability to seek and adapt to new markets. (This often occurs on a macro-scale, as in the restructuring of, say, a country's state apparatus after IMF debt intervention, but it can happen also on a micro-scale, as in the more recent targeted advertising which takes up increasing space on social media feeds.) What ought to be emphasised, however, is that this neoliberal dispossession reaches all aspects of life in neoliberal society, so that it reaches the area of artistic and cultural production as well. In the 1980s, in particular it seems, at the dawn of neoliberalism, there was a strong wave of mergers and acquisitions between publishers. Albert Greco, in his history of publishing, writes that 'Between 1984 and 1988, there were 151 mergers, almost as many as in the entire 1960s.' He goes on, 'A small number of firms in the 1980s carefully crafted media empires that were positioned to withstand the ravages of recession and political unrest and capture global business opportunities.' This analysis is unsurprising given neoliberalism's free market competition and its tendency to redistribute wealth unevenly. What McInerney's novel picks up on is the proliferation of this trend in the mid-1980s, but for McInerney, the superficiality of cultural production as a means to capital accumulation as an end in itself is played off against the broader atmosphere of literary realism and literary experimentalism in which he learnt to write, where the latter is viewed as being coterminous with surface capitalism.

In order to fully understand how McInerney develops these ideas in the novel it is worth pausing briefly to quickly assess the fictional history of Russell and Corrine Calloway, the two principle characters in *Brightness Falls*. The creation of the Calloways – McInerney's perennial couple – denotes a notable shift away from McInerney's early trilogy. Their emergence in 'Smoke', a story published in *Atlantic Monthly* in 1986, preceded their fuller exposition in *Brightness Falls*. Its sequel, *The Good Life*, was published in 2006 and situated Russell and Corrine amongst the aftermath of September 11, before they resurfaced more recently in 2009 in another story called 'The March'. They made what appears to be their final appearance in 2016 in McInerney's latest novel, *Bright, Precious Days*.

Their fictional debut, under the guise of the Callahans in the story 'Smoke', predominantly concerns their fledging marriage as they attempt to negotiate the strains and complexities of New York City life. Framed within this context is the retelling of their time at college, in which their first encounter was signified by an inexhaustibly long conversation where they 'talked about everything', Russell unable to 'stop thinking about her mouth, her lips on a cigarette', before the words stopped only to be replaced by 'a crisis of lips and tongues' – a suitable metaphor for a relationship marked by a failure to understand and embody a Carveresque idea of linguistic accuracy.[86] Once an aspiring poet, Russell, constrained by the financial burden of the city, has taken an editorial job with a publisher. Presiding over a 'series of travel books composed of plagiarism and speculation in equal parts', his move to publishing symbolises, in the narrator's mind at least, the beginning of a descent from the 'Byronic tradition' to literary bureaucrat. His current work is now only a formulaic production in which 'adjectives became severely dog-eared', which leaves him feeling 'queasy and unclean'.[87] His wife, Corrine, a recent convert to investment banking, tempers Russell's cynicism:

> Certain dates and names were fraught with unlikely significance for her, and, much more than Russell, the class poet, she believed in the power of words. When, after a week, Russell asked her to marry him, she made him solemnly promise never to use the word divorce, even in jest.[88]

The characterisation of the Calloways in 'Smoke' indicates that McInerney is using them to embody something of the opposition between those like Gardner and Carver – who viewed the writers' task as having some kind of orthodox moral obligation tied to the inherent power of language – and postmodernists like Barth and Gass who emphasised experimentation and a more decentred linguistics. McInerney reveals something of his belief when he opens his reminiscence by describing Carver's voice:

> As I say, he mumbled, and if it once seemed merely a physical tic, akin to cracking knuckles or the drumming of a foot, I now think it was a function of a deep humility and a respect for language bordering on awe, a reflection of his sense that words should be handled very, very gingerly. As if it might be almost impossible to say what you wanted to say. As if it might be dangerous, even.[89]

It seems only natural therefore that when Russell and Corrine try to quit smoking – ostensibly the primary theme in the story – Corrine is keen that they work on their communicative network, surmising that talking about it would make it easier to quit and making Russell agree that they call each other 'whenever they are feeling weak'.[90] However, under pressure at work and fortifying their stress with a string of social commitments, Russell and Corrine separately succumb to their cravings. Gradually the couple's schedule moves out of sync. Corrine finds solace in her long hours and an attentive colleague and Russell in parties and alcohol. The blurred boundaries between the temptation to smoke and the temptation of infidelity are rife in the story and it is Russell and Corrine's inability to articulate these problems that proves their downfall. Such reticence, both when Russell fantasises of an affair with an ex-girlfriend and when Corrine dreams of smoking, ignites a downward spiral that leads to real – rather than imagined – infidelity. Despite Corrine's confession at the end of the story that she has smoked, it is Russell's eventual unfaithfulness at a party that make him the greater sinner. His lack of integrity with words, both written and spoken, are clearly analogous with the dishonesty of his actions and his relationships; his inability to confess to Corrine, symbolically recalls that, of course, there is no smoke without fire.

Clearly, then, there are parallels between McInerney's view of Carver and Carver's own view of Gardner – that words have the capacity to 'improve life' and 'inspire and incite human beings toward virtue'.[91] Carver famously wrote in 'On Writing' that 'At the first sign of a trick or a gimmick in a piece of fiction, a cheap trick or even an elaborate trick, I tend to look for cover.'[92] He continued, with particular reference to John Barth, 'Too often "experimentation" is a license to be careless, silly or imitative in the writing.' And as if to cement his idea in Gardner's 'moral fiction' he concluded, 'Even worse, [it is] a license to try to brutalize or alienate the reader. Too often such writing gives us no news of the world.'[93] While the veracity of Carver's argument is, as I have already indicated, debatable, and while it is not my intention to analyse it in detail right now, it is worth noting that, for better or worse, McInerney appears to have taken on the ideas proposed by Carver about this opposition and used them as the basis for his characterisation of the Calloways in *Brightness Falls*.

In order to understand, then, how this idea plays out in *Brightness Falls* it is helpful to begin by analysing Victor Propp, a novelist that Russell edits. Propp, who begins as an ostensibly minor character, soon becomes the hub on which the novel's plot turns when he suggests, in a move that will propel both men's careers, that Russell should attempt to leverage financial control of Corbin, Dern, Russell's employer. The attempted buyout in turn marks the beginning of a concomitant decline in Russell's employment, his marriage and his literary standing as one of New York's rising editors, until eventually – and perhaps inevitably – all three collapse at once with the rest of the financial market in the 1987 crash. Propp, a synecdoche for the anti-realist novelist of the 1970s and 80s, and therefore presented by McInerney as the antithesis of Carveresque realism, is satirised throughout the novel. Suitably enough Propp claims he was 'spawned' in Boise, Idaho, a 'product' of a Swedish mother and a Russian father.[94] In his own mind he had never been 'particularly American', and only began to find his place when he 'discovered Europe in the comp lit department' at Yale when he was sixteen.[95] It is because of this that he came to view himself as 'outside the culture, critical and aloof, quarantined at an Ellis Island of the spirit with the disease of his art'.[96] Thus Propp's self-diagnosis – that his identity is in the texts of the comparative literature department at Yale – exposes the fault line between foundational realist principles and decentred worldview of post-structural experimentalism. McInerney elaborates:

> A hundred years after Henry James had fled the raw continent, Victor mused, the consciousness of his native land remained barely half forged. Americans were still radical materialists. More innocent than Kalahari bushmen, who were adepts at reading signs and symbols, Americans took everything at face value – words, signs, rhetoric, faces – as if reality itself were so much legal tender. For Victor it was a treacherous text composed by a necromancer, diabolically resistant to analysis. Even the phrase 'face value' suggested to a mind like Victor Propp's a labyrinth of interpretation, of masks and falsity and deceit, divergences of appearance and reality, rancorous divorces between signifier and signified, the apparent solidity of the words collapsing underfoot, feathering out and deliquescing into Derridean twilight, surfaces giving way suddenly.[97]

Seen within the context of the whole novel McInerney's analysis is deeply ironic. And while McInerney shows awareness of the risks of unmediated realism – an American consciousness 'barely half forged' – the stronger critique appears to be of Propp's decentred worldview; an author who has taken Derrida's famous maxim that there is nothing outside of the text to its logical conclusion.[98] Thus, in what is meant to be an ironic comment, for Propp, even the phrase 'face value' emits a plethora of disjunctive, slippery definitions. In the novel, and, it seems, in McInerney's mind, this post-structural ideal, where everything is a 'treacherous text' firmly 'resistant to analysis', opposes Carveresque realism, which purports that the ability to craft one true sentence presents, on some level, a valuable engagement with reality. This idea is reinforced later in the novel when one fictional commentator describes Propp's prose as, 'Henry James with bowel movements'.[99]

Propp's hypothetical masterpiece, then, becomes a metaphor for what McInerney sees as superficial literature. The unfinished novel appears to be a deliberate attempt by Propp to maintain a high level of literary stature while the fame of his contemporaries diminishes according, McInerney is quick to point out, 'to conventional market principles as they predictably published fifth, sixth and seventh novels'.[100] Still, fragments of Propp's novel are intermittently published in literary journals in order to continue the facade. One of the most famous passages, McInerney explains is, 'the heroic monologue of the embryonic protagonist recounting the tides, rhythms and developmental struggles of the amniotic world as he delivered himself from the womb by sheer force of will'.[101] If the description of Propp's fiction is laughable it is because there is a strong element of reality in his landscapes, for the extreme caricature would seem implausible if it were not for Harold Brodkey, a Propp-like figure, whose semi-mythical novel, *A Party of Animals*, was also in production for decades, and also reportedly increased in value year-on-year. And yet McInerney is doing more than merely caricaturing, for he is attempting to present a pertinent critique. Russell, who has a history of adhering to the 'Byronic tradition', begins to be taken in by Propp's ideology, and puts immutable faith in the unfinished novel, which, consistent with his obfuscatory character and typical Pascalian nature, and despite its deadline receding 'gradually into a semi-mythical future', he considers, 'worth the wager of belief'.[102]

Later, Russell puts his faith into action and agrees to arrange a publicity reading at the Y for Propp, but when Jeff Pierce, a younger novelist that Russell edits, fails to show up to give the introduction, Propp becomes furious and leaves. Thus Propp and his novel remain suitably inconspicuous and cause a minor media storm. 'Propp's dusty, enigmatic legend grew immeasurably', McInerney writes, 'burnished with a shiny coat of scandal.' The resulting rumours inevitably became, 'much more interesting than any possible response to an actual reading'.[103] McInerney takes pains to invent an elaborate quote from a 'downtown weekly', which calls Propp the, 'quark and the black hole of contemporary American literature, a nearly theoretical entity whose size and shape and importance can be deduced only partly from visible manifestations', before the fictional review seals the synopsis of Propp's ambition:

> Derrida having made the author obsolete in favour of an endless scrim of écriture and intertexuality, Propp apparently means to erase even the text with his long silences, punctuated by glimpses of dazzling prose – the silence assuming legendary proportions, the long-unfulfilled promise of the novel, which we register in pieces, like glimpses of flesh beneath a hem, this deferred gratification perhaps the very point of the enterprise.[104]

Thus Propp's novel becomes the extreme parody of art in the postmodern or neoliberal era. It is a novel which, to coin Jameson's earlier critique 'does not really speak to us at all'.[105] Propp's novel speaks even less, considering its non-existence. This kind of world offers little problem for someone like Propp who lives 'as if in a maze of conspiracy', a world where he cannot trust 'the evidence of his senses', and is unable to 'take reality for granted'.[106] But for McInerney – who holds to Carveresque realism – Propp's disdain is an affront, a pernicious attack even, on its foundations. In this sense, the constant satirising and elaborate parodying by McInerney appears to be a defensive manoeuvre – perhaps even a retreat in the face of an incomprehensible postmodern experimentation towards a more orthodox form of writing. In any case, McInerney is clearly implying that he holds faith in the values that Propp opposes, and in doing so demonstrates an acute consciousness of what he deems to be the forces ranged against Carveresque values, but ultimately, he fundamentally proposes that these values are still the best way to understand reality.

It is highly significant therefore, that Russell's belief in Propp's artificial reality – a world which is inextricably linked to the unsteady foundation of the financial markets – leads to his downfall. Appropriately enough the events that propel the plot towards their inevitable end are ignited by Propp. Attending one of their monthly lunch meetings with the preconceived idea that 'Russell might just accomplish something noteworthy or even spectacular, particularly if given a push', Propp proposes that Russell mount a financial coup at Corbin, Dern.[107] In what becomes a rather self-serving conversation, Propp, who seems to know Russell's job prospects, solicits his feeling of presentiment:

> 'Everybody's getting rich, Russell', Victor confided, leaning forward and engaging him with that toilet-plunger gaze, which was unsettling and flattering in equal measure. 'Every remotely sentient being except for you and me. If you were in any other business right now, you'd be making twice, ten times what you do now.'[108]

In a scene that recalls the mythic appeal of urban excess, Propp proposes, 'Do you remember what Nick Carraway said as he was driving into Manhattan?' – a question as much rhetorical as it is meant to conjure romantic notions of the lost American dream – 'Anything can happen now that we've slid over this bridge ... anything at all.'[109] Russell is almost convinced, but in one last appeal to the vestige of reality he counters with his inability to raise capital. 'That doesn't matter', Propp's responds, 'All you need is ambition, imagination and leverage', before concluding his pitch, 'Credit, Russell, the philosopher's stone of our era. You can turn the lead of wage slavery into golden destiny – if you have the courage.'[110] Propp's mischief should be viewed as the ignition for Russell's ambitions – although not the source, for McInerney explains that 'the idea was not so wild or remote that it had not occurred to Russell' – ambitions which appeal more to the 'artifice' of Propp's decentred world than any foundation of 'reality'.[111]

It is in this way that McInerney symbolically aligns his novel with a critique of the neoliberal financialisation.[112] It is Russell's hostile takeover of his employer, Corbin, Dern, that simultaneously exposes the unethical foundations of the financial sector and the superficiality of literary culture. Firstly, not only has Russell symbolically moved from an idealised view of literature to the world of administrative publishing, but he is now about to attempt to leverage financial control of an artistic institution by taking advantage of a corrupt financial system. Supposedly more concerned with 'Literature and socially conscious publishing', the chance of a quick profit is too great a temptation for Russell to resist.[113] During the negotiations he brokers a 10 per cent cut of equity based on sales targets and buys $100,000 worth of undervalued stock on borrowed credit.

In the novel the attempted acquisition of Corbin, Dern soils everything (and everyone) that comes into contact with it, and, to reiterate, it is Russell's faith in Propp's artificial premise that begins this series of events. Despite Russell's protestations of literary purity, the acquisition of Corbin, Dern is the culmination of a line of smaller instances that exhibit his tendency towards McInerney's cultural analysis that 'debt is good, equity bad'.[114] Three years before he orchestrates the deal, he purchases a fur coat for Corrine, which 'cost twice as much as they'd planned to spend', but the thrill of the purchase exhibits a physical response which parallels the ephemeral buzz of substance abuse elsewhere in the novel. 'Russell insisted in spite of, or perhaps precisely because of, the syncopated flutter of his heartbeat, the hollow vertiginous feeling in his stomach, the sweat on the palms of his hands.'[115] It is an addiction that even the acquisition of a $70 million company cannot quench, for Russell soon becomes a man 'chummy with the four-and-five-digit numbers', considering a house in Southampton that 'went for ten thousand a month', when, as Corrine thinks, 'they didn't have a liquid nickel'.[116]

It is only a small step then, it seems, once Russell has instigated the attempted acquisition and succumbed to the speculation of the financial markets to his infidelity with Trina Cox. And while Trina becomes the object of Russell's affections, his predisposition to infidelity – which, again, is symptomatic of the infiltration of the markets into aesthetic production – can be traced to the very opening of the novel.[117] It is indicative, then, of the novel's wider critique that the main sexual temptation that Russell faces is intertwined with the fiscal world and it is therefore entirely appropriate that Trina, who is an up-and-coming operative in Mergers and Acquisitions, works in the field of financial services, which is the very personification of McInerney's critical maxim earlier in the novel. The night of Russell's first sexual episode with her represents the integration between infidelity and commodity production appropriately. Lying on her bed in her apartment as she pours them both champagne she explains the principles of the fiscal system, '"Well, anyway, a beta of one is the market rate. Oops, little spillage, here." Licking her wet wrist, she said, "A high beta, like two, indicates high risk and a higher required rate of return. See?"'[118]

Russell, of course, has seen, and before long the inevitable happens, and ever the pragmatist he seeks to internally justify the sequence:

> Even when she twisted over on top of Russell to pour him another glass and kissed him instead, as if merely because she chanced to be in the immediate vicinity – this was harmless enough. Why should anybody object to this pressing together of lips, which felt so good, after all? Why should pleasure be a zero-sum commodity, when the store of it could be so easily expanded, the wealth increased by sharing?[119]

The reification of pleasure in this passage – only one of the many instances when emotion or sensation is commodified in the novel – more broadly represents McInerney's attempt to expose the omnipresence of capital in the neoliberal era.[120] This influence, as we have seen already, appears to be viewed negatively by McInerney in the novel and is closely intertwined with a rejection of Carveresque literary principles. It is significant then, that McInerney characterises Corrine as a figure who resists its presence. At their lunch meeting, Propp asks Russell how Corrine is progressing as a stockbroker, interested to find out if the recent rise of women in the financial service industry has tempered the traditional bravado and risk that its masculinity exudes. Russell explains that Corrine is cautious about the financial outlook. 'Women are cautious', Propp interrupts, before offering a prescient contrast, 'Men are the great romantics, the dreamers and fools. Women are realists.'[121] Her description as a 'realist', places her in conflict with Propp's decentred universe, and indicates that McInerney is using her to embody those principles most clearly associated with Carver. It might be tempting, then, to view Russell and Corrine rather simplistically, as representative of opposing poles, that one is compromised by commodity production and the other disassociated from market influences, but this is not the case. In fact the Calloways often present an entirely ambiguous analogy. However, rather than view them as a confusing model, we might better see them as reflecting the nuances and intricacies insistent in a more pragmatic view of literary realism.

Corrine, in particular, finds herself conflicted between the two values. On the one hand, she respects what McInerney calls 'the power of language', has a strong social conscience and eventually rejects the corrupt financial system, but on the other, she works as a stockbroker, covets the affluent lifestyle of her friend, Casey Reynes, and succumbs to frequent retail impulses. The dialectic is exposed after one of her many arguments with Russell when she flees to the sanctuary of Fifth Avenue in a state, 'almost mad enough to go into Bergdorf's and charge up one of these nice Donna Karen ensembles with all the accessories'.[122] Her temperament betrays her weakness for the fleeting pleasures of consumerism, but it is quickly tempered by a lucid anthropological assessment that suggests a deeper understanding of the forces that oppose Carveresque realism:

> Dioramas of late-twentieth-century Manhattan chieftains and their women, the windows at Bergdorf's displayed extravagantly costumed mannequins in the postures of revel and feasting. Having swindled the original inhabitants out of the land and then exterminated them, this tribe flourished until shortly before the millennium ... Pausing in her commentary, Corrine, as anthropologist of the future, tried to decide what form of doom had befallen – would befall – her own. For lately it seemed to her that the horsemen of the apocalypse were saddling up, that something was coming to rip huge holes in the gaudy stage sets of Ronald McDonald Reaganland. Meanwhile she was selling stocks, a glorified Fuller Brush Girl. Hi, I'm Corrine, can I interest you in a sexy growth stock or maybe a cute little annuity?[123]

Corrine's prediction is symptomatic of the broader critique of commodity production in the novel. On a practical level her premonition that some kind of 'doom had befallen – would befall – her own' is proved right in the 1987 market crash and also the concomitant failure of her marriage. Still, what signifies a weightier perception is that her presentiment is not restricted to her personal experience. Her description of America as 'Ronald McDonald Reaganland' – a dual rebuff which denotes capitalist greed and a shallow politics where a Hollywood actor was president – pairs her admission as a 'glorified Fuller Brush Girl', criticising the superficiality of the financial industry which was becoming increasingly prevalent in neoliberal society.

To conclude: these ideas are combined in a key set piece in the novel. During their weekly Sunday visit to the Museum of Modern

Art, Russell and Corrine find themselves in a post-impressionist exhibition when Russell notices a French woman in a nearby gallery. Perhaps indicating McInerney's broader point of aesthetic corruption he writes, 'Amidst the rocks and trees of Cézanne's Provence, this French girl was shaped like something dreamed by Brancusi, Russell thought, a piece that would be called *Sex Moving Through Space*.' As if reading Russell's thoughts, Corrine interrupts his fantasy by saying, 'At least Cézanne doesn't let his ego into the painting.' Surprised, Russell challenges her comment. Corrine continues:

> 'I was thinking about Hemingway saying he learned how to write from Cézanne', she said. 'His descriptions of nature have that same solidity of depth, but it's like all the trees in Hemingway's forest have his initials carved in them, and his brooks burble "Me! Me! Me!"'[124]

Frustrated by this apparent 'shopworn revisionism', Russell begins to raise his voice and their argument fills the gallery. He notices the French woman move into another room – infuriating him further:

> 'When was the last time you read "Big Two-Hearted River"?' Russell boomed, his voice filling the small gallery. Feeling absurd even as he spoke – defender of truth, the mot juste and American literature. 'Read it and weep. Then tell me about ego.'[125]

Corrine, in response, flees from the gallery and Russell is left alone. 'Why do we even come here?' he wondered. 'Usually they made it to Synthetic Cubism before they started to argue.'[126]

Distinguished by its dynamic rather than its critically perceptive qualities, Russell's defence of Hemingway's fiction is, of course, sharply ironised by his actions in the novel. For, far from being the 'defender of truth, the mot juste and American literature', as he claims, the surrender of his poetic ambition in pursuit of financial success embodies his failure to uphold any kind of Hemingwayean, or even, Carveresque code of realism. His allusion to 'Big Two-Hearted River' is significant too, for Carver's first publication in *Western Humanities Review* in 1963, 'Pastoral' (later published as 'The Cabin' in *Fires*) was, as Stull notes, a 'Hemingway imitation' that is 'closely modelled on "Big Two-Hearted River"'.[127] Carver's story is, significantly, an ironic imitation of Hemingway's Nick Adams stories and centres on Mr Harold, a middle-aged man who goes on a fishing retreat to a place where he and his wife had earlier enjoyed a holiday together. But his trip is interrupted by a gang of teenage boys who are hunting deer and threaten to shoot him while he's fishing. Mr Harold only survives by pleading for their mercy and leaves the retreat feeling, as Stull summarises, contra-Hemingway, 'unheroic, homeless, and alone'.[128]

The argument in the museum, and the literary and critical context in which it occurs, is significant because it reflects McInerney's own judgement that reading Carver's fiction in the 1970s was a seminal experience for his own literary development. Writing in *The New York Times Book Review*, he describes his early engagement with Carver's work as 'comparable to discovering Hemingway's sentences in the twenties', and, in a short comparison between the two, argues that Carver's fiction supplants Hemingway's idiomatic style by dispensing with his 'romantic egoism'. He writes, 'The cafés and *pensions* and battlefields of Europe were replaced by trailer parks and apartment complexes, the glamorous occupations by dead-end jobs . . . The good *vin du pays* was replaced by cheap gin, the romance of drinking by the dull grind of full-time alcoholism.'[129] In other words, what made Carver's fiction so attractive for McInerney is that it revealed a type of American experience in a particularly authentic way that was at once illuminating but also creatively liberating. And here, it seems, is the nub. Corrine's opinion of Hemingway's egoism in *Brightness Falls* echoes McInerney's own reading. In its critical denial, it alludes to McInerney's view of Carver: that through his perceived authentic working-class content, his refusal – in his published fiction, at least – to accept the debonair idealism implicit in Hemingway's masculinity and in his emphasis on craftsmanship over innate talent and experience, Carver sidestepped what McInerney sees as a limited literary model and presented, in the form of this realist revisionism, an attractive retreat from the world of postmodern literary experimentation. 'What Carver seemed to say to us', McInerney concludes, 'was that literature could be fashioned out of strict observation of real life, wherever and however it was lived. This was news at a time when academic metafiction was the regnant mode. His example reinvigorated realism.'[130]

Notes

1. For various accounts of their first meeting, see McInerney, 'Raymond Carver: A Still, Small Voice', 6 August 1989; Halpert, *Raymond Carver*, pp. 132–41; Sklenicka, *Raymond Carver*, p. 364; Wittman, 'Jay McInerney, The Art of Fiction No. 231'.
2. Halpert, *Raymond Carver*, p. 138.
3. Ford, 'Good Raymond', 5 October 1998.
4. McInerney, 'Raymond Carver: A Still, Small Voice', 6 August 1989.
5. For more on the urban crisis, bankruptcy and subsequent implementation of neoliberal financialisation in New York City in the late 1970s see Harvey, *A Brief History of Neoliberalism*, pp. 44–8.
6. Sklenicka, *Raymond Carver*, p. 364.
7. Halpert, *Raymond Carver*, p. 135.
8. Usery, 'A Very Close Deal'. It is hard to fully scrutinise the veracity of McInerney's narrative here, but it is interesting to note that his convenient discovery, and its association to ideas of innate natural talent, contradicts the notions of craft and labour that Carver later attempts to instil through his mentorship.
9. McInerney, 'I Miss You George'.
10. Carver, *Call If You Need Me*, p. 111.
11. Fisketjon, 'Normal Nightmares', p. 132.
12. Carter, 'Leading the Gliterary Life', p. 165.
13. Girrard, 'Vintage Contemporaries, *Bright Lights, Big City*, and the Problems of Betweeness', p. 166.
14. Sklenicka recounts that *Will You Please Be Quiet, Please?* only sold 1,500 paperback copies. Sklenicka, *Raymond Carver*, p. 339.
15. Sklenicka, *Raymond Carver*, pp. 423–4; Girard, 'Vintage Contemporaries', p. 167.
16. Girard, 'Vintage Contemporaries', p. 168.
17. McGuane wrote, 'Terrific: remarkable, funny writing, a perfect power-to-weight ratio.' The quote that Carver gave for the front cover still remains on the current edition, 'A rambunctious, deadly funny novel that goes for the right mark – the human heart.'
18. Wolff wrote, 'In its depiction of youth striving mightily to amuse itself, in the exuberance of its language and antic shamelessness of its tale, Jay McInerney's novel calls to mind such classics of knight-errantry as *The Ginger Man* and *The Bushwhacked Piano*. It is a dazzlingly debut, smart, heartfelt, and very, very funny.'
19. As Appelbaum reports, the prospect of low inflation, low interest rates, the strengthening of the dollar and increased sales in all major segments of the publishing industry caused widespread optimism for publishers at the end of 1983. 'In 1987', she predicts, 'publishers will sell 786.19 million more books

than they did in 1982 and take in an additional $6.171 billion.' Citing John P Dessauer, the director of the Centre for Book Research at the University of Scranton: 'Focusing on books for the general public, he projected sales of 681.6 million units of trade titles and 1.034 billion units of mass market paperback titles in 1987, compared with 433.8 million units of trade books and 668.07 million units of mass market paperbacks in 1982'. See Appelbaum, 'Paperback Talk', 4 September 1983.
20. In this sense the series appealed to consumer trends in the mid-1980s. Appelbaum also reports that Charles Newman, a bookstore owner in New York, thought that consumers were '"looking for value and quality," and as books compete with television, computers and the like for the public's attention, the "aesthetic appeal of a well-made book is becoming increasingly important"'. Appelbaum, 'Paperback Talk', 4 September 1983.
21. Girard, 'Vintage Contemporaries', p. 169.
22. Halpert, *Raymond Carver*, p. 137.
23. *Dreams Are What We Wake Up From*, TV, directed by Daisy Goodwin. UK: BBC, 1989.
24. McInerney, 'Raymond Carver: A Still, Small Voice', p. 25.
25. Halpert, *Raymond Carver*, p. 135.
26. *Dreams Are What We Wake Up From*, TV, directed by Daisy Goodwin. UK: BBC, 1989.
27. McInerney, 'Raymond Carver: A Still, Small Voice', p. 25.
28. The other three essays are 'My Father's Life', 'Fires' and 'John Gardner: The Writer As Teacher'.
29. Carver, *Collected Stories*, pp. 728–33.
30. Many of the positions are, of course, politically driven, and, at the risk of oversimplification, see realism as either being part of or opposed to the political status quo. Erich Auerbach and Ian Watt provide the seminal assessments of realism's poetics. See Auerbach, *Mimesis*; Watt, *The Rise of the Novel*. The realism versus modernism debates between Adorno, Brecht and Lukács in the 1930s, 40s and 50s have been compiled in a useful edition by Ronald Taylor. See Taylor, *Aesthetics and Politics*. Roland Barthes's essay 'The Reality Effect' regards realism as a distinctly bourgeois aesthetic. See Barthes, *The Rustle of Language*. In the 1980s Catherine Belsey continued the critical attack on realism by arguing that post-structuralism undoes any notion of the conservative universality of language representation. See Belsey, *Critical Practice*.
31. Woolf, 'Mr Bennett and Mrs Brown', in Bowlby (ed.), *A Woman's Essays: Selected Essays*, p. 70.
32. McHale claims that Chapter 8 is where the significant break occurs when he argues that Sutpen murder-mystery is solved 'not through epistemological processes of weighing evidence and making deductions, but through the imaginative projection of what *could* – and, the text insists, *must* have happened'. McHale, *Postmodernist Fiction*, p. 10.
33. McGuire, *Richard Ford and the Ends of Realism*, p. xiii.
34. Bradbury and Ro, *Contemporary American Fiction*, pp. x–xi.
35. Barth, 'The Literature of Exhaustion', p. 32.

36. Vonnegut, *Slaughterhouse-Five*, p. 87.
37. In 'Surfiction' Raymond Federmen attempts to defend a similar accusation claiming that no writer ever says to himself, 'I am going to experiment with fiction', and concludes that the label is applied post-production to whatever, 'is difficult, strange, provocative, and even original'. This is, perhaps, a helpful, if slightly conspicuous, observation. As Federman continues, he argues for a more subtle approach in the assessment of writers such as Gass, Barth and Burroughs whose fiction is not, he suggests, exceptionally experimental, but rather an exploration of the limits of fiction, a challenge to tradition and an example of imagination. Federman, 'Surfiction', in Federman (ed.), *Surfiction*, p. 7.
38. Carver, *Collected Stories*, p. 729.
39. Sklenicka argues that in light of the battle and compromise that Carver underwent with Lish over the publication of *What We Talk About When We Talk About Love*, 'On Writing' makes for equivocal reading. Sklenicka, *Raymond Carver*, pp. 364–5.
40. In 'Literature of Exhaustion' Barth writes that 'it's dismaying to see so many of our writers following Dostoevsky or Tolstoy or Flaubert or Balzac, when the real technical question seems to me to be how to succeed not even Joyce and Kafka, but those who've succeeded Joyce and Kafka'. Barth, 'Literature of Exhaustion', p. 33.
41. It is unsurprising that Carver's reminiscence of Gardner, 'John Gardner: Writer as Teacher' is an antecedent to McInerney's reminiscence of Carver, 'Raymond Carver, A Still, Small Voice'. Both are written after their respective mentors' deaths and are remarkably similar in tone and form, each recounting early impressions of their mentors at an early point in their career.
42. Carver, *Call If You Need Me*, p. 108.
43. Carver, *Call If You Need Me*, p. 107.
44. Carver, *Call If You Need Me*, p. 108.
45. Carver, *Collected Stories*, p. 739.
46. Tromp, '"Any Good Writer Uses His Imagination to Convince the Reader"', in Gentry and Stull (eds), *Conversations with Raymond Carver*, p. 77.
47. O'Connell, 'Raymond Carver', in Gentry and Stull (eds), *Conversations with Raymond Carver*, pp. 141–2.
48. As well as *On Moral Fiction*, two writers handbooks, *On Becoming a Novelist*, which Carver's 'John Gardner, Writer as Teacher' was a foreword for, and *The Art of Fiction: Notes on Craft for Young Writers* were published posthumously in 1983. Sklenicka claims that 'Carver believed that Gardner's ideas about fiction had not changed a great deal between the year he had him as a teacher and the years when he began publishing them in his two handbooks and *On Moral Fiction*.' See Sklenicka, *Raymond Carver*, p. 508.
49. In the opening pages of his book Gardner wrote:

> No one is more cranky, more irascible, more quick to pontificate on the virtues of his effort than the artist who knows, however dimly, that he's gotten off the track, that his work has nothing to do with what Shakespeare did,

or Brahms, or Rembrandt. Having gotten into art for love of it, and finding himself unable to support, in his own art, what true art has supported since time began, he turns defensively on everything around him. He becomes rabid, often rabidly cynical, insisting on the importance of his trivia. He sends to his fellow artists sharply worded notes: 'Literature is exhausted'. Gardner, *On Moral Fiction*, p. 7.

50. Gardner, *On Moral Fiction*, p. 5.
51. Gardner, *On Moral Fiction*, p. 5.
52. Gardner, *On Moral Fiction*, p. 18.
53. Gardner, *On Moral Fiction*, pp. 65, 67.
54. Gardner, *On Moral Fiction*, p. 69.
55. Gardner reserves his most disparaging criticism for William Gass, a writer that becomes a synecdoche for a generation of anti-realists who are, in Gardner's damning estimation, 'short of significant belief ... and short on moral fibre'. According to Gardner, Gass and his contemporaries are 'more in love, on principle, with the sound of words – or with newfangledness – than with creating fictional worlds', which, principally is a rejection of the conservative position that literature ought to communicate – what might pragmatically be referred to as – some kind of truth. 'The fact remains', Gardner concludes, 'that the search for opacity has little to do with the age-old search for understanding and affirmation' (p. 71). See Gardner, *On Moral Fiction*, pp. 69–71.
56. Carver, *Call If You Need Me*, p. 110.
57. Carver, *Call If You Need Me*, p. 112.
58. Carver, *Collected Stories*, p. 744.
59. Gardner, *On Moral Fiction*, p. 107.
60. McCaffery and Gregory, 'An Interview with Raymond Carver', in Gentry and Stull (eds), *Conversations With Raymond Carver*, p. 109.
61. Sennett, *The Craftsman*, p. 9; Carver, *Call If You Need Me*, p. 113.
62. Schumacher, 'After the Fire, into the Fire: An Interview with Raymond Carver', in Gentry and Stull (eds), *Conversations with Raymond Carver*, p. 220.
63. McInerney, 'Raymond Carver: A Still, Small Voice', 6 August 1989. Also see Tromp, '"Any Good Writer Uses His Imagination to Convince the Reader"', in Gentry and Stull (eds), *Conversations with Raymond Carver*, p. 78.
64. McInerney, 'Raymond Carver: A Still, Small Voice', 6 August 1989.
65. McInerney, 'Raymond Carver: A Still, Small Voice', 6 August 1989.
66. James Annesley notes that *Bright Lights, Big City* is part of this broader trend of New York novels about affluent urbanites; a trend that mutates from the more satirical slant of McInerney's novel and those by Ellis and Tama Janowitz to the light comedy of Chick Lit. 'Clear continuities can be traced', Annesley argues, 'both in terms of setting and with regard to the ways in which they display brands and logos in their prose.' See Annesley, *Fictions of Globalization*, p. 33.
67. In true postmodern artifice the Literary Brat Pack were just a mirage of a mirage. The original 'Rat Pack' had emerged thirty years earlier, now replaced by the Brat Pack, a group of young actors and actresses who symbolised the

hedonism, consumerism and glamour of 1980s America. Blum, 'Hollywood's Brat Pack'.
68. Hendin, 'Fictions of Acquisition', in Mills (ed.), *Culture in an Age of Money*, p. 219. Linsey Abrams similarly argues that McInerney's novel is a story without subtext, 'an endorsement of things as they are'. Abrams, 'A Maximalist Novelist Looks at Some Minimalist Fiction', p. 26.
69. Jameson, *Postmodernism, or, the Logic of Late Capitalism*, pp. 8-9.
70. Kotzwinkle, 'You're Fired, So You Buy a Ferret', 25 November 1984; Anon., 'Bear in Mind: Editor's Choice for Particular Interest', 2 December 1984.
71. Garrett, 'American Publishing Today', p. 516.
72. Pinsker, 'Soft Lights, Academic Talk: A Conversation with Jay McInerney', p. 108.
73. McInerney, *Bright Lights, Big City*, p. 4.
74. Kaufmann, 'Yuppie Postmodernism', p. 102.
75. McInerney, *Bright Lights, Big City*, p. 3. It is also worth pointing out that Carver saw something of value in McInerney's novel, as his blurb quotation indications. While his comments ought to be tempered by a certain amount of nepotistic scepticism, Carver's selection of an extract for *Ploughshares* and his willingness to be publically associated with the novel suggests that he saw, at the very least, some level of worth in McInerney's text.
76. McInerney, *Bright Lights, Big City*, p. 180.
77. McInerney, *Bright Lights, Big City*, p. 180.
78. McInerney, *Bright Lights, Big City*, p. 182.
79. William L. Stull was the first critic to notice the difference between the two versions. His essay also provides a convincing argument in favour of interpreting the end of 'A Small, Good Thing' in religious terms – although (and in an attempt to push back slightly on Stull's analysis) whether it is possible to read something deeper into Carver's personal state from this observation is decidedly ambiguous. Stull, 'Beyond Hopelessville: Another Side of Raymond Carver', pp. 1-15.
80. Carver, *Collected Stories*, p. 425.
81. Kaufmann, 'Yuppie Postmodernism', p. 97.
82. Kaufmann, 'Yuppie Postmodernism', p. 109. Also see Habermas, 'The New Obscurity: The Crises of the Welfare State and the Exhaustion of Utopian Energies', pp. 1-18.
83. Kaufmann, 'Yuppie Postmodernism', pp. 99, 101.
84. Kaufmann, 'Yuppie Postmodernism', pp. 108-9.
85. McInerney, *Brightness Falls*, p. 143.
86. McInerney, *How It Ended*, p. 109.
87. McInerney, *How It Ended*, p. 102.
88. McInerney, *How It Ended*, pp. 109-10.
89. McInerney, 'Raymond Carver, A Still, Small Voice', 6 August 1989.
90. McInerney, *How It Ended*, p. 111.
91. Gardner, *On Moral Fiction*, pp. 5, 18.
92. Carver, *Collected Stories*, p. 729.
93. Carver, *Collected Stories*, p. 729.

94. McInerney, *Brightness Falls*, pp. 70-1.
95. McInerney, *Brightness Falls*, p. 70.
96. McInerney, *Brightness Falls*, p. 71.
97. McInerney, *Brightness Falls*, p. 71.
98. Derrida, *Of Grammatology*, p. 158.
99. McInerney, *Brightness Falls*, p. 74.
100. McInerney, *Brightness Falls*, p. 73.
101. McInerney, *Brightness Falls*, p. 74.
102. McInerney, *Brightness Falls*, pp. 21, 242.
103. McInerney, *Brightness Falls*, p. 242.
104. McInerney, *Brightness Falls*, pp. 242-3.
105. Jameson, *Postmodernism*, p. 9.
106. McInerney, *Brightness Falls*, p. 23.
107. McInerney, *Brightness Falls*, p. 72.
108. McInerney, *Brightness Falls*, p. 78.
109. McInerney, *Brightness Falls*, p. 79.
110. McInerney, *Brightness Falls*, pp. 79-80.
111. McInerney, *Brightness Falls*, p. 80.
112. One thinks, for instance, of Jameson's comment that the 'frantic economic urgency' of Wall Street has infiltrated the 'essential structural function' of aesthetic production. Jameson, *Postmodernism*, pp. 4-5.
113. McInerney, *Brightness Falls*, p. 207.
114. McInerney, *Brightness Falls*, p. 143.
115. McInerney, *Brightness Falls*, p. 373. Ace's drug abuse is described in a similar way earlier in the novel, 'The buzz enters through his lungs and spreads like an electric current into the bloodstream, passes Go and collects two million dollars, rockets up the spine, deposits it at the back of the skull, where it explodes in a burst of white phosphorescence.'
McInerney, *Brightness Falls*, p. 211.
116. McInerney, *Brightness Falls*, p. 220.
117. The perennial problem is, at first, tempered by, 'a nagging inner voice acquired via the *Times* op-ed and the higher media, progressive girlfriends and old New England schools', but soon gives way, first during a trip to the Museum of Modern Art, then when the Calloways go on holiday to the Caribbean, then at a party in New York when Russell is approached by a model and finally, and significantly, through his relationship with Trina. McInerney *Brightness Falls*, p. 61.
118. McInerney, *Brightness Falls*, p. 257.
119. McInerney, *Brightness Falls*, p. 258.
120. Elsewhere, for instance, the Calloway's marriage is compared to a 'corporate debt restructuring deal'. McInerney *Brightness Falls*, p. 276.
121. McInerney, *Brightness Falls*, p. 77.
122. McInerney, *Brightness Falls*, p. 66.
123. McInerney, *Brightness Falls*, p. 66.
124. McInerney, *Brightness Falls*, p. 61.
125. McInerney, *Brightness Falls*, p. 62.

126. McInerney, *Brightness Falls*, p. 62.
127. Stull, 'Raymond Carver Remembered: Three Early Stories', p. 466.
128. Stull, 'Raymond Carver Remembered', p. 466.
129. McInerney, 'Raymond Carver: A Still, Small Voice', 6 August 1989.
130. McInerney, 'Raymond Carver: A Still, Small Voice', 6 August 1989.

CHAPTER 3

'The Transpacific Partnership': Raymond Carver and Haruki Murakami

In his reminiscence of Carver, Haruki Murakami – a modern-day international literary phenomenon – inextricably ties his fiction to Carver, and claims him as his 'greatest literary comrade'.[1] Murakami's claim to Carver's legacy might seem conceited for those who are unfamiliar with the close connection between the two writers. In 1982, early on in his writing career, Murakami first encountered Carver's fiction when he read the story 'So Much Water So Close To Home' in the anthology *West Coast Fiction*. Writing after Carver's death he described the experience in this way:

> The story literally came as a shock to me ... There was the almost breathtakingly compact world of his fiction, his strong but supple style, and his convincing story line. Although his style is fundamentally realistic, there is something penetrating and profound in his work that goes beyond simple realism. I felt as though I had come across an entirely new kind of fiction, the likes of which there had never been before.[2]

For English language readers who are familiar with Murakami's fiction, his admiration of Carver's writing might come as a surprise. His lengthy and complex novels embody a kind of postmodern surrealism – one that blends the ubiquitousness of life in late capitalism with the distinctly American styles and modes of detective writing and science fiction.[3] Carver's style on the other hand, as I have already highlighted, is distinctly minimal and distinctly realist – a form that still has its proponents but which has also come under increasing critical scrutiny in recent decades. Murakami himself offers a rebuff to those critics when he claims that Carver's fiction goes 'beyond simple realism' – and by that, surely he means, beyond its supposed minimalist limitations – that beneath the surface of Carver's fiction are important, communicable and relevant truths, even for the postmodern, neoliberal age. For Carver this conservative view of literature finds its root, as I suggested in the previous chapter, in Gardner's ideological pedagogy (that 'true art is moral: it seeks to improve life, not debase it'), and this idea finds an analogous outlet in Murakami's own writing, through which he feels he has a 'vested duty' as a popular Japanese author to improve Japanese society.[4] Moreover, while a major strand of my argument in this chapter is that the influence of Carver on Murakami is seen most strongly in their responses to their specific socio-economic conditions, it does appear that Murakami – especially in his short stories – often borrows from Carver's fascination with the uncanny strangeness of everyday life. In his more surreal writing, this appropriation of the quotidian and ubiquitous existence of late capitalism – from shaving and dressing to dull work and empty materialism – is given free reign, and often turns into moments of explicit psychological distress. However, in his more realistic writing, such as his story collection *After The Quake* (2002), this quotidian world more simply reflects Carver's own fiction, exploring, as his translator Jay Rubin describes, 'the lives of realistic people in realistic situations, people whose outwardly satisfactory lives leave them feeling unfulfilled and who live on the edge of some devastating discovery'.[5]

If the connection between Carver and Murakami is less apparent for English language readers, then in Japan, Murakami has undoubtedly had a significant influence on how people experience Carver's writing. He has translated all of Carver's fiction, including his posthumous stories, and also published interviews and articles about him.[6] And even though Murakami's translations and fiction are distinct entities, there is clearly a relationship between the two outputs. In May 1983, only a year after he had read Carver for the first time, Murakami published his first translation, *Boku ga denwa o kakete iru baso* [*Where I'm Calling From and Other Stories*], in the same month that he published his own first collection of short stories, *Chugoku-yuki no suro boto* [*A Slow Boat To China*]. This pattern continued for the early part of his career, demonstrating the close correlation between the two processes.[7] The strong synergy is further emphasised by Murakami's translation technique which is painstakingly meticulous, working word by word, so that his translation, in his opinion, personifies the deceased writer and conveys 'the rhythm of his breathing, the warmth of his body, and the subtle wavering of his emotions'. Murakami refers to this process as 'experiencing Raymond Carver', a feeling so powerful that he claims he becomes one – 'body and soul' – with Carver.[8] One of Murakami's English translators, Jay Rubin, supports this idea. At a symposium on Murakami's fiction at – of all places – the University of California, Berkeley in 2008, Rubin, in response to a question about Murakami's translation technique said, 'I remember reading a Raymond Carver story twice in one day – once in English, once in Japanese – and it was like reading the same thing twice.'[9]

While Carver is a central influence for Murakami, it is worth pointing out that the development of his distinctive literary style has a broader base than just one man. Born in 1949, Murakami made a notable diversion from his ancestral past when he was young. It was possibly his proximity to Kobe and Osaka – two east-coast mercantile port cities – that began to shape his sensibility for Western culture. Discovering English language paperbacks in second-hand bookshops when he was a teenager, he began to immerse himself in the fiction of Raymond Chandler, F. Scott Fitzgerald and Kurt Vonnegut, Jr. Evidence of the influence of those American writers can be found in his first two novels *Hear The Wind Sing* and *Pinball, 1973*.[10] Both novels found a small but committed audience among the young, post-war generation, but conservative Japanese critics denigrated their explicit references to Western pop culture and condemned them as items for popular consumption.[11] It was not until 1982 when he published his third novel, *A Wild Sheep Chase* – significantly, the year he first encountered Carver's fiction – that his writing reached a wider audience. The commercial success of the novel allowed Murakami the financial stability to immerse himself further in his writing. His fourth and fifth novels, *Hard-boiled Wonderland and the End of the World* (1985) and *Norwegian Wood* (1989), bear the hallmarks of his early Americanised fiction, but also denote a shift towards the exposition of a clearer critical evaluation of the contemporary Japanese experience.

Brian Seemann recently offered a thought-provoking analysis of what he considered to be an existential connection between Carver and Murakami's short fiction.[12] And while there is value in pursuing this line of enquiry – one that finds its precursor in the foundational Carver scholarship of David Boxer and Cassandra Phillips – it is the proposition of this chapter that Carver's influence on Murakami resides most powerfully in the example or model which he set of how to negotiate, for better or worse, the complex and shifting neoliberal foundations of late twentieth-century capitalist society. This chapter argues, therefore, that the process of reading (and later meeting) Carver enabled Murakami to engage with, and think through, his own similar yet distinct socio-economic experience. Murakami is, I propose, a good candidate for this influential model because he is not only clearly influenced by Carver but he is also consciously working within, and often against, the boundaries of late capitalism. I will present my argument through a number of comparative close textual readings, positioning each in its relevant socio-economic context, before judging the extent and limitation of Carver's influence. Ultimately my readings suggest that Murakami's acceptance of Carver's influence rests in a corresponding desire to depict a pervasive societal humiliation and dislocation, one that is distinctly tied to each author's experience of the trends towards short-term flexibility in the labour market in America and Japan in the late twentieth century.

In David Harvey's account of the socio-economic transformation that occurred in the US in the late twentieth century, he argues that working life in America was marked by the inability of the hegemonic Fordist system to contain the inherent contradictions of capitalism.[13] The Fordist principles that had dominated since the early 1900s, designed on the premise of the mass production and mass consumption of goods, led to a post-war boom and eventual market saturation. As a result, the long-term, large-scale fixed capital investments that had proved stable in the past became increasingly profitless. The labour force, instead of adapting to new markets, became rigid – reallocation was problematic – and any attempt to overcome these rigidities were opposed by the immovable force of working-class power. Unable to maintain the compromise, the capitalist system shifted, as Harvey describes, to a system of flexible accumulation.[14] Resting not on the premise of rigidity but flux, this new system was designed to promote flexibility in labour markets, labour processes and consumption. As a result, those attempting to achieve socio-economic prosperity through a Fordist mentality of constant work and consumption were blocked by a system designed to directly confront the rigidity of the Fordist narrative. These new socio-economic circumstances were reinforced by the breakdown of Bretton Woods, the subsequent liberalisation of currency markets and a new focus on foreign investment. Corporations which, under the Fordist system, had focused on domestic investment were now turning to an increasingly international clientele who focused on short-term profits in share prices. When this new economic context was combined with the time-space compression provided by technological advances in telecommunication and computing, the old system in which individuals or workers found a defined sense of self in their commitment to a long-term institution, an idea which is closely tied to the acquisition of the American dream of socio-economic prosperity, was quickly eroded. In his account of the period, Sennett describes this damaging affect. Most people, he argues, 'need a sustaining life narrative, they take pride in being good at something specific'. He goes on to write that the new 'cultural ideal required in new institutions thus damages many of the people who inhabit them'.[15] While this new, dynamic capitalism might seem technologically progressive, Sennett argues that it directly opposes any sense of sustained occupational pride, what he refers to as craftsmanship. This situation extends to the broader socio-economic context of working life in the US more generally. Sennett continues:

> The more one understands how to do something well, the more one cares about it. Institutions based on short-term transactions and constantly shifting tasks, however, do not breed that depth. Indeed the organization can fear it; the management code word here is *ingrown*. Someone who digs deep into an activity just to get it right can seem to others ingrown in the sense of fixated on that one thing – an obsession is indeed necessary

for the craftsman. He or she stands at the opposite pole from the consultant, who swoops in and out but never nests.[16]

For Americans, men and women like Carver, who are tied rather rigidly to the idea of sustained hard work, or craft, as a route to socio-economic, even artistic, success, the move towards dynamic capitalism in the neoliberal period marks a particular moment of crisis. Instead of long-term narratives, which offered delayed gratification, institutions – more broadly labour, education and consumption – began to focus on short-term plans and short-term goals. In what amounts to a rather perverse paradox, then, despite rising economic expectations, many Americans did not actually see an increase in long-term personal prosperity.[17] In fact, as Sennett argues in *The Culture of New Capitalism* and earlier in *The Corrosion of Character*, the fragmenting of institutions left large groups of Middle Americans feeling distinctly alienated. For many, the advent of neoliberalism destroyed the hopes of attaining the American dream.

Growing up in the post-war period, Carver felt the effect of this transition. As I noted in my introduction, in his essay 'Fires', Carver recalls the moment when he realised the illusory nature of his long-term plans for economic and social mobility. While the essay does not reveal the precise nature of his plans – although one imagines they most likely involved education, movement out of the working class and a successful writing career – what his account reveals, at the very least, is a *ressentiment* that failed to account for any reality beyond their control. Harker unpacks this idea when he suggests that:

> They invested in the hegemonic narratives of contemporary consumer society – working hard, loyalty, trying to advance themselves through education, doing the right things. But the socioeconomic world inflicted experiences – bankruptcy, unemployment, and working hard and getting nowhere – about which these hegemonic narratives had little or nothing to say.[18]

One need only spend a short time studying Carver's early life to find a number of pertinent examples to illustrate this. Take, for instance, the account of their first bankruptcy in 1967. Carver, who had just completed his undergraduate degree at Humboldt State, was honing his writing while working a variety of low-paid jobs, most notably as a night janitor at a local hospital. His wife, Maryann, on the other hand, was beginning to earn a dependable salary as a saleswoman. Still, despite a level of financial security, Carver found a number of outstanding debts – mainly college loans and credit cards – to be a daily burden. After meeting a bankruptcy attorney at a bar, he decided that the easiest way to escape from their onerous loans would be to declare bankruptcy and start afresh. What is particularly interesting about the situation is that Maryann opposed Carver's plan. Sklenicka records that, from Maryann's point of view, they both had steady employment and, with time, was sure they would have been able to pay back their creditors. Her embrace of America's new debt economy can be seen as being tantamount to an acceptance of the forthcoming neoliberal economic era. Carver's attitude, and fear of debt, on the other hand, reflects the rigidity of the Fordist narrative. This small anecdotal example serves to illustrate Carver's struggle to adapt to the transition from embedded liberalism to neoliberalism – and might also be understood as a reflection of the difficulties faced by many Americans trying to adjust to a new era of capital in this period. The humiliation that he faced before the facts of working life in the neoliberal era – or as he put it in his laconic prose, 'the imminent removal of the chair from under me' – reveals the flaw of the Fordist principle, or, what we might better understand as an orthodox American narrative of hard work, in a society shifting towards neoliberal ideals.[19]

It is unsurprising therefore that Carver's early fiction represents a wide spectrum of Middle American jobs and documents much of this humiliation. Often caught 'in-between' circumstances, Carver's characters are humiliated because of joblessness, unable to improve their lot through hard work, and left yearning for a missing 'something' in their lives. The working life that his first collection *Will You Please Be Quiet, Please?* depicts – waitresses, students, teachers, writers – does not represent a demeaning life in itself; rather it is the threat of fragmenting institutions and fragmenting lives that weakens his characters' long-term socio-economic plans and causes humiliation.[20] For Carver and for many Americans it was *hard* work that was the vehicle for long-term social and economic prosperity; joblessness, bankruptcy, or even the prospect of either, therefore, reflected a weakening of that American dream. This, in turn, led to a dislocation that Sennett argues was emblematic of late twentieth-century capitalism where 'institutions no longer provide a long-term frame' and individuals have to 'improvise his or her life-narrative, or even do without any sustained sense of self'.[21]

Carver's story 'What Is It?' deals with the humiliation of broken socio-economic aspirations. The opening sentence reveals an ultimatum, 'Fact is the car needs to be sold in a hurry.'[22] After a period of uncontrollable consumption, Leo and Toni have been forced to declare bankruptcy. They are advised by their lawyer to sell their most expensive possession: the convertible, 'today, *tonight*'. Such insistence calls for urgent action and, in a darkly equivocal manner, 'Leo sends Toni out to do it.'[23] This action marks a significant moment in their lives. As the desperate couple part company amid empty promises of an unrealistic future – 'I'll get out of it' and 'Things are going to be different!' – they let go of their final vestige of consumer addiction, the yardstick by which they measure socio-economic success.[24] This humiliation is underlined a few hours later when Leo, after contemplating their predicament considers whether 'he should go to the basement, stand on the utility sink, and hang himself with his belt'.[25] Pulled out of his suicidal thoughts by Toni who rings from a restaurant, where she is with the salesman who is buying the car, Leo verbalises his chief concern a number of times, 'Did somebody buy the car?'[26] Toni reveals she has sold the car for 'six and a quarter', which she counts as lucky – although it is not the $900 Leo wanted – and, after repeating the salesman's opinion that, 'he'd rather be classified a robber or a rapist than a bankrupt', she hangs up the phone.[27] In a moment of subtle ambiguity, Carver underlines Leo's humiliation. Not only has his economic situation drawn him to suicidal thoughts but it is now compounded by the salesman's opinion that bankruptcy is worse than robbery and rape – two crimes which, it seems almost certain, are about to be committed in one form or another. When Toni returns, the two lie in bed and Leo feels the 'stretch marks' on her body, a physical reminder of their distorted ambition, which seem like 'roads', and finally thinks of the lost convertible, 'He remembers waking up in the morning after they'd bought the car, seeing it, there in the drive, gleaming.'[28]

The foundational problem to Leo and Toni's predicament is that they have bought into the hegemonic narrative that work and consumption lead to long-term economic and social success:

> She wanted something to do after the kids started school, so she went back selling. He was working six days a week in the fiber-glass plant. For a while they didn't know how to spend the money. Then they put a thousand on the convertible and doubled and tripled the payments until in a year they had it paid.[29]

Their embodiment of the Fordist principles of mass production and mass consumption belie a contradiction that cannot be contained by their belief in the hegemonic narrative, for soon they enter a period of overwhelming consumption. They spend their money on their children, buying them bicycles, clothes and food. Their actions are motivated in large part by a desire to escape their working-class roots through consumption and Toni's admission that she had to, 'do without when I was a kid' confirms this.[30] Their acquisition of books and records is a symbol of an attempt at a cultural education before they buy the obligatory consumer capitalist appliances and luxury goods that denote graduation to Middle America. Their compulsive spending reflects the consumer zeitgeist described by Sennett:

> In using things we use them up. Our desire for a dress may be ardent, but a few days after we actually buy and wear it, the garment arouses us less. Here the imagination is strongest in anticipation, grows ever weaker through use.[31]

For Leo and Toni the initial freedom offered by an expendable income in consumer-capitalist America mutates into a consuming addiction. The convertible is a significant symbol in this regard.[32] Its symbolism is concomitant with Gareth Cornwall's notion that Carver's characters have 'no limit to the range and scale of their desire' and therefore presents a defining paradox for Leo and Toni.[33] One might expect the acquisition of their most notable consumer item, the convertible (the sky's the limit), to be the catalyst to release them from the confines of their working poor life, but instead, it becomes a prison of consuming addiction. Consequently it is *that* addiction and the impending humiliation of bankruptcy that leads to the collapse of their upward economic and social mobility. For Leo and Toni hard work and consumption does not lead to the acquisition of long-term socio-economic dreams. The sky is *not* the limit. Instead they are caught in the dark side of America, where, just like Carver's experience in real life, hegemonic narratives are undermined by a capitalist society in transition.

If 'What Is It?' explores the failure of Carver's orthodox work ethic as a means to socio-economic security and prosperity, then another story in his first collection, 'What Do You Do In San Francisco?', explores the flipside of that narrative, the unattractiveness of idleness, or, the lack of any work ethic. Narrated by Henry Robinson, a mailman in the small northern Californian town of Arcata, the story revolves around the arrival of the Marstons, a small family who move to the town from San Francisco. Whatever their reasons for moving to Arcata, the Marstons buck small-town convention. They keep to themselves, take a long time to move their belongings from their U-Haul trailer, and fail to keep up the appearance of the house. As weeds grow and the lawn turns yellow, their idleness, or lack of small-town American work ethic, is reinforced by the term that Robinson uses to describe them: beatniks. Marston's wife, who remains nameless throughout the story, is a painter and Robinson supposes that Marston does something similar, which, importantly for Robinson, does not count as real *work*. Real work, he claims, has 'value' – but the only value Robinson advocates is, 'the harder the better'.[34] Soon rumours abound in the small town as to who the Marstons really are and what they are doing in Arcata. Sallie Wilson, a member of the Welcome Wagon, claims 'the worst story', Marston's wife is a dope addict and the family are trying to escape their past.[35] In the narrative, the reason for their move to Arcata is never revealed, and eventually Marston's wife and the three children leave him, leaving Marston in limbo, unemployed, waiting daily on the porch for news from his wife until he too disappears from Arcata altogether.

Throughout the story it is Marston's inactivity that is scrutinised the most. Robinson's narrative stems from a murder he reads about in the newspaper. 'It wasn't the same man', he assures the reader, 'though there was a likeness because of the beard.'[36] The beard is an important aspect of Marston for it symbolises his idleness. 'People here aren't used to seeing men with beards – or men who don't work for that matter', Robinson states.[37] Whether the beard reflects a lack of work-readiness or a lax attitude towards personal hygiene (or both), one thing is certain: it becomes his distinguishing feature. As the drug-related rumours settle down, the only time anyone in Arcata takes notice of Marston is when they stare at his beard in the supermarket. This is conjoined with the gender ambiguity of how his wife dresses, in 'a man's undershirt', and together represents a subversion of traditional American values.[38] If there is anyone more likely to work in the sense that Robinson sees it, it is Marston's wife, it seems – her appropriation of masculine apparel perhaps denoting that she is dressed for action.

These ideas are only reinforced by a lack of urgency in Marston's actions. Not only does it take them over fourteen hours to drive the three hundred miles from San Francisco to Arcata, their U-Haul trailer sits half-emptied outside their house for several days. Marston fails to rename his mailbox – an (in)action that suggests impermanence – and he remains in a state of befuddled transience at the end of the story after his wife leaves him. Coinciding with these smaller incidences is Marston's refusal to look for paid employment. The reason for his ideological aversion to work is never fully revealed by Robinson – a sign that he finds Marston's idleness incomprehensible – but the story's narrative suggests that Carver does not view it as an attractive option. Whatever the cause, Marston's one notable action early in the story is to refuse the job opportunity offered to him by Robinson:

> I tapered off, seeing how they didn't look interested.
> 'No, thanks', he said.
> 'He's not looking for a job', she put in.[39]

Marston's inactivity is, of course, a point of contention for Robinson who views it as a violation of the American ideal of hard work. His values are in line with those that were influential for the rise of productivity and development of the US in the early to mid-twentieth century (the very ideals that, as we shall see later in this chapter, the Japanese sought to imitate in the post-war years). And while Robinson's attitude is hardly designed to be an emulative model, the flipside, Marston's idleness, or refusal to engage in any meaningful work or activity is an equally unattractive option. The climax of the story occurs when Robinson attempts to pull Marston out of his inactivity by espousing his American work ethic. He does it the day he delivers a letter with a Portland postmark that he imagines is from his wife:

> She's no good, boy. I could tell that the minute I saw her. Why don't you forget her? Why don't you go to work and forget her? What have you got against work? It was work, day and night, work that gave me oblivion when I was in your shoes and there was a war on.[40]

Of course, Robinson's appeal does not result in any change in Marston's attitude. Rather, the opposite happens: on the run from his failure, a feeling seemingly cemented by joblessness, he is left in stasis, in a state of humiliation. He retreats into his house and does not come out to meet Robinson anymore. Instead, he waits for the mail inside, looking out of the window. The final scene depicts Marston staring beyond Robinson as he delivers the mail, his eyes fixed over 'the rooftops and the trees, south', (towards San Francisco), apparently watching something. But when Robinson looks all he can see is 'the same old timber, mountains, sky'.[41] Of course, we are witnessing the most Carveresque of motifs. David Boxer and Cassandra Phillips argue that it is 'a symbol of voyeurism'. That is, what Marston is staring at is not the scenery but the 'hideously clear vision' of himself, distant, in the words of Boxer and Phillips, and unattainable.[42] This 'hideously clear vision' is the reality of his joblessness, and his isolation, displacement and dissociation from society and himself. While Robinson's presence implies the existence of an intact Fordism, it does not provide a valuable alternative for Marston. The dislocation of the neoliberal era has begun to have an affect on him. Marston has been cast adrift. Even the confrontation with Robinson fails to buoy him into action, and Marston is left to wander, like a peripatetic loner in small town America.

The effect of Carver's literary response to his socio-economic situation on Murakami's own fiction can only be understood with clarity by placing it within the context of the social and cultural crises that Murakami's fiction depicts in late twentieth-century Japan. Prior to the dramatic socio-economic changes after 1955, Japanese life was defined by the humiliating defeat in the Pacific War, the emperor's surrender and the subsequent military occupation by the US. The level of poverty in immediate post-war Japan was high, but advances in industrial technology and procurement orders from the US military during the Korean War ignited economic recovery. From 1955 onwards, consumption of traditional necessities declined as the country began to adopt the ideals of Western embedded liberal capitalism, most notably increasing expenditure on education, the financial sector and the leisure industry. This coincided with Prime Minister Ikeda's income-doubling plan in 1960 which began a period of huge economic growth. In an effort to improve exports many companies moved towards the Pacific coast causing significant migration. In Murakami's home region, Kyoto-Osaka-Kobe, for example, the population increased by 62 per cent.[43] The movement towards the Pacific was significant in a cultural sense, too, as television ownership increased and imported American films and television programmes began to have an impact. The media became American-centred – the material and social success of the post-war period in the US became an emulative model – and depictions of American families surrounded by consumer goods had a powerful impact on the Japanese mindset. Marilyn Ivy recognises that 'The middle-class "American way of life" became the utopian goal and the dream of many Japanese in the 1950s', a goal tied to the orthodox American (even Fordist) conviction that unflagging hard work is the basis for commodity acquisition.[44] Crucially this positive impression was passed on to Murakami and his post-war generation. 'When I was in my teens in the sixties', Murakami told one interviewer, 'America was so big. Everything was shiny and bright.'[45]

The specific boom period between 1966 and 1970, known as the Izanagi Boom, paved the way for a swift change in lifestyle priorities for the Japanese people in two distinct ways. Those who were older, who were tied to corporate infrastructure and could remember Japan's immediate post-war poverty, embraced their new prosperity with vigour. They became intensely proud of their achievements, and began to enjoy their gains in an increasingly materialist society. Commodities such as electrical appliances and cars became common among the masses. If the 'American way of life' was their goal then the pre-war generation was coming close to achieving it. The post-war generation however, like Murakami himself, had a different attitude to Japan's rise. Many of them, embedded in Japanese universities, began to harness a particularly strong grievance against the established priority given to the economy and industry, which they viewed as leading to an excessive level of corporate control on individuals. This came to a head in 1968 with widespread rioting at the universities.

Writing two decades after the event, Murakami's novel, *Norwegian Wood*, gives a fictional account of the riots:

> The lecture was about half over and the professor was drawing a sketch of a Greek stage on the blackboard when the door opened again and two students in helmets walked in. They looked like some kind of comedy team, one tall, thin and pale, the other short, round and dark with a long beard that didn't suit him. The tall one carried an armful of political agitation handbills. The short one walked up to the professor and said, with a degree of politeness, that they would like to use the second half of his lecture for political debate and hoped that he would cooperate, adding, 'the world is full of problems far more urgent and relevant than Greek tragedy'.[46]

Murakami's farcical descriptions in the novel undermine the protesters' attempt at revolution. The protagonist, Toru Watanabe, unimpressed with their propaganda, claims that 'The true enemy of this bunch was not State Power but Lack of Imagination.'[47] He immediately leaves the lecture with his friend Midori. When outside, she suddenly asks, 'Are we going to be strung up on telephone poles if the revolution succeeds?' To which Toru replies, 'Let's have lunch first, just in case.'[48] The novel's mocking tone belies the fact that Murakami initially became involved in the riots. However, he came to view the political organisations that erected barricades and pursued a violent agenda as hypocritical. When the police were called in to break up the students the revolutionaries gave in easily and the Establishment claimed victory. After almost a year of closures, universities began to reopen and the majority of students came back the following semester, and student radicals, who had once thrown rocks and handed out propaganda, began to prepare for life in Japanese society. 'The mood of excitement and idealism collapsed', Rubin writes, 'leaving in its wake a terrible sense of boredom and politeness.'[49]

This widespread sense of societal disillusionment (or boredom and politeness) is paramount in *Norwegian Wood*. The novel opens in 1987 with Toru sitting on a plane in Hamburg airport. The weary tone of post-1970s Japan is implied by his tone at the very opening of the narrative, 'So – Germany again'.[50] Tired from years of Establishment living and the prominence of empty materialism he begins to recall his (free) student days between 1968 and 1970. It is within this temporal frame that the contrast between the reality of post-1970 Japan and the idealistic world of the 1960s is considered, and yet, as Matthew Strecher argues, 'Murakami's parody of the 1960s is not entirely nostalgic, for it is tinged with a critical scorn for the politics and moralism of the student movement of the late 1960s.'[51] The distinction that results from the protesters' failed idealism and their eventual adherence to Establishment living is played out in the novel. Talking in an interview with Larry McCaffery a number of years later, Murakami summed the feeling up in the following way:

> I belong to a generation of Japanese people who grew up during the counterculture era and the revolutionary uprisings of 1968, 1969, and 1970. The Japan when I was a child was poor, and everybody worked hard and was optimistic that things were getting better. But they are not. When we were kids, we were a poor country but very idealist. That began to change in the sixties; some people just got rich and forgot their ideals, while other people struggled to save idealism ... Then, very quickly, all that simply disappeared. The uprisings were all crushed by the cops and the mood became bleak. The whole sense of the counterculture rebellion seemed finished.[52]

In *Norwegian Wood* this sense of loss – loss of idealism, loss of autonomy – finds itself most expressed in the series of events that lead to Naoko's suicide: the loss of virginity, the loss of youth, the loss of mental stability, the loss of Toru's fidelity, until finally her suicide completes the loss of innocence. It is this sense, then, of humiliation before the hegemonic narrative of Japanese life that Murakami is responding to in much of his fiction. Like Carver's bleak depiction of the ubiquitous humiliation of Middle Americans caught in a world where full-time work is in decline and low-paid, irregular work is increasing, Murakami's portrayal of the boredom and politeness of corporate work and consumption in post-1970s Japan represents a national sentiment. It is a feeling that is still so pervasive that Rubin recognises that Murakami's fiction continues to 'attract readers too young to have experienced the events themselves, but who respond to the lament for a missing "something" in their lives'.[53] The crux of Murakami's fiction is often found when characters, distracted by corporate conformity or a consumerist mentality – a way of life that Murakami clearly depicts as an unfit antidote for the prevalent malaise in late twentieth-century Japan – realise they are still suffering from the debilitating burden of post-1970s humiliation. For, in Murakami's fiction of the 1980s we frequently meet characters who are awkwardly and painfully caught between the failed idealism of the 1960s and the materialism of the 1970s and 1980s. The resulting sense of humiliation, as characters reflect on their lost idealism, echoes very clearly the kinds of humiliation present in Carver's America.

While *Norwegian Wood* reflects the post-war generation's struggle to come to terms with post-1970s humiliation, I want to suggest that it is in Murakami's short fiction that we find the clearest exposition of this theme.[54] Boku, the narrator of Murakami's story 'The Second Bakery Attack', is symptomatic of his generation's situation.[55] One night he wakes up suffering from 'tremendous overpowering hunger pangs'.[56] Sitting at the kitchen table with his wife he reveals that he suffered a similar feeling when he protested as a student. His resistance to corporate infrastructure was so firm at the time that he refused to get a job, even to buy food. So, in order to eat he and a friend decided to attack a bakery. Their folly is underlined when the baker deflates the situation by offering no physical resistance and instead gives them free bread on the condition that they sit and listen to an album of Wagner overtures. The students decide to accept the deal because it was not work 'in the purest sense of the word'.[57] For another writer the failed bakery attack might not hold much more significance, but in Murakami's fictional world Boku's failed idealism mutates into a humiliating reality, and marks victory for the Establishment in his life. Talking to his wife he concludes:

> It was a kind of turning point. Like, I went back to the university, and I graduated, and I started working for the firm and studying for the bar exam, and I met you and got married. I never did anything like that again. No more bakery attacks.[58]

The return of Boku's hunger pangs, then, cannot be coincidental, for they correspond with his move into the Establishment – he has only been married two weeks and recently passed the bar exam – and reflect the re-emergence of old countercultural desires. The inability of the hegemonic narrative of corporate work to satisfy the humiliation of his lost idealism is indicative of its failure. His justification for his conformity is merely a reticent 'Times change. People change', a declaration that reflects something of the socio-economic transitions in twentieth-century Japan, one that is reminiscent of Sennett's argument that 'the normal path of the adult's "sentimental education" is meant to lead to ever greater resignation about how little life as it is actually conducted can accord with one's dreams'.[59] In light of this, then, we might consider the humiliation of failed Japanese idealism exhibited in much of Murakami's fiction as being correlative with the humiliation Carver felt when he realised the failure of the Fordist narrative in 1970s America.

To view 'The Second Bakery Attack', then, as being influenced by – or even developing – Carver's fiction is to notice a number of interesting points. The first is that the couple in Murakami's story do not attempt to overcome their problem alone, like the rather autonomous actions of Leo and Toni, or Marston and his wife, but express their solution through communal activity. It is Boku's wife who deems that the only way to resolve the 'curse' of the first failed bakery attack is to implement another, more successful raid – an indication that familial community is an important ideal in combatting corporate conformity. She loads up their Toyota Corolla – the most ordinary of Japanese cars – with the extraordinary: a Remington shotgun, ski masks, rope and cloth-backed tape, and the newly weds set off into the Tokyo night. However, unable to find a bakery, Boku's wife decides that a McDonald's will suffice and the pair enter the restaurant and hold up the staff. The only other customers are a couple of students who are asleep at their table and are oblivious to the attack. It is worth pausing on this point briefly, for there is a significant distinction between Boku's student idealism and that of the post-post-war generation; the former were defined by a principled refusal to enter the corporate structure (even if they eventually compromised their ideals), while the latter are defined by a pervasive sleep; Boku characterises the students like 'a couple of deep-sea fish', before rhetorically asking, 'What would it have taken to rouse them from a sleep so deep?'[60] Disaffected by the example of failed idealism set by the post-war generation, the students of post-1970 (who incidentally represent the core of Murakami's readership) have succumbed to the failed promise of consumerism and entered a symbolic boredom expressed through inactivity.

Managing to escape with thirty Big Macs, Boku and his wife drive half an hour away to a deserted car park where they consume a third of their spoils. The result and conclusion of the story is significant. As the couple's insatiable hunger begins to fade they have an epiphany, symbolised by dawn breaking over the Tokyo skyline. As they look out of the windows of their car they notice, for the first time, the 'filthy walls' of the urban environment around them, the huge Sony Beta ad tower glowing with 'painful intensity', and the 'whine of highway truck tires' as ubiquitous as the dawn chorus. The scene is reminiscent of another Murakami story, 'A Slow Boat To China', in which the narrator describes Tokyo as a place full of dirty facades, nameless crowds, unremitting noise, packed trains, grey skies, billboards on every square centimetre of space, hopes and resignations; and the crux, 'everywhere, infinite options, infinite possibilities. An infinity, and at the same time, zero.'[61] The failed ideology of 1960s Japan, and post-1970s conformity, which may have initially appeared hopeful, has mutated into resignation – 'zero' – a parallel of the humiliation felt by many of Carver's characters in his fiction. This idea is only reinforced by the very close of Murakami's story, in which both Boku and his wife attempt to overcome their resignation through extreme consumption. The absence of a bakery, their magnetism to McDonald's, the thirty stolen Big Macs, and the capitalist cityscape symbolise as much. The sleep that Boku's wife succumbs to in the final scene after she has consumed the hamburgers is reminiscent of the 'deep-sea' sleep of the students in McDonald's. This sleep, which was so elusive at the beginning of the story, has finally come, but with it a menacing undertone. For the couple are left isolated in the capsule of their car, with the looming narrative of materialism rising high in the filthy urban environment around them.[62]

If the societal shift towards trends of overconsumption in Japan in the late twentieth century were determined by the country's rising economic prospects, then on a personal level they also represented a distraction from post-1970s humiliation. If yuppie culture was prominent in America in the 1980s, then the Japanese had their own version: *shinjinrui* (the new species). Their lifestyle, described by Gary D. Allinson as 'a parody of materialism in its own right', mirrored the increasingly fragmenting social fabric of Japan during the decade.[63] If the student riots highlighted growing intergenerational differences in the 1960s, then the post-post-war generation's materialism was their way of rebelling against the post-war generation's lost idealism and conformist living. They rejected the pattern of their workaholic parents, and instead sought the part-time service sector work that was becoming increasingly prevalent in free market capitalism. After short, intense periods of effort, and after amounting a pile of expendable income, they'd quit their jobs and go on spending sprees. When the money ran out, they simply repeated the cycle. Allinson writes:

> The uneasiness, anxieties, and contention that appeared in the 1970s and 1980s were a by-product of this increasing dividedness, if not divisiveness. Individuals, families, business firms, interest groups, and others seemed preoccupied with their own concerns ... A more dissenting, self-centred atmosphere promoted greater flux, less cohesion, and diverging goals.[64]

If, on the one hand, Murakami suggests that failed Japanese idealism has mutated into a humiliating, debilitating conformity, then he also suggests, on the other hand, that the answer to that problem is not the overconsumption indicative of the post-post-war generation. The Boku in the story 'Family Affair' is, then, in this sense most clearly representative of this new species. He conducts a decidedly autonomous lifestyle, and the phrase 'it's my life, not yours' is his mantra in the story.[65] While on the surface this kind of idea might seem reminiscent of the post-war generation's anti-establishment ideals, it is really a distortion of that reality, for his autonomy, has more do with his amoral lifestyle than any principled refusal to conform.[66] When his sister, who is four years younger than him, begins to take her life more seriously, Boku's self-interest becomes the point of contention for the pair. His sister's passage to the Establishment is well documented by Boku in the story, who recognises early on what he calls her 'dangerous symptoms' – cleaning, cooking and organising.[67]

The biggest change to their relationship occurs when his sister meets her fiancé, Noboru Watanabe, on holiday. When they return to Japan they begin to date and straight away Boku notices that she has begun to 'glow'.[68] The introduction of light is no coincidence, for 'Family Affair' is suffused with images of light that appear to be an attempt by Murakami to highlight, or illuminate, negative aspects of Boku's life. Coming home from work one day, he tries to listen to his records but then remembers that his amplifier has recently broken. He tries watching television instead but the same amplifier powers the speakers so the sound doesn't work:

> This also made it impossible to watch TV. I have one of those monitors without any sound circuitry of its own. You have to use it with the stereo. I stared at my silent TV screen and drank my beer. They were showing an old war movie. Rommels Afrika Korps tanks were fighting in the desert. Their cannons shot silent shells, their machine guns shot silent bullets, and people died silently, one after another.[69]

Like the interconnectivity of Boku's consumer devices, when one component fails the rest fail too. His sister's impending marriage appears to be one such broken component that threatens to break his aimless consumerist drifting. The problem is compounded for Boku by Noboru, who seeks to impose conformity onto his life.[70] When Noboru comes round to Boku's flat to have dinner with his sister he takes the chance to look at Boku's broken amplifier, and quickly diagnoses the problem, 'The connecting cords between the preamp and the power amp. The connection's been broken at the plugs on both channels.'[71] He promptly runs out to the hardware store to buy a soldering iron and fix the amplifier. Reconnecting the circuitry is important because it allows the three of them to play music again, and, as Rubin explains, 'Music is, for Murakami, the best entry into the deep recesses of the unconscious mind.'[72] This leads to an important moment for Boku at the end of the story. That same evening he meets a girl at a bar and the two go back to her apartment where they have sex, according to Boku, as a 'matter of course':

> 'Put the light out', she said, so I did. From her window you could see the big Nikon ad tower. A TV next door was blasting the day's pro-baseball results. What with the darkness and my drunkenness, I hardly knew what I was doing. You couldn't call it sex.[73]

The conformist capitalist institutions that infiltrate the darkness of the bedroom, and, also what is typically in Murakami's fiction a moment of love, intimacy and human connection, suggests that Boku's countercultural ideals have been corrupted. The subsequent re-emergence of sound in connection with his failed sex signifies the crux of the story and implies that the principled opposition to the status quo has lapsed into a kind of amoral decadence. This point in the story marks a noteworthy parallel with 'The Second Bakery Attack'. The Nikon ad tower is reminiscent of the Sony ad tower, and both emit an intense glow that illuminates warped countercultural idealism. In 'The Second Bakery Attack' this emerges as excessive materialism which leads to inactivity and sleep – a wholly unattractive option – and in 'Family Affair' it has become an amoral, self-absorbed ideal – another wholly unattractive option. By extension there is a similarity to Carver's 'What Do You Do In San Francisco?' too, in that Marston's countercultural ideals translate into isolation and dislocation and become, like the examples found in Murakami's short fiction, again, wholly unattractive.

After the failed sex, Boku begins his journey home. As he walks he begins to think about Noboru Watanabe:

> Then, with no connection at all, I thought about Noboru Watanabe and the soldering iron he had brought me. 'You really ought to have a soldering iron in the house. They come in handy', he said. What a wholesome idea, I said to him mentally as I wiped my lips with a handkerchief. Now, thanks to you, my house is equipped with a soldering iron. But because of that damned soldering iron, my house doesn't feel like my house any longer.[74]

Now it is the lack of connection that binds these two men together. A wholesome idea, perhaps, and admirable for its attempt to bridge the gap between the poles of Japanese society, but it is unsuccessful. The final line of the story (which is reminiscent of 'The Second Bakery Attack' and also Carver's 'What Is It?') presents a world still waiting for an effective answer, 'When I closed my eyes, sleep floated down on me like a dark, silent net.'[75] While there is no obvious solution offered, like much of Carver's early fiction Murakami's early fiction highlights the unattractiveness of dominant ideology: a zone where the difference between hegemonic narratives and lived experience is explored.

If Carver and Murakami present corresponding ideas on the failure of both orthodox narratives and their alternatives, then they offer, I want to suggest, a somewhat similar solution, too. The themes found in their early fiction are cemented in their response to the personal and social conditions that they saw around them. For Carver this was struggling to maintain financial stability, sobriety and a marriage. For Murakami it was the lost idealism of the post-war generation and their conformity to the Establishment. It is in the same, consistent manner then, that their later work reflects the changing of those personal and social conditions. Carver's late fiction, for example, is characterised by a readjustment of aims. The orthodox narrative of hard work as a means to social and economic prosperity (which lost out to alcoholism, bankruptcy and broken relationships) gave way to what might be thought of as more objective, down-to-earth aims: the restoration of personal relationships, recovery from addiction, and modest artistic creation. Likewise Murakami responded to the life-altering events of the Kobe earthquake and Tokyo gas attack in 1995 by attempting to present what he calls a 'new narrative'; an answer to the conformity of the post-war generation and the hyper-consumerism of the post-post-war generation. For the rest of this chapter, then, I want to explore Carver's late work, after his recovery from alcohol addiction, and then assess how this acts as a model for Murakami as he seeks to create his own new narrative for the Japanese people after 1995.

The date 7 June 1977 was, famously, when Carver stopped drinking. Almost a decade of alcoholism had ruined his marriage, crippled his fledgling career and almost ended his life. Slowly beginning to recover from this destructive cycle, his writing appeared to change. His fiction, once described by Donald Newlove as 'sparingly clear as a fifth of iced Smirnoff', began to intimate signs of embellishment and growth.[76] At the time, critics viewed the transformation as part of a wider development in Carver's *oeuvre*. Writing in 1985, William L. Stull claimed that Carver's fiction was beginning to embody a metamorphosis from 'sorry tales more transcribed than told' – the Carvers' first bankruptcy and 'What Is It?' is a premium example of this – to a more generous realism in 'a spirit of empathy, forgiveness and community'.[77] The idea of positive progression and development fast became the prevailing opinion and was backed up by critical approaches that emphasised his formal expansion. While this view remained dominant among scholars through the 80s and 90s, it was superannuated when D. T. Max published his article on Lish's editing in 1998. Those loyal to the Carver cause rushed to the archives to invalidate the journalist's claims, only to be disappointed and find that, yes, it seemed Lish had played an important role in shaping Carver's formal aesthetic. The evolution theory had been disproved. His early writing was, in its original form at least, as generous as his late writing. In an attempt to preserve the purity of Carver's work, a move soon followed to establish and publish Carver's original manuscripts. William L. Stull and Maureen P. Carroll completed *Beginners*, the original and unedited text of *What We Talk About When We Talk About Love* in 2007.[78]

The situation regarding Lish is complicated by Carver's lack of denial concerning Lish as a negative influence. In fact, more often than not, despite their fractious relationship, he tended to present a positive front and praise Lish for his editorial involvement – or at least for giving him the opportunity to begin his career.[79] A second factor further obfuscates the issue: Carver's relationship with Tess Gallagher. It seems to be no accident that Carver's publication of longer, generally positive and more expositional stories coincides with the reduction of Lish's editorial control *and* the development of his relationship with Gallagher. Chad Wriglesworth is convinced that Carver's relationship with Gallagher 'remains the most significant influence on his spiritual and relational recovery'.[80] Evidence of this abounds, Wriglesworth claims, not only in Carver's late fiction and poetry, but also his non-fiction prose. He offers Carver's final piece of writing, a short essay written for the University of Hartford's 1988 graduation ceremony, at which he was due to receive an honorary doctorate, as an apposite example. Sklenicka reinforces Wriglesworth's claim when she notes a strong undertone of Gallagher's vision in the text, 'the Hartford speech moves in a rhythm that sounds more like Gallagher's than Carver's', although she does concede that 'there's a definite Carver touch in his valedictory paragraphs'.[81] The address echoes a religious belief that Carver claimed to hold towards the end of his life, and turns on a phrase he borrows from Saint Teresa: 'Words lead to deeds ... They prepare the soul make it ready, and move it to tenderness.'[82] In what amounts to a short sermon, Carver moves on to describe the phrase as being 'mystical' and focuses particularly on the words 'soul' and 'tenderness', finally exhorting his audience to 'remember that words, the right and true words, can have the power of deeds'.[83] Such power comes, by Carver's own admission, from a spiritual place, especially in a time 'less openly supportive of the important connection between what we say and what we do', a sentiment that, since Carver's death, Gallagher has placed as a template for Carver's second-life recovery:

> [Carver] never heaped credit upon himself for having overcome his illness. He knew it was a matter of grace, of having put his trust in what AA identifies as a 'higher power', and of having miraculously been given the will to turn all temptation to drink aside.[84]

It is easy to be sympathetic towards Wriglesworth's argument that Carver's post-alcoholic life and work evinces a spiritual recovery – one, in particular, 'not bound by orthodox creed or specific doctrine'.[85] This idea is perhaps most clearly reinforced by the posthumous publications that Gallagher has commissioned – *Call If You Need Me, Carver Country, Soul Barnacles, A New Path To The Waterfall* – which contain a particularly overt spiritual resonance. Gallagher concludes her foreword to *Call If You Need Me*, for example, by asserting that Carver's writing holds an almost scriptural property, one that 'we can dip into at any point and find something to refresh and sustain us'.[86] And yet, given the intensely material world of Carver's earlier fiction, Gallagher's remarks obscure as much as they illuminate. Indeed, whether or not we choose to accept or deny what Wriglesworth calls a 'manifestation of a sacred reality' in Carver's second-life fiction, it is interesting to note that Murakami's more recent publications offer a correlative proposition to the idea that words have the power to provoke actions of tenderness and spirituality.[87] This idea is very much part of his response to the post-war obsession with corporate identity and materialism and post-1970s malaise. Perhaps unsurprisingly too, Murakami's move to a clearer critical response is marked – much like Carver's – by a profound real-life experience.[88]

After the extended economic boom in the 1970s and 80s, Japan's economy finally came to a halt in 1991 with the widespread collapse of the financial sector. The long bust that ensued sapped the self-assurance of the 1980s and replaced it with serious anxieties about the future. The period, which has been defined as being 'synonymous with prolonged malaise', extended beyond the economic instability and political stasis to the general populace. Sociologists have reported the rise in unemployment, suicides, divorce and domestic violence. Jeff Kingston states, '[w]ith the misery index rising, the swaggering self-confidence of the 1980s gave way to sweeping anxieties that extend well beyond the economy'.[89] And so The Lost Decade began, ten years of malaise among the Japanese that carried them from shattered 1960s idealism, the boredom of conformity and the excesses of materialism to disaster. Kingston notes that the outcomes of these economic and social conditions were twofold. First, there was, 'a pervasive social malaise in contemporary Japan', and secondly, it was 'generating a sense of looming catastrophe'.[90]

Eventually catastrophe struck twice in the first three months of 1995. In January an earthquake struck the city of Kobe and killed over 6,000 people, and in March the cult Aum Shinrikyo dropped multiple bags of sarin gas in the Tokyo subway which killed thirteen people and injured over 1,000. These two events led the Japanese to become even more introspective, and Kingston notes that 'some analysts suggested they [cultists] were reacting against the materialism and spiritual void that permeate contemporary Japan'.[91] Murakami was one of those analysts. In his fiction and non-fiction writing he pulls both events together; for Murakami, both disasters – one natural, one man-made – act as wake-up calls. He describes the events as, 'the gravest tragedies in Japan's postwar history', and spent the latter half of the 1990s working on two projects in connection with them.[92] The first, *Underground* (1997), focused on the gas attack and presented a series of interviews with the victims alongside cult affiliates. This non-fiction project allowed Murakami to explicitly diagnose the social conditions that he saw in Japan at the time, while continuing to explore similar themes with those in his early fiction – lost 1960s idealism, conformity to the Establishment and an acceptance of hyper-materialism. Murakami finally draws the following conclusion:

> What have we learned from this shocking incident? One thing is for sure. Some strange malaise, some bitter aftertaste lingers on. We crane our necks and look around us, as if to ask: where did all *that* come from? If only to be rid of this malaise, to cleanse our palates of this aftertaste, most Japanese seem ready to pack up the whole incident in a trunk labelled THINGS OVER AND DONE WITH. We would rather the meaning of the whole ordeal was left to the fixed processes of the court and everything was dealt with on the level of 'the system'.[93]

This, of course, is not a satisfactory answer for Murakami. Writing with a rhetoric which curiously reflects Carver's in a 'Meditation on a Line from Saint Teresa', Murakami calls for 'words coming from another direction, new words for a new narrative' that will have the power to 'purify the [old] narrative' of mindless conformity to work and consumption.[94] The (new) task that Murakami sets is to present a narrative that leads towards a sustained, complete, fulfilling life in contemporary Japan. He compares the feeling to, 'a gigantic sword dangling above my head. It's something I'm going to have to deal with much more seriously from here on.'[95] Now accepting that he is in 'the ranks of that generation with a "vested duty" towards Japanese society', Murakami recognises that 1995 symbolises a new period in his writing; a time for a more sincere fiction – a more viable narrative – that seeks to answer the problems of lost idealism, conformity and materialism that he presented in his early fiction.[96]

The second project, a series of short stories published as *After The Quake*, was a response to the Kobe earthquake in January 1995. Set in February 1995, the month between the earthquake and the gas attack, the context of this series is fundamental to the predicament that its characters find themselves in. They are literally caught 'in between' two disastrous events. Perhaps deliberately reminiscent of the paradigm that many of his characters are stuck between in his early fiction (Establishment and non-conformity), the characters in *After The Quake* are still coming to terms with the disastrous impact (both nationally and personally) of the earthquake. It is not long, then, until the man-made disaster, the Tokyo gas attack, will present the Japanese people with a problem: how to cope with what Murakami calls the 'darkness' that is inside. This is, perhaps, the real leitmotif of the series and yet, much like Carver's unorthodox spirituality, its exact nature and origin is hard to pinpoint. Murakami provides a fictional illustration in 'UFO in Kushiro' in which the story's protagonist, Komura, is asked by a colleague to deliver a box to the northern island of Hokkaido. His colleague's sister and her friend, Shimao, meet Komura at the airport. Later Shimao takes him to a love hotel where she attempts to sleep with him. But the couple fail to have sex (Komura, whose wife has recently left him, cannot go through with the act), and instead Shimao begins to question Komura about his life. She asks him what he thinks is inside the box that he has delivered – its contents were unknown to Komura – and she suggests that the parcel contained, '*something* that was inside you'. This causes a violent reaction in Komura who is overcome with disgust at her suggestion. 'For one split second', Murakami writes, 'Komura realised that he was on the verge of committing an act of overwhelming violence.'[97] The act, however, is never committed. Shimao pulls out of her comment by suggesting that she was only joking, but the phrase has stuck with Komura and he begins to make a profound discovery. Jonathan Boulter recognises that the box which, 'weighs practically nothing', and which Komura surmises might be 'used for human ashes', becomes, 'a portentous emblem, a physical object correlative to Komura's own emptiness'. This emptiness, Boulter suggests, is the result of Komura's 'loss of his own wife, but also the massive loss initiated by the quake'.[98] This emptiness also, it appears, has the capacity for what Murakami might term 'darkness' – violence and destruction. *After The Quake*, then, documents how characters face the wake-up call of the natural earthquake without succumbing to the internal darkness that threatens to usurp any attempt to purify the old-narrative. The stories also mark a notable change in direction for Murakami's short fiction. Abandoning his recognisable – and popular – Boku narrator, the series is written in the third person. Rubin acknowledges the significance of this change, 'By abandoning the limited focus of Boku, Murakami implies that the malaise he is diagnosing goes beyond the privileged few who live on the periphery of national events.' The series also marks an important reflection of how Murakami saw life in Japan at the time. 'The result', Rubin says, 'is a glum panorama of mid-1990s Japan in which the earthquake is a wake-up call to the emptiness of their lives.'[99] This emptiness, Rubin argues, may also reflect what Murakami saw in the ordinary people he interviewed for *Underground*: that there is some indefinable thing missing from their lives. The result is that the characters that feature in *After The Quake* are, often, similar to the sort of peripatetic loners found in Carver's (or Murakami's) early fiction. There is an overriding sense of the banal in this series – Murakami's talismanic surreal world is absent. Paramount too is the consumer-capitalist culture that permeated Japan up to that point. The recession of the early 1990s may have caused an economic and social malaise, but the characters in *After The Quake* still work in electronics, medicine and banking. This is a collection, then, that seeks to explore the realistic lives of people in everyday situations. These are the quintessential

Murakami characters, ordinary Japanese people whose outwardly satisfactory lives hide a deeper sense of incompleteness and malaise.

The series of narratives that make up *After The Quake* document how the natural earthquake acts as a wake-up call for characters caught in the net of post-1970s despondency. The severe hangover that Yoshiya, the protagonist of 'All God's Children Can Dance', is suffering from is surely the physical symptom of what Murakami sees as an increasingly 'spiritual' void amongst the young, post-post-war generation. Attempting to regain some kind of psychological normality after a hedonistic night, Yoshiya epitomises the addiction to hyper-consumerism in post-1970s Japan. He elicits a plea to the heavens, 'Please, God, never let this happen to me again', a cry, which is uttered more in despair than in genuine petition.[100] Yoshiya's mother, who he still lives with, conducts, in contrast, a religious but hypocritical life. On the one hand a devout member of a Christian cult, she holds to the purity of a works-based religion, and on the other succumbs to the depravity of her sexual desires for her own son. With the perverse, organised religion of his mother offering no real alternative to his hyper-consumerism, Yoshiya embarks on a series of sexual encounters, but these also fail to remedy the void of his spiritual nature. Claiming that Yoshiya has no biological father – an ideology proffered by her cult – his mother one day describes a string of sexual experiences she had with an obstetrician before his birth. Spotting a man on the train that matches the obstetrician's description the day of his severe hangover, Yoshiya begins to trail him. When he alights he follows him in a taxi before pursuing him on foot and losing him in a series of dark alleys. Left in a void of blindness and silence, Yoshiya's quest represents a broader search for meaning in 1990s Japan:

> What was I hoping to gain from this? he asked himself as he strode ahead. Was I trying to confirm the ties that make it possible for me to exist here and now? Was I hoping to be woven into some new plot, to be given some new and better-defined role to play?[101]

It is at this point in the narrative that Murakami grants Yoshiya a strong element of self-perception. His internal questioning enables him to understand his situation. His denial, therefore, that his current void is the result of past collective experience (mixed identity or unanswered cultural guilt) makes him realise the insufficiency of the orthodox narrative offered by the Establishment. In discussing Murakami's post-1995 fiction, Stephen Snyder and Philip Gabriel argue that 'Murakami turns not to collective myth and memory but to the inviolateness of the individual and the insistence on the right of the individual to loneliness and separation', and it is this persistence of autonomy that allows Murakami to pinpoint the source of the void in 1990s Japanese society.[102] This, then, is a quest of serious consequence; Murakami's reference to the 'tail of the darkness inside' is clearly a synonymous phrase for his conjecture in *Underground* that the Tokyo subway attack and the Aum phenomenon revealed the 'distorted image of ourselves'.[103] While Yoshiya's quest to fill the void in 1990s Japan may be commended, the dangers for a wrong turn are profound. As such, the problem does not stem from the past but from inside. The 'darkness' is symbolised by the metaphor of the alley in which Yoshiya chases the man – it is 'dark as the bottom of the night-time sea' – and Yoshiya can only follow the man based on the sound of his footsteps.[104] The re-emergence of the sound – reminiscent of Rubin's comment that music is the best entry into the deep recesses of the mind in Murakami's fiction – points towards a significant moment in the story. Murakami describes Yoshiya as 'clinging to the sound' of the man's footsteps until eventually even that begins to fade and 'there is no sound at all'.[105] Left in a void of blindness and silence, Yoshiya continues down the alley until he comes to the end and manages to escape and finds himself on an empty baseball field. The pursuit has ended. The man who Yoshiya thought was his father has mysteriously disappeared. The self-perception that Yoshiya shows at this point is important because it represents an awareness of the danger that lurks in the quest for release from the void in 1990s Japan. Forced to confront the emptiness that has been inside him for his twenty-five years, Yoshiya is at a crux.

In many ways whether the man was Yoshiya's father or not is irrelevant to the plot of the story. The point is that he represents an outside guiding force that leads to a moment of perspicuity. Murakami writes, '[n]ow the stranger had disappeared, however, the importance of the succeeding acts that had brought him this far turned unclear inside him. Meaning itself broke down and would never be the same again.'[106] Having begun to realise the brokenness of the 'old' narrative, Yoshiya is at a point of self-diagnosis, and his next act embodies a kind of generic spiritual solution:

> Unable to think of a song to match his mood, he danced in time with the stirring of the grass and the flowing of the clouds. Before long, he began to feel that someone, somewhere, was watching him. His whole body – his skin, his bones – told him with absolute certainty that he was in *someone's* field of vision. So what? he thought. Let them look if they want to, whoever they are. All God's children can dance.[107]

This closing moment, an example of what Rubin in a BBC documentary calls Murakami's 'down to earth spirituality', is, I am tentatively suggesting, Murakami's solution to the hangover-malaise of the orthodox narratives of corporate conformity and materialism. If Yoshiya's quest reveals a longing to fill the internal void present in The Lost Decade, then his improvised dance, in time with nature, reveals a kind of independent pantheism that frees him from the constraints of the post-war Establishment and protects him from the darkness of the post-post-war generation.[108] And yet, this new narrative mirrors what some critics view as Carver's non-creedal spiritualism in that it is enacted out in the presence of a benign guiding force – analogous to the 'higher power' that Gallagher claims that Carver believed in after his recovery from alcoholism. Rubin continues to explain Murakami's spiritual solution by suggesting that his fiction is 'dealing with religious themes without the remotest appeal to established religion. He's getting into those things that you can call spiritual without any spiritual nonsense.'[109] The success of Murakami's solution is, of course, far more equivocal. If, for instance, Rubin's definition seems a little vague, it is, perhaps, because it fails – much like the definitions that describe Carver's second-life spirituality – to mirror the specificity of the strongly materialist, socio-economic diagnosis found in both writers' early fiction. In this way it is perhaps better viewed not as a definitive model, but an idealistic one; an undogmatic solution that presents fleeting moments of connection and fulfilment to a society steeped in orthodoxy.

While Gallagher's notion that Carver evinced a spiritual answer to the material diagnosis of his early life goes some way to explaining the more 'generous' aspects of his late fiction – and while I think this idea is picked up by Murakami in his response to the events of 1995 – I want to conclude by suggesting that this is really a rather limited view of Carver's final years. In the introduction to this book I suggested that Carver's work is better viewed as embodying a return to a kind of residual narrative associated with ideas of craftsmanship, one that is nominally seen as being more authentic and supplying a more sustained sense of self and purpose in the neoliberal era. It is to this idea that I now return. Elements of Carver's craftsmanship are depicted in his very late fiction and while some of his ideas are perhaps not as fully developed as they might be – in part due to his death in 1988 – the notion of craftsmanship is a large part of Carver's response to the socio-economic problems that he saw around him in the early neoliberal era. With this in mind I want to return in more detail to his story 'Kindling'.

'Kindling' was, as I have already noted, published posthumously by *Esquire* in 1999 and, as such is unlikely to have offered an example for Murakami's immediate post-1995 fiction. The purpose of looking at this story now, however, is that I want to suggest that it indicates the trajectory that Carver's fictional vision was taking before his death. The story principally concerns Myers who has just got out of rehabilitation. The story opens, 'It was the middle of August and Myers was between lives.'[110] If, as I have already intimated, there are moments of incomplete recovery from socio-economic demise in some of his other fiction (particularly in stories like 'Where I'm Calling From', 'Chef's House' and 'A Small, Good Thing') then 'Kindling' fulfils something of the promise of those early partial optimistic fictional visions. In the story, Myers is beginning a new life – a second-life, we might say – he has left his wife and her boyfriend, he has left his alcoholism, and he is starting out again in small-town America. He moves in with Sol and Bonnie, a childless couple with a spare room looking for a lodger. While Sol might be read as an invocation of Carver's call in 'A Meditation On A Line By Saint Teresa' for the value of spiritual belief – the name, of course, suggests spiritual life, hope and vivacity – his actions also suggest that he operates as an extension of other characters in Carver's fiction who have a positive impact on the protagonist's problems. Like Frank Martin in 'Where I'm Calling From' or Chef in 'Chef's House', Sol provides a deeper meaning to the start of Myers's second-life, pushing him towards the cultivation of social and labour-related responsibility:

> What kind of work do you do? he wanted to know. I'm just curious. This is a small town and I know people. I grade lumber at the mill myself. Only need one good arm to do that. But sometimes there are openings. I could put in a word, maybe. What's your regular line of work?[111]

Readers who are familiar with Carver's fiction will know the answer to Sol's questions. Myers is, of course, an aspiring writer; a man now between narrative lives and likely feeling despicable. In another story, 'The Compartment', he is attempting to repair his broken relationship with his son, but ends up on the wrong train heading in the opposite direction. But something has changed in Myers's life. While he still finds himself, as Carver puts it, between lives, he now has a more sustained sense of purpose; his aim for the time being is to find some way to be reconciled with his wife. In a scene that significantly evokes the actions of the estranged husband in 'Intimacy', Carver writes:

> Myers kept to his room, where he was writing a letter to his wife. It was a long letter and, he felt, an important one. Perhaps the most important letter he'd ever written in his life. In the letter he was attempting to tell his wife that he was sorry for everything that had happened and that he hoped someday she would forgive him. *I would get down on my knees and ask forgiveness if that would help.*[112]

Myers is a character quite distinct from any other in Carver's fiction. Where Carver's early fiction was noted for its stasis and idleness, Myers is decidedly active and his attempt to write a letter to his wife reflects something of his desire to craft for himself some kind of new social ideal. What Myers more broadly represents in 'Kindling' is a character intent on pursuing, in all areas of his life, the ideals of craftsmanship argued for by Sennett as a means to providing a solution to the problems that he is encountering in life in neoliberalism. Sennett writes, '*Craftsmanship* is a term most often applied to manual labourers and denotes the pursuit of quality.' But, he goes on, 'This is too narrow a view.' For mental and social craftsmanship are equally valid pursuits. 'An embracing definition of craftsmanship would be', Sennett concludes, 'doing something well for its own sake. Self-discipline and self-criticism adhere in all domains of craftsmanship; standards matter, and the pursuit of quality ideally becomes an end in itself.'[113] While Myers's ability to craft a letter is important in the narrative, and in Myers reaching some level of emotional closure, it is not where the crux of the narrative lies. Instead, it lies in the work that Myers completes while he is staying with Sol and Bonnie:

> The next morning it was all he could do to wait until they'd left the house before he went out back to begin work. He found a pair of gloves on the back step that Sol must have left for him. He sawed and split wood . . . His shoulders hurt and his fingers were sore and, in spite of the gloves, he'd picked up a few splinters and could feel blisters rising, but he kept on. He decided that he would cut this wood and split it and stack it before sunset, and that it was a matter of life and death that he do so. I must finish this job, he thought, or else.[114]

As the sun sets, Myers finishes work. In Carver's early stories the close of day often marks a point of psychological distress or the oncoming of a menacing future. But in 'Kindling' Myers's work leads to a distinctly positive ending. 'Just as the sun went down and the moon appeared over the mountains, Myers split the last chunk and gathered up the two pieces and carried the wood over to the garage . . . Then he went inside.'[115] Myers appears to be embodying the essence of Sennett's craft. Here is work done 'well for its own sake'. It is a 'self-discipline', where 'standards matter' and the 'pursuit of quality ideally becomes an end in itself'. Part, then, of what makes craftsmanship so appealing for Sennett as a means to escape the futility of working life in the neoliberal era is that it emphasises objectification. In other words something is made to matter in and of itself. 'This objectifying spirit can give even low-level, seemingly unskilled labourers pride in their work', Sennett argues. And then illustrates this point by drawing upon his research of Bostonian bakers in the 1970s (an appropriate illustration for Carver), 'in a family run bakery where the most junior members were treated roughly and pressed too hard by fathers and uncles, the results in the early morning similarly salved some of the upset: the bread was good'. Sennett concludes his point with this observation:

> While it's important not to romanticise the balm of craftsmanship, it matters equally to understand the consequence of doing something well for its own sake. Ability counts for something, by a measure which is both concrete and impersonal.[116]

To recall, once more, the socio-economic context in which Carver is writing, the distinctly short-term aims of institutions in late capitalism, the flux and flexible accumulation opened up by the liberalisation of international currency markets, the requirements for labourers to be constantly shifting tasks with transferable skills, and the avoidance of anything, to borrow the management term, ingrown, then the idea that Myers would complete a seemingly low-level, unimportant task such as splitting wood, a task that offers no financial remuneration, with the sole purpose of doing it well for its own sake, seems deeply countercultural. The personal affirmation and sense of fulfilment that the action leads to at the end of the story, the promise of a pastoral landscape, is a place reminiscent of residual values – Myers writes, 'It reminds me of someplace I've read about but never travelled to before now' – and suggests that this kind of craftsmanship is Carver's answer to the problems he experienced in his socio-economic context.[117]

The strong literary influence between Carver and Murakami was reflected in a trip that Murakami and Yoko, his wife, took in 1984 to meet Carver and Gallagher at their home in Port Angeles. The four spent their time together discussing Carver's fictional depiction of the many humiliations in daily life, something, Murakami thought, that made Carver's fiction particularly appealing across the Pacific. By the end of the afternoon Gallagher recalls that she and Carver recognised they had 'met an extraordinary couple to whom they felt somehow connected'.[118] Near the end of his life, Carver recalled the meeting in the poem 'The Projectile', which he dedicated to Murakami. The poem opens by recalling their time together in which they 'sipped tea, politely musing on possible reasons for the success of my books in your country', before Carver writes about the apparent coincidence that the 'pain and humiliation' in his stories 'translates in terms of sales'.[119] Carver continues to describe how their conversation triggered an adolescent memory of a snowball fight which ended in a broken eardrum after a snowball fluked its way through a three inch gap in his car window. The pain, Carver writes, was 'stupendous', but more pertinently, so was the humiliation as Carver began to weep in front of his peers. While the poem is an interesting account of their time together, its content is more than anecdotal and acts as an ironic commentary on the influence and impact of Carver's early-life humiliations, which, in Murakami's hand translate – pun intended – into book sales. While Carver could not have read Murakami's fiction at the time (it was yet to be translated into English) Carver's recollection of their conversation neatly encapsulates the close association between his and Murakami's fiction. In this sense then, the problems that Carver faced early in his life – the impact of the socio-economic transition from embedded liberalism to neoliberalism – and which, in turn, contributed to the production of his fiction are the very characteristics which drew Murakami, who saw similar trends reflected in Japanese society, to his writing. The poem reveals that Carver realises the irony of this, that when that same experience was commodified through Murakami's translations, the popularity of Carver's work contributed to bringing about the very socio-economic mobility and artistic posterity which had seemed so inaccessible early in his life.

Notes

1. An earlier version of Chapter 3 appeared in *The Raymond Carver Review*, 5/6 (2017), 58–78. For more on Murakami's claim see Murakami, 'A Literary Comrade', in Stull and Carroll (eds), *Remembering Ray*, p. 132.
2. Murakami, 'A Literary Comrade', p. 130.
3. Although it ought to be noted that there are strong realist elements to Murakami's fiction which are often overlooked by critics. His first bestselling novel in Japan, *Norwegian Wood*, for instance, is devoid of fantasy elements. Likewise, so are many of his short stories, particularly those featured in *After The Quake*. It is also worth pointing out that Murakami has published two less-read books that link him to Carver. The first, in 2004, an anthology of

selected stories, which features Carver's 'The Bath', titled, *Birthday Stories*. The second, in 2008, a book on running titled *What I Talk About When I Talk About Running*.
4. Gardner, *On Moral Fiction*, p. 5; Murakami, *Underground*, p. 204.
5. Rubin, *Haruki Murakami and the Music of Words*, p. 258. At the outset of this chapter it is worth highlighting that while I intend to deal with some of the stylistic connections between both writers, as my analytical approach is heavily socio-economically mediated, I will stop short of any thorough exploration. For more on the stylistic similarities between the two writers see Matsuoka, 'Murakami Haruki and Raymond Carver: The American Scene'.
6. It is worth pointing out that Murakami is a prolific translator. The list of authors he has translated aside from Carver includes: F. Scott Fitzgerald, Truman Capote, Raymond Chandler, J. D. Salinger, John Irving, Tim O'Brien, Grace Paley, Denis Johnson, Thom Jones, Mark Strand and Paul Theroux.
7. From the mid-1980s to the year 2000, Murakami published the following translations of Carver's fiction (publication dates given in parentheses after the title): *Boku ga denwa o kakete iru baso* [*Where I'm Calling From*] (1983), *Yoru ni naru to sake wa …* [*At Night The Salmon Move*] (1985), *Sasayaka da keredo, yaku ni tatsu koto* [*A Small, Good Thing and Other Stories*] (1989), *Carver's Dozen: Reimondo Kava kessakusen* [*A Dozen of Raymond Carver's Best Stories*] (1994), the eight-volume *Reimondo Kava zenshu* [*Complete Works of Raymond Carver*] (1990–7) and finally Carver's posthumous collection *Hitsuyo ni nattara denwa o kakete* [*Call If You Need Me: The Uncollected Fiction and Other Prose*] (2000). Note the dates of Murakami's own story collections in the same period: *Chugoku-yuki no soro boto* [*A Slow Boat To China*] (1983), *Kangaru-biyori* [*A Perfect Day For Kangaroos*] (1983), *Hotaru, Naya o yaku, sono-ta no tanpen* [*Firefly, Barn Burning and Other Stories*] (1984), *Kaiten mokuba no deddo hiito* [*Dead Heat on a Merry-Go-Round*] (1985), *Pan'ya saishugeki* [*The Second Bakery Attack*] (1986), *TV Piipuru* [*TV People*] (1990), *Murakami Haruki zensakuhin 1979–89* [*Murakami's Collected Stories 1979–89*] (1990–1), *Rekishinton no yurei* [*The Lexington Ghost*] (1996), and *Kami no kodomotachi wa mina odoru* [*After The Quake*] (2000).
8. Murakami, 'A Literary Comrade', p. 131.
9. Available at <http://ieas.berkeley.edu/cjs/50th_ann_2008.10.10.html> (last accessed 11 April 2019).
10. Both novels were published in 1979 and 1980 in Japan, but because Murakami viewed them as ostensible 'apprentice novels' they were only published in the US and UK in English translation for the first time in 2015.
11. Miyoshi, *Off Center*, p. 234.
12. Seemann argues that inarticulateness and inaction in both writers' work exemplifies a struggle to determine individual essence. He writes, 'this failure to connect ultimately serves as the existential foundation for many Carver stories as his characters strive to relate in environments that may prevent the acts of discovery and engagement'. Seemann, 'Existential Connections: The Influence of Raymond Carver on Haruki Murakami', p. 77.
13. Harvey, *The Condition of Postmodernity*, pp. 141–2.

14. Harvey's term is used tentatively in his account, and I would suggest is now more broadly recognisable as being in line with neoliberal free market principles. For a more in-depth account, see Part II of Harvey *The Condition of Postmodernity*, pp. 121–97.
15. Sennett, *The Culture of New Capitalism*, p. 5.
16. Sennett, *The Culture of New Capitalism*, pp. 105–6.
17. One way that neoliberal policy makers sought to combat this problem was to introduce a debt-based economy; an idea that still operates to this day. In the 1980s in particular, and as I explored in Chapter 2, credit became easily available for many.
18. Harker, 'Raymond Carver and Class', p. 720.
19. Carver, *Collected Stories*, p. 737.
20. Carver's tone makes this clear. These are jobs that any American might hold, and which Carver, as he documented in 'Fires', did at one time. Later, in an interview with Bruce Weber, Carver claimed that 'the country is filled with these people. They're good people. People doing the best they could.' Weber, 'A Chronicler of Blue-Collar Despair', in Gentry and Stull (eds), *Conversations with Raymond Carver*, p. 92.
21. Sennett, *The Culture of New Capitalism*, p. 4.
22. Carver, *Collected Stories*, p. 157.
23. Carver, *Collected Stories*, p. 157.
24. Carver, *Collected Stories*, p. 159.
25. Carver, *Collected Stories*, p. 159.
26. Carver, *Collected Stories*, p. 161.
27. Carver, *Collected Stories*, p. 162.
28. Carver, *Collected Stories*, p. 164.
29. Carver, *Collected Stories*, p. 159.
30. Carver, *Collected Stories*, p. 160.
31. Sennett, *The Culture of New Capitalism*, pp. 137–8.
32. To illustrate this kind of consuming purchase Sennett uses the example of an iPod whose 'commercial appeal consists precisely in having more [memory] than a person could ever use'. The car that Leo and Toni buy therefore reflects this desire. 'Buying a little iPod similarly promises to expand one's capabilities', and here is the crux, apt to the point of cliché, 'As the salesman who flogged my iPod said, without any embarrassment, "The sky's the limit".' Sennett, *The Culture of New Capitalism*, pp. 153–4.
33. Cornwall, 'Mediated Desire and American Disappointment in the Stories of Raymond Carver', p. 346.
34. Carver, *Collected Stories*, p. 85.
35. Carver, *Collected Stories*, p. 89.
36. Carver, *Collected Stories*, p. 85.
37. Carver, *Collected Stories*, p. 86.
38. Carver, *Collected Stories*, p. 86.
39. Carver, *Collected Stories*, p. 87.
40. Carver, *Collected Stories*, pp. 91–2.
41. Carver, *Collected Stories*, p. 92.

42. Boxer and Phillips, 'Will You Please Be Quiet, Please?: Voyeurism, Dissociation, and the Art of Raymond Carver', pp. 75, 77.
43. Takafusa, *A History of Showa Japan, 1926–1989*, pp. 322, 379.
44. Ivy, 'Formations of Mass Culture', in Gordon (ed.), *Postwar Japan as History*, p. 249.
45. Kelts, *Japanamerica: How Japanese Pop Culture Has Invaded the US*, p. 38.
46. Murakami, *Norwegian Wood*, p. 74.
47. Murakami, *Norwegian Wood*, p. 75.
48. Murakami, *Norwegian Wood*, p. 75.
49. Rubin, *Music of Words*, p. 23.
50. Murakami, *Norwegian Wood*, p. 1.
51. Strecher, 'Beyond "Pure" Literature: Mimesis, Formula, and the Postmodern in the Fiction of Murakami Haruki', p. 370.
52. McCaffery, Gregory and Miyawaki, 'It Don't Mean A Thing, If It Ain't Got That Swing: an Interview with Haruki Murakami', p. 117.
53. Rubin, *Music of Words*, p. 29.
54. Murakami's short fiction is also where he admits to feeling Carver's influence most strongly:

    Raymond Carver was without question the most valuable teacher I ever had and also the greatest literary comrade. The novels I write tend, I believe, in a very different direction from the fiction Ray has written. But if he had never existed, or if I had never encountered his writings, the books I write (especially my short fiction) would probably have assumed a very different form.' Murakami, 'A Literary Comrade', p. 132.

55. Boku is the Japanese word for the 'I' that Murakami chooses to narrate the majority of his short stories. It positions Murakami's stories in a canon of Japanese 'I-novels'. For more on the use of Boku in Murakami's fiction, see Rubin, *Music of Words*, p. 37.
56. Murakami, *The Elephant Vanishes*, p. 36. It is worth noting that *The Elephant Vanishes* was Murakami's first collection of stories published in English and was compiled and commissioned by Gary Fisketjon. In a publicity move reminiscent of his Vintage Contemporaries series, Fisketjon had McInerney provide a quote for the back cover.
57. Murakami, *The Elephant Vanishes*, p. 40.
58. Murakami, *The Elephant Vanishes*, p. 41.
59. Murakami, *The Elephant Vanishes*, p. 40; Sennett, *The Culture of New Capitalism*, pp. 182–3. Boku's declaration is also a notable reflection of Mike's acceptance of neoliberal 'common sense' in Carver's story 'The Student's Wife'.
60. Murakami, *The Elephant Vanishes*, p. 48.
61. Murakami, *The Elephant Vanishes*, p. 238.
62. It's worth noting that Murakami's story also presents a gross mutation of Carver's story 'A Small, Good Thing'. 'The Second Bakery Attack', which was published in 1986, three years after Carver published 'A Small, Good Thing' in *Cathedral*, alters Carver's optimistic vision of a reformed baker. In Carver's story the reconciliatory ending reveals the baker's humble and deindustrial-

ised 'dark loaf' which is 'heavy bread, but rich' (the indication being that *this* bread has a powerful capacity to enrich social interactions). In Murakami's story, the second bakery attack takes place in a McDonald's, a symbol of US capitalist imperialism, where the taste of 'molasses and coarse grains' is replaced by the grease of a Big Mac patty.

63. Allinson, *Japan's Postwar History*, p. 154.
64. Allinson, *Japan's Postwar History*, pp. 166–7.
65. Murakami, *The Elephant Vanishes*, p. 160.
66. In the story Boku has several girlfriends at one time – his sister describes them simply as 'a body you sleep with' – he drinks copious amounts of alcohol, and generally shirks any familial, occupational or collective responsibility. He has no serious career ambitions, only working at his particular company because, as his sister again points out, 'It just so happened he had an in with that particular company', before adding, 'He's not particularly interested in anything that's of benefit to society.' Murakami, *The Elephant Vanishes*, pp. 160, 178.
67. Murakami, *The Elephant Vanishes*, p. 166.
68. Murakami, *The Elephant Vanishes*, p. 165.
69. Murakami, *The Elephant Vanishes*, p. 163.
70. Noboru is a computer engineer who Boku describes as working for 'one of those three-letter places – IBM or NEC or TNT. I don't know.' Like Murakami's use of McDonald's in 'The Second Bakery Attack' the abbreviated company name represents the prevalence of global capitalist conglomerates in Japan in the late twentieth century. And while Noboru has a kind of Fordist stability to his life – the polemic opposite of Boku's lifestyle – I don't think Murakami is suggesting it as a viable alternative or answer to post-1970s humiliation. Both characters represent two extremes – conformity and distorted autonomy. I will suggest in my forthcoming discussion that Murakami seeks to present a balance between both extremes as a viable narrative for life in late twentieth-century Japanese capitalism. Murakami, *The Elephant Vanishes*, p. 167.
71. Murakami, *The Elephant Vanishes*, p. 176.
72. Rubin, 'Murakami Haruki's Two Poor Aunts Tell Everything They Know About Sheep, Wells, Unicorns, Proust, Elephants, and Magpies', in Snyder and Gabriel (eds), *Oe and Beyond: Fiction in Contemporary Japan*, p. 180.
73. Murakami, *The Elephant Vanishes*, p. 182.
74. Murakami, *The Elephant Vanishes*, p. 182.
75. Murakami, *The Elephant Vanishes*, p. 185.
76. Newlove, 'Fiction Briefs', p. 77.
77. Stull, 'Beyond Hopelessville', pp. 1, 6.
78. *Beginners* was first published in Japan in 2007, of course, translated by Murakami.
79. In 'Fires', writing only months after Lish had severely cut *What We Talk About When We Talk About Love*, Carver writes that Lish was one of two individuals who held irredeemable notes of influence on his work. A fact hardly worth contesting, and one stated, I think, by Carver with a note of affirmation. Carver, *Collected Stories*, p. 745.

80. Wriglesworth, 'Raymond Carver and Alcoholics Anonymous', in Kleppe and Miltner (eds), *New Paths to Raymond Carver*, p. 149.
81. Sklenicka, *Raymond Carver*, p. 469.
82. Carver, *Call If You Need Me*, p. 123.
83. Carver, *Call If You Need Me*, p. 125.
84. Carver, *Call If You Need Me*, p. 123; Gallagher, *Soul Barnacles*, p. 199.
85. Wriglesworth, 'Raymond Carver and Alcoholics Anonymous', p. 133.
86. Gallagher, 'Foreword', in Carver, *Call If You Need Me*, p. xv.
87. Wriglesworth, 'Raymond Carver and Alcoholics Anonymous', p. 139.
88. One of Murakami's English translators, Philip Gabriel, argues that 1995 marks a significant turning point in Murakami's fiction, when his writing began to show the 'beginnings of a serious critique of contemporary Japan'. Gabriel, *Spirit Matters: The Transcendent in Modern Japanese Literature*, p. 89.
89. Kingston, *Contemporary Japan*, p. 23.
90. Kingston, *Contemporary Japan*, pp. 255, 38.
91. Kingston, *Contemporary Japan*, p. 30.
92. Murakami, *Underground*, p. 206.
93. Murakami, *Underground*, p. 196.
94. Murakami, *Underground*, p. 197.
95. Murakami, *Underground*, p. 202.
96. Murakami, *Underground*, p. 204. I am not suggesting that Murakami's writing pre-1995 was not 'sincere' – this would undermine my argument – rather, I am seeking to demonstrate that the events of early 1995 affected Murakami in a such a way that he began to attempt a more complete and fulfilling answer to the problems that he saw around him.
97. Murakami, *After The Quake*, p. 19.
98. Boulter, *Melancholy and the Archive: Trauma, History and Memory in the Contemporary Novel*, p. 87; Murakami, *After The Quake*, p. 19.
99. Rubin, *Music of Words*, p. 256.
100. Murakami, *After The Quake*, p. 43.
101. Murakami, *After The Quake*, p. 56.
102. Snyder and Gabriel, 'Introduction', in Snyder and Gabriel (eds), *Oe and Beyond*, p. 8.
103. Murakami, *Underground*, p. 198.
104. Murakami, *Underground*, p. 54.
105. Murakami, *Underground*, p. 54.
106. Murakami, *Underground*, p. 56.
107. Murakami, *Underground*, p. 58.
108. Matthew Strecher reinforces this idea when he argues that 'the point of this story is the process by which a young man discovers and acknowledges his proper place in the world. The story illustrates and celebrates spiritual awakening to the internal narrative and to the omnipresent Narrative.' See Strecher, *The Forbidden Worlds of Haruki Murakami*, p. 136.
109. *A Wild Sheep Chase: In Search of Haruki Murakami*, TV. UK: BBC, 2008.
110. Carver, *Collected Stories*, p. 654.
111. Carver, *Collected Stories*, pp. 660–1.

112. Carver, *Collected Stories*, p. 661.
113. Sennett, *The Culture of New Capitalism*, pp. 103–4.
114. Carver, *Collected Stories*, pp. 664–5.
115. Carver, *Collected Stories*, p. 665.
116. Sennett, *The Culture of New Capitalism*, pp. 104–5.
117. Carver, *Collected Stories*, p. 666.
118. Rubin, *Music of Words*, pp. 98–9.
119. Carver, *All Of Us*, p. 146.

CHAPTER 4

'Why Raymond Carver?':
Neoliberal Authenticity and Culture in Alejandro G. Iñárritu's *Birdman*

In Alejandro G. Iñárritu's 2014 feature film *Birdman or (The Unexpected Virtue of Ignorance)*, the protagonist, a once successful Hollywood actor called Riggan Thomson (Michael Keaton), explains to his co-actor in the film, Mike Shiner (Edward Norton) why he has chosen to adapt Raymond Carver's story 'What We Talk About When We Talk About Love' into a Broadway play. Handing him a crumpled napkin, Riggan says, 'When I was in high school, I was in a play up in Syracuse and Carver was in the audience. He sent that back to me afterwards.' Written in an almost indecipherable scrawl, the napkin reads, 'Thanks for an honest performance. Ray Carver.' After reading the message aloud, Mike begins to laugh. When Riggan asks him why, Mike says, 'It's written on a cocktail napkin. He was fucking drunk, man.'[1]

Mike's question – 'Why Raymond Carver?' – exposes a pointed critical angle towards Carver's work in Iñárritu's film. Carver, it seems, has influenced both actors in very different ways and both, therefore, have divergent impressions of Carver's work and persona. Riggan holds Carver as a paragon of authenticity – an idea that is linked in his mind to 'honesty'. He views Carver as a writer of enduring artistic integrity, whose work transcends all social, political and historical concerns – namely, his own past commercially orientated Hollywood career – and holds deeper, universal truths and meanings imperative for human connection and love. Mike, on the other hand, holds a more radical position towards Carver's work. He views him as a working-class alcoholic who suffered in much the same way as his characters. In this sense, Mike's opinion presents a deliberate challenge to Riggan's ideals. It denotes admiration for Carver's artistic sacrifice, in which the reality of his historical experience produced an authentic form of literature. This chapter argues that this dialectic forms the basis for a critical discussion about Carver's work and persona in *Birdman* that has deeper implications for artwork in the neoliberal era. While Iñárritu's early multi-protagonist trilogy – *Amores Perros* (2000), *21 Grams* (2003) and *Babel* (2006) – depict the alienation and dislocation prominent in neoliberal societies, by casting Carver as the axis for a discussion around authenticity and artistic legacy in *Birdman*, Iñárritu begins to explore the impact of recent neoliberal cultural developments and questions whether it is possible to create authentic artwork in a contemporary neoliberal society.

Born in a small barrio in Mexico City in 1963, Alejandro G. Iñárritu is a filmmaker concerned with the specific socio-economic trends of his homeland over the past three and a half decades.[2] He began his career in the media industry in his twenties as a disc jockey for WFM, one of Mexico's most popular radio stations, before becoming an artistic director for Televisa in 1990. A year later he founded his own production company, Zeta Films, and began making short films and commercials. During this same period he partnered with the novelist Guillermo Arriaga to develop his first feature-length production, *Amores Perros*. The film, with a reported budget of $2.4 million, was the most expensive privately funded Mexican film when it was made, and was released only weeks before the political establishment, *Institutional Revolutionary Party* (PRI), lost the general election for the first time in seventy-one years.[3] Their defeat at the polls indicated a significant shift in the sociopolitical structure of the country. Since the revolution in 1920, the PRI had governed on a broadly socialist protectionist trade and investment basis. However, the onset of the 1982 debt crisis – brought on by the neoliberal turn in the US – resulted in the IMF instigating a support package of neoliberal structural reforms.[4] Democratic capitalism was introduced to the country, business and manufacturing was agglomerated and centralised, and anarchic urban growth began to ensue in the capital city.[5]

Iñárritu's *Amores Perros*, a multi-protagonist film that portrays social divisions in Mexico City, attempts to represent the increasingly uneven and fragmented existence in Mexico's new neoliberal era. The film's representation of extreme violence, severe disparity of wealth and lack of social justice are encompassed by a pervasive feeling of alienation and dislocation that prefigure motifs found in Iñárritu's later work. These concerns find their specific context within the expansion of availability of technology in Mexican neoliberal society – media that Néstor Canclini describes as having 'vertical and anonymous logic', and that Iñárritu views as prioritising capital (or commodification) over community and human relationships. It is through the prevalence of television, celebrity culture, advertising, mobile phones and global banking that *Amores Perros*, as Julie Minich highlights, offers 'a critique of consumer culture [and] also a sense of how thoroughly it permeates our lives'.[6]

Equally notable for their critique of late capitalism are Iñárritu's subsequent English language films. His second and third feature films, *21 Grams* and *Babel*, along with *Amores Perros*, form a trilogy of multi-protagonist pieces that concomitantly represent the complex relationships between people (labour), goods and capital within the increasingly compressed global existence in neoliberalism. A real-world parallel to these films is found in the socio-economic effect of the North American Free Trade Agreement (NAFTA) on his homeland, and as a Mexican filmmaker working in the US, it is firmly within this context that Iñárritu is making his films. While its proponents argued that the treaty would instigate national economic progression, in turn curing Mexico's debt overhang and improving social problems, in reality the result of NAFTA and the affiliated liberalisation has been – in vast contrast to regional economic convergence – dramatic uneven geographical development, in the vein of other neoliberal economies.[7] Strong and lasting economic growth has not ensued in Mexico, particularly in the labour market, and the lack of internal innovation and investment has caused analysts to project poor prospects for sustainable development in the country.[8]

Iñárritu's third feature film, *Babel*, is particularly significant in this regard. Set on three separate continents, the film traces the movement of people and goods across geographic borders and draws attention to the contemporary issues of nation-state sovereignty and social injustice that Iñárritu sees in neoliberal Mexico. The narrative follows the movement and impact of a hunting rifle, a gift from a Japanese tourist to a Moroccan guide, which ends up being involved in the accidental shooting of an American tourist in the Moroccan desert. The central image in the film, the hunting rifle, denotes the ease with which foreign goods and services move between nation-state borders and the potent impact that they have on the local population. The shooting of the American tourist sets in motion a series of dramatic global events – buoyed by the dominance of US foreign policy – which leads to the death of children in Morocco, the deportation of unofficial Mexican workers from California, and the near-suicide of the Japanese businessman's daughter.

Notable in this multi-protagonist piece is the narrative of Amelia (Adriana Barraza), an undocumented Mexican nanny, who looks after Richard (Brad Pitt) and Susan Jones's (Cate Blanchett) children while they are travelling in Morocco. When Susan is shot and left stranded in a remote Moroccan village, their delayed homecoming creates a conflict of interest between Amelia's responsibility as a nanny and her own son's wedding in Mexico. Intent on not missing the wedding, Amelia resolves to take the two children with her across the border for the day, and asks her nephew, Santiago (Gael García Bernal), to drive them. While their exit from the US is markedly uneventful – as they cross the border, one of the children ominously says, 'My mom said Mexico is dangerous.' 'Yes', Santiago responds in Spanish, 'it's full of Mexicans' – their return is dramatically different. Stopped at a US border checkpoint after an increase in security – due in part to the shooting in Morocco and the perceived global terrorist threat on US citizens – Amelia, with no official documents and two American children in the back of the car, is thoroughly scrutinised. Her nephew, still drunk from the wedding, anxious and seeing no obvious escape from the police, drives through the checkpoint. He leaves Amelia and the children by the side of the road in the remote wilderness and drives off into the desert.

The moment is keenly symbolic, for Amelia's excursion in the US / Mexico hinterland overtly embodies the soul of the film: the diasporic effect felt by many Mexicans in contemporary America.[9]

In the morning the police eventually find Amelia, and the dehydrated and exhausted children are saved from their life-threatening situation. Amelia, however, despite living in the US for many years, is deported back to Mexico. The border porosity, which allows the unimpeded movement of goods between nation-states, clearly does not extend to the movement of people groups – even to those who are willing to offer social and economic support to the country. The defining summary indicated by the film's biblical title is that while there are intricate and global connections between people groups in contemporary society, ultimately there is still no effective form of communication, and the impact of neoliberalism and NAFTA remains: the primacy given to the movement of capital is a process which reifies the Mexican populace and leaves them alienated.[10]

Despite the fact that *Babel* predates the recent rise of US racial and nativist ideologies, the film continues to speak into the current policy of border control and migrant detention. This more recent political nativism clearly grates against neoliberal commitments to free trade – embodied, for instance, in Executive Orders to Buy American and Hire American, and Maximising Use of American-Made Goods, Products, and Materials – and yet in both instances Iñárritu's presentation of the overwhelmingly negative impact of millennial neoliberal politics on Hispanic migrants is presciently applicable. Whether Iñárritu's personal beliefs are aligned with the strongly polemic writing of David Harvey cannot be ascertained for certain, but his films do reveal support for a set of values that are analogous to Harvey's call in *Spaces of Global Capitalism* for 'open democracy dedicated to social equality coupled with economic, political, and cultural justice'.[11] As I have suggested, this idea is clearly present throughout Iñárritu's work – including in his feature *The Revenant* (2015) which portrays the excesses of capitalist accumulation by dispossession in the US at the beginning of the nineteenth century – but it is particularly explicit in *Babel*, which pits the dominance of American capital against the welfare of humanity. Harvey's analysis is of significant help when seen within this context, for he argues:

> Almost everything we now eat and drink, wear and use, listen to and hear, watch and learn comes to us in commodity form and is shaped by

divisions of labor, the pursuit of product niches, and the general evolution of discourses and ideologies that embody precepts of capitalism. It is only when daily life has been rendered totally open to the circulation of capital and when political subjects have their vision almost entirely circumscribed by embeddedness in that circulation that capitalism can function with affective meanings and legitimacy as its support.[12]

It is the impact and effect of capitalism's embeddedness in daily life that Iñárritu's early multi-protagonist trilogy explores.[13] As Deleyto and Azcona usefully elaborate:

> In them, time expands and contracts, becomes distorted and repeats itself ad infinitum, moves around in circles and branches off in unexpected directions – constituting, in sum, a powerful symptom of the ways in which contemporary experience has been shaped by economic, cultural, and technological phenomena.[14]

For Iñárritu the result of capital's primacy is a fragmented existence that makes effective human interaction and community ephemeral, transient and fragile. Such obvious cinematic mapping marks *Babel* as the cornerstone of his work, as well as a platform from which he is able to progress towards more nuanced and specific contemporary issues to do with artistic authenticity, legacy and influence in the neoliberal era, and it is exactly these kinds of problems that Iñárritu seeks to address in *Birdman*.

A relatively detailed description of the opening sequence of *Birdman* will give an idea of the distinctive manner in which Iñárritu tackles these themes and how they relate to Carver's literary afterlife. The film's epigraph, Carver's poem 'Late Fragment', appears letter by letter at random intervals on a black screen and remains only long enough to be read briefly before it disappears. The poem's transient appearance prefigures broader motifs of cultural ephemerality in the film, but its ostensible randomness (like his early multi-protagonist films) is countered by Iñárritu's subtle orchestration – the letters actually appear in alphabetical order and when they disappear they leave, for a microsecond, the word 'amor'. In a film that is not only concerned with the broader implications of maintaining loving relationships in a contemporary society, but also, on a diegetic level, a film about an adaptation of a story called 'What We Talk About When We Talk About Love', this opening shot carries meaningful overtones that connect it to the themes of Iñárritu's earlier work. Notwithstanding this interesting allusion, the poem's poignancy is heightened by its context. Written only weeks before Carver's death, it also appears on Carver's gravestone – perhaps the ultimate indication of the universality of life's fragility and ephemerality. The text has strong elegiac connotations and its title echoes back, as Sandra Lee Kleppe points out, 'to antiquity and the heart of the Western love poem tradition as represented by Sappho's *fragments*'.[15] And yet, despite the poem's compact nature, it encapsulates much of Riggan's predicament in the film. The antipophoric effect in particular – which is emphasised by left and right justification on screen – not only reflects Carver's poetic voice, but also interplays with Riggan's alter ego, a character who performs the role of internal interrogator in the film.

Even at the outset, then, the link between Carver's writing and Iñárritu's film is intricate. In the film, Riggan's main preoccupation is the creation of a critically respected piece of art that he hopes will ensure his posterity. This aim is ultimately tied to a recent epiphany that his personal life and acting career have been a failure, and that his past Hollywood work is disposable, ephemeral and ultimately worthless. ('I'm disappearing', he says at one moment of particular desperation in the film.) Concerned, and often reminded by other characters, that the commercial success of his early career is firmly rooted in the past, his adaptation, production and performance of Carver's story becomes an attempt to fix some kind of longevity to his name. But the purity of Riggan's motivation is a moot point. His estranged wife, Sylvia (Amy Ryan), makes the perceptive observation that Riggan has confused love for admiration – a notable reason for their initial break-up, it seems – and so, in light of her comment we might view Carver's conclusion to 'Late Fragment' ('To call myself beloved, to feel myself beloved on the earth') as being tantamount to Riggan's situation.[16] In fact, it is precisely this personal conflict that is explored in the film. Carver's poem presents an interesting, if slightly ambivalent, conclusion. The first clause of Carver's final sentence, 'To *call* myself beloved' (emphasis added), appeals to Riggan's search for critical admiration, but the phrase is spontaneously broken off by the poem's final phrase, 'to *feel* myself beloved' (emphasis added), which aligns more clearly with the need for experiential love and community. As I will argue later, the conflict is ultimately resolved in the film's conclusion, for Riggan finally – and unwittingly – gains critical recognition for his play and in the process restores his filial relationships.

The rest of the opening sequence continues to build on these ideas. The appearance of the epigraph coincides with Antonio Sanchez's erratic and inimitable drum score. The percussive accompaniment, which continues throughout the film, is a subtle reflection of Riggan's chaotic production as well as his increasing inner turmoil. Its menacing rhythm is also tantamount to Carver's prosaic specificity, and aids the transition from the epigraph into the opening shot – after a short prelude of a shooting star, yet another potent motif that reiterates notions of transience and intense ephemerality – which begins in Riggan's dressing room.

Riggan is alone, wearing a pair of white briefs and sitting in the Lotus Position – apparently levitating in mid-air. His bare back fills the screen. Backlit by a bright white light from an opaque sash window – a feature evocative of the bleach by-pass effect prevalent in Iñárritu's early films – Riggan's skin is the same colour of the walls: an off-white shade reminiscent of dirty snow. This decidedly intrusive moment recalls many of Carver's stories, forcing the viewer into Riggan's intimate space. The quietness is oppressive – a ticking clock, the only indication that time is actually passing. Faint sirens and traffic noise place the scene in an unidentified metropolis. Unable to see Riggan's front, his physical condition remains undetermined, but his broad shoulders and the visible portion of his slight thighs suggest a middle-aged man who was once physically active. A half-hidden Buddha's head and some obscured pictures (photographs of Carver, Tess Gallagher, and a print of Alfredo Arreguin's *Ray's Ghost Fish*) reinforce the initial element of spirituality and community, while the defunct lightbox in the bottom left-hand corner denotes depressive tendencies. It is the latter sensibility that pervades, the peeling white paint on the radiator, outdated decor, wonky clothes rack, and empty paper towel dispenser recalling a dilapidated school restroom more than the comfortable dressing room of a Hollywood star.

While the opening shot prefigures Riggan's failures in the film, the mobile video call from his daughter, Sam (Emma Stone), which follows, prefigures ideas that relate more specifically to Iñárritu's critique of neoliberalism. The mobile phone, as Deleyto and Azcona have noted, is a prominent motif in Iñárritu's early films, especially in relation to the notion of ephemerality or the fragility of human relationships, and so its early appearance in *Birdman* is unsurprising.[17] Set against the wider socio-economic context of the film, the early appropriation of mobile video calling – a noticeably contemporary technological phenomenon – is noteworthy. Iñárritu's adoption of the form (as opposed to a regular phone call) not only allows Sam to infiltrate Riggan's dressing room through the transmission of sounds, but also allows her to see *into* Riggan's absolute space. Sam is 'present' in the dressing room without actually being there. As I will argue later on, the appearance of technology, especially social media, is particularly important in relation to broader ideas that Iñárritu expresses concerning technology's inability to compensate for what he sees as authentic, real experience.[18] This idea is underlined in the film's opening by the fleeting temporality of the video call – particularly in how abruptly Sam is able to start and, most significantly, end it – and also by its incapacity to offer an effective means of communication. For despite the dominance of technology, neither the absolute space of the florist nor that offered through cyberspace affords an effective avenue for communication. Sam, who is trying to buy Riggan flowers, cannot understand the Korean florist behind her, nor her father, and ends up buying his least favourite flowers – roses.

While the opening sequences of *Birdman* help contextualise the film within Iñárritu's broader critique of neoliberal capitalism, it is worth asking at this point, how Carver – an artist whose own work retreats from definitive critical perspectives towards a consolatory craftsmanship – fits into Iñárritu's film, and why, therefore, Iñárritu chose to employ him as the film's central artistic figure. Perhaps the most conspicuous reason is that Iñárritu claims to have been an admirer of Carver since he was a young man. But to rely solely on that idea would belie the complexity with which Iñárritu treats Carver. In an interview with Jeff Goldsmith, Iñárritu reveals that the reason he chose Carver was 'not only because I was a fan, but also because I thought it was the best bad idea ever to adapt Raymond Carver for the theatre'.[19] In other words, Iñárritu chose Carver because he was *not* an appropriate figure for theatrical adaptation, an admission that suggests that Carver's influence on the film is more mediated than it may first appear. I will develop this idea later on in this chapter, especially when I consider how Riggan appropriates Carver's text in the film, but Iñárritu's initial suggestion is that Riggan's misreading of Carver's story is an integral element to the film; that Riggan's attempt to attach himself to Carver's legacy through his theatrical adaptation is not necessarily an efficacious route for negotiating and conquering the ephemerality and surface of his early Hollywood career.[20]

While these ideas add to the interesting associations between Carver and Iñárritu, a more complex reason for choosing Carver lies in the significance of Carver's fictional napkin note to Riggan. For Riggan, it seems, sees a strong correlation between a conservative element that communicates some kind of transcendental truth about the human condition in Carver's fiction and his own critical success and longevity. This version of Carver is revealed most clearly in Carver's own personal essays. The bulk of his essay 'On Writing', for instance, is dedicated almost paragraph by paragraph to the exposition of writing dictums borrowed from other (notably realist) writers that reinforce this conservative view: 'avoid weak specification' – Henry James; 'no cheap tricks' – Geoffrey Wolff; 'no iron can piece the heart with such force as a period put just in the right place' – Isaac Babel; 'and suddenly everything became clear to him' – Anton Chekhov; 'fundamental accuracy of statement is the ONE sole morality of writing' – Ezra Pound.[21] Carver, the essay reveals, wrote these mottos on three-by-five cards and pinned them to his noticeboard. As I noted in Chapter 2, Carver's emphasis on carefully chosen vocabulary, usage and grammar, while in itself not distinguishing his writing from postmodern experimentalism, does clearly associate him with the tenets of orthodox literary realism. The link is clarified when considered in light of his personal essays, which were written in the background of the radicalism posited by writers like John Barth and William Gass. And while Carver was clearly mistaken in some opinions – take, for instance, the fact that he thought experimentation was a 'license to try to brutalise or alienate the reader' – 'On Writing' reveals that he thought that *his* art was doing something very different; that it held some kind of communicable essence that was antithetical to what he saw as the surface of experimentalism; that it transcended the historical and political conditions in which it was produced; that it was, what might pragmatically be called, serious or meaningful art.[22]

It is this image of Carver that holds particular significance for Riggan, because in the bottom right-hand corner of his dressing room mirror is his own three-by-five motto, which reads 'A thing is a thing, not what is said of that thing', a phrase that appears to reflect a firmly Carveresque, even anti-Saussurean, understanding of reality. Not only does the tone of Riggan's motto stand in line with Carver's rhetoric – the phrase is noticeably reminiscent of Carver's stylised titles – it also represents the axis upon which much of the film turns. For the world that Riggan inhabits is one ruled by a warped, decentred intellectualism. Truth and even the very notion of reality are, for Riggan, slippery properties. He is able to use the superpowers of his fictional alter ego Birdman – the superhero character that he played decades ago in a once commercially successful comic-book film franchise – to telekinetically open doors, move objects and even, in one scene of euphoric triumphalism, fly through the streets of Manhattan.

And yet, in the film there is a strong tension between the phantasmagoric world inhabited by his alter ego – one associated with the transience of Riggan's commercial success – and the reality of his current existence and his aim of artistic posterity. Riggan's motto, therefore, interplays with Carver's elegy in the film's epigraph. For the distinction that the poem places between 'calling' and 'feeling' loved reflects the contrast between 'what is said' and simply 'what is', and reflects Carver's idea – most obviously sourced from John Gardner – that what is most important in writing is the communication of some kind of immutable truth rather than the language in and of itself. The motto's appeal then, to this kind of Carveresque view of reality has a broader impact on Riggan's metaphysical nature in its attempt to pull him away from the illusory surface of his alter ego and the commercialised – and ephemeral – art he is associated with, and draw him towards a more serious, lasting and transcendent art form.

If the reason that Iñárritu uses Carver is founded on a representational view (that is, what Carver is seen to symbolise), then I want to develop this idea further by considering how Carver is used in the film. As the discussions between Riggan and Mike, and their divergent interpretations of Carver, plays a central part in the film, I want to start by analysing their critical antagonism, before moving on to assess Riggan's play in relation to Carver's text, and then conclude by considering the role of Riggan's alter ego and the film's ending.

The critical antagonism between Mike and Riggan begins early in the film when Mike joins Riggan's production as a replacement for Ralph (Jeremy Shamos) the day before the play's first preview. While the backstory reflects the chaotic nature of Riggan's production, it is important to bear in mind because it usefully foregrounds the film's exploration of authentic artwork in the neoliberal era. Ralph is forced to leave the production after a stage light falls on his head during rehearsal. (The moment is suitably caustic, as Ralph cries out the line, 'Son of a bitch, your days are numbered!' the light falls and knocks him to the ground.) After the accident, Riggan diminishes the seriousness of the situation by telling his agent, Jake (Zach Galifianakis), 'That guy's the worse actor I've ever seen in my life. The blood coming out of his ear was the most honest thing he's done so far.' He then begins an unceremonious search to find a better actor – that is, someone capable of performing with a deeper sense of honesty – and finds a replacement in Mike, who another cast member, Lesley (Naomi Watts), reveals has recently become unattached to his current project. His surreptitious departure ('Quit or fired, which is it?' Riggan asks Lesley. 'Well with Mike it's usually both', she replies) indicates Mike's disruptive nature, but buoyed by his joint commercial and critical appeal ('He sells a shit load of tickets', Jake argues. 'They [critics] want to spooge on him.') Jake begins contract negotiations. Compared with Ralph, Mike initially appears capable of providing a performance filled with the authenticity that, up until that point, had been missing from Riggan's play. Impressed after just one reading, Riggan tries to justify Mike's salary demand to Jake by describing him as 'the real deal'. The exact definition of Riggan's riposte is not entirely clear, but Mike's 'real' acting comes at a price – a point that is not entirely serendipitous – and it is four times more expensive than Ralph's 'dishonesty'.

If Riggan, the A-List Hollywood star, is introduced in his dressing room, then Mike, the critically respected actor, is, appropriately enough, introduced on the theatre stage. In their opening conversation, Mike's dialogue is presented with pointed derision, 'Do you have any idea who walked on these boards before you? Geraldine Page, Marlon Brando, Helen Hayes, Jason Robards and now you, Riggan Thomson.' Could Riggan, the one-time 'Hollywood clown in a Lycra jumpsuit' – as he is described at one point in the film – be antecedently connected to Page, Brando, Hayes and Robards? The answer, found in the subtext of Mike's next line, is clear, 'So, you wrote this adaptation. And you're directing and starring in the adaptation. Ambitious.' Mike's reference is heightened within the context of the film because all four actors, who are nominally respected for their theatre acting, made the successful transition to the Hollywood backlot. (In fact, it is probably generally accepted that they stand for a time when Hollywood studios were still concerned with creating what Riggan would think of as authentic art.) Riggan, of course, embodies a reversal of sorts and *Birdman* makes a major point out of this distinction. Mike later tells Riggan that the play is a risk-free endeavour for him because if it fails he can simply go back to his 'studio executive pals' and continue to commit 'cultural genocide'. He, on the other hand, as a theatre actor will always be out on the stage 'baring his soul'.

Mike, then, challenges Riggan's view of Carver with his own, very different, portrayal. The result is that while one might be tempted to, like Riggan, affirm Carver as an authentic and transcendent artist, Iñárritu treats Riggan's play with a deliberate irony that indicates certain limitations to its capacity. This idea is reinforced by Mike's characterisation, which challenges Riggan's belief in Carver with a very different portrayal. Mike's hostility is presented in a progressive manner through a number of important scenes in the film. The first (part of which I have already considered) occurs during their initial meeting on the theatre stage. Uncertain that Mike will be able to rehearse without a copy of the script, but provoked by Mike's insistence that he knows the lines, Riggan launches into his dialogue:

I'm the wrong person to ask. I didn't know the man. I've only heard his name mentioned in passing. I wouldn't know. You'd have to know the particulars. But I think what you're saying is that love is absolute.

Mike stares at Riggan. Ruminating, he says, 'Am I saying that love is absolute? "Yeah. The kind of love I'm talking about is. The kind of love I'm talking about you . . . Well, you don't try to kill people".' Mike's performance, even in this impromptu rehearsal, contrasts starkly with his predecessor's. Ralph's version of Mel (the character that he and Mike play in the production) was contrived, factitious even; distinctly separate from the required method that Riggan is searching for in his direction. Mike's performance, on the other hand, appears spontaneous. This impression comes as much from Mike's process as it does from his actions – he only follows Riggan's script after he has cross-examined his character's motivation. His interior questioning ('Am I saying that love is absolute?') is not only rhetorical, it is a focused internalisation that reveals his methodology: he is *becoming* Mel McGinnis. Of course, considering the cynical tone of the film, it is not hard to see beyond Mike's characterisation. If Riggan is an ironised version of a failed Hollywood actor attempting to resurrect his career, then Mike is an ironised version of the American method actor. In fact, Mike fits this mould so well it is hard not to see something more significant in Iñárritu's causticity. For the film suggests, as I will argue in more detail later, that both characters' artistic approaches undermine their search for artistic authenticity. For now, though, it is enough to note that Mike's minor critique, and the subsequent interaction, reveals a more rigorous textual questioning and an astute critical objective. After suggesting they rehearse the scene again, Mike interrupts Riggan's speech and begins to challenge the adaptation:

Can I make a suggestion? Do you mind? Forget that, just stay with me. *'I'm the wrong person to ask'*, he says, but what is that? What's the intention in that? Is he fed up with the subject, so he's changing it? Is he deflecting guilt over the marriage? And here's the thing, you got four lines after that, that all say the same thing: *'I didn't even know the man.' 'I've only heard his name mentioned in passing.' 'I wouldn't know.' 'You'd have to know the particulars.'* And the particulars, I mean, it sounds like my grandmother, but the point is, you don't know the guy, we fucking get it, make it work with one line: '*I didn't even know the man*', right?

The significance of Mike's editorial suggestion is heightened by the fact that the section he insists on breaking up is taken, verbatim, from Carver's published text. When Mike accuses Riggan of ambiguity, tautology and archaism he is, by association, accusing Carver too. And while, on the one hand, Mike is pursuing Carver's own economic line – which, conversely enough, is found most clearly in 'On Writing', the essay which is so clearly aligned to Riggan's own artistic philosophy – his appeal to 'cut it down' is a conspicuous assault on Carver's text.

This first critical antagonism is followed by other, more explicit, interventions later in the film. The following night, Mike disrupts the play's first preview when – drunk because he has been drinking real gin rather than the water provided by the prop team – he interrupts the story's central anecdote about the elderly couple. Breaking out of character, Riggan turns to Mike and says, 'Take it easy. You're drunk.' Mike responds:

> I'm drunk? Yes, I'm drunk. I'm supposed to be drunk. Why aren't you drunk? This is Carver. He left a piece of his liver on the table every time he wrote a fucking page. If I need to be drinking gin, who the fuck are you to touch my gin, man!

While Riggan idolises Carver for what he sees as a set of enduring artistic principles, Mike's monologue reveals that he values Carver because he sees Carver's work as authentically reflecting Carver's own historical experience. (That is, that Carver was an alcoholic, who wrote about alcoholics, and whether knowingly or not, sacrificed his body for the sake of his art.) Despite his apparent antagonism towards Carver, in many ways Mike's opinion fits neatly with the general perception that Carver's work was a product of his working-class life. And yet, while he accepted the influence of his upbringing, as I considered particularly in relation to Carver's time in Iowa reaching with John Cheever in Chapter 1, Carver always denied any relationship between his addiction and his artwork. In an interview with Kay Bonetti, Carver said, 'There's a myth that goes along with writing and alcohol. But purely and simply, drinking is *not* conducive to artistic production.'[23] Neither does the connection exist in relation to the composition of 'What We Talk About When We Talk About Love', which was written in the early 1980s, when Carver was sober. But if Mike's opinion on Carver can so easily be debunked, what is the point of Iñárritu utilising it? My proposition is that Mike's opinion is connected less with his idea of Carver (although this is certainly part of it), and more closely connected with the debate about what it means to be a truthful or authentic artist in the neoliberal era. As Mike continues his onstage interruption the audience becomes hysterical and dozens of cell phones begin to film the spontaneous performance. Addressing the audience, he says, 'Oh, come on, people. Don't be so pathetic. Stop looking at the world through your cell phone screens – have a real experience. Does anybody give a shit about truth other than me?'

This point is clarified when viewed in light of the climax of his opposition with Riggan, which occurs when Riggan reads Mike's interview on the front page of *The New York Times'* Art Section. The headline reads, 'Carving Out His Place In Theatre History: Shiner says Raymond Carver is the reason he became an actor.' History, again, plays an important role in validating the experience of the present, this time though (the viewer knows because they have been privy to the conversation earlier in the Rum House) in a fallacious manner. For Mike, a method actor who purports to uphold truth, has stolen Riggan's backstory, appropriated Carver's reputation and used it to propagate a myth about his own artistic ambitions.

Mike's plagiarism is a turning point for Riggan who, after reading the interview, bursts into his dressing room, throws open his sunbed (bought under the pretence that Mike needs a tan because his character is a 'red neck') and attacks him with the rolled-up newspaper. Wearing nothing but a pair of grey camouflage briefs and conspicuously reading a copy of Borges's *Labyrinths*, Mike gets up and the pair begin to argue.[24] 'So, Carver is the reason you became an actor?' Riggan says. 'I said – I don't know, I said the first thing that came to mind', Mike replies. 'The first thing that came to mind? Right. Cause that's you. Mr. Natural. Mr. Fuck the scene, just stare at my massive hard-on because that's the truth of the moment', Riggan says, before closing his tirade by saying,

'Everybody says, "Mike is so honest, so truthful"', and then pinning him to a dressing room locker.

It is important to remember that this scene is positioned within the context of a broader debate about what being truthful, or authentic, really means. Not only does it occur after Mike's onstage pronouncements about truth, but earlier, during one of the previews, as Mike and Lesley prepare for the motel sex scene, Mike – now playing Mel – reveals that he is aroused and suggests that they 'really do it', justifying his idea by saying, 'It'll be so real.' Attempting to resist, Lesley pleads with Mike to stop. 'Don't call me Mike. Call me Mel. Mel', he insists. Interrupted by Riggan's character, Lesley manages to free herself, and when Mike stands up his erection is prominent. Offstage the couple fight about the incident. 'I needed it to be real', Mike insists again after Lesley reveals, 'You can't get it up in six months and now you want to fuck me in front of eight hundred strangers!' Mike's reality, in other words, only exists on the stage set of the Broadway theatre; all other reality has collapsed into a world of simulation and any distinction between reality and representation is blurred, a fact which undermines his claim of artistic authenticity. This idea is reinforced later in the film when Mike plays a game of 'truth or dare' with Sam and she asks if he wants to fool around. 'No', Mike replies, 'I'd be afraid I couldn't get it up.' 'That didn't seem to be a problem for you on stage', Sam says, before Mike reveals the underlying issue, 'Nothing's a problem for me on stage.'

Riggan and Mike's physical fight – which, of course, represents a broader ideological battle over their interpretation of Carver and, by proxy, their opinions on artistic authenticity – begins to unpack the oppositions in these ideas. Mike's response to Riggan's accusations is that his 'hard-on already has fifty-thousand views on YouTube', and reveals a solipsistic rationale that denotes Mike's partiality for virtual admiration. The point is not entirely lost on those who are aware of Iñárritu's earlier critiques of multinational capitalism. Not only does the virtual space to which Mike aligns himself typically dominate the contemporary neoliberal era, but it is also a space in which reality (or truth) is often replaced by image and illusion. In fact, the proliferation of references to social media is a notable feature of Iñárritu's film, not only connecting it to his earlier critiques of neoliberal technology, but also presenting an example of the personal impact of the embeddedness of capital in neoliberal life. This is an idea that needs to be contextualised alongside broader socio-economic critiques. David Harvey, writing recently in *Seventeen Contradictions and the End of Capitalism*, explores this phenomenon, which he terms 'spectacle':

> Everything from TV shows and other media products, films, concerts, exhibitions, sports events, mega-cultural events and, of course, tourism is included in this. These activities now dominate the field of consumerism. Even more interesting is how capital mobilizes consumers to produce their own spectacle via YouTube, Facebook, Twitter, and other forms of social media. All of these forms can be instantaneously consumed even as they absorb vast amounts of what might otherwise be free time. The consumers, furthermore, produce information, which is then appropriated by owners of the media for their own purposes.[25]

As a filmmaker who is highly conscious of the neoliberal boundaries in which he is working, and also interested in the capacity and creation of human communities and relationships, it is unsurprising to find Iñárritu's film reflecting something of these concerns. When Riggan and Sam argue over Riggan's motivation for producing the play, Sam says:

> Let's face it, Dad, it's not for the sake of art. It's because you just want to feel relevant again. Well, there's a whole world out there where people fight to be relevant every day. And you act like it doesn't even exist! Things are happening in a place that you wilfully ignore, a place that has already forgotten you. I mean who are you? You hate bloggers. You make fun of Twitter. You don't even have a Facebook page. *You're* the one who doesn't exist.

Taken within the wider context of the film, Sam's rebuke, which is delivered with deliberate exaggeration, becomes a subversive critique of the integration between virtual and absolute space – that is, between illusion and reality or inauthenticity and authenticity – in neoliberal culture. Of course Riggan 'exists'. But Sam's assertion is tantamount to the neoliberal experience in which everything is subsumed by the ideological status quo; where existence is focused on the virtual arena of the spectacle. This idea can be applied more widely to the integration of virtual commodification with the absolute space of real life. In an era in which virtual identities are constantly created or re-created, where relationships are only official if they are confirmed in the virtual arena, and where, at a click of a mouse, friends can be requested, accepted or even deleted, it is hard to imagine – for many individuals – life outside of this virtual reality. Later, as if to cement this idea, Riggan is locked outside the theatre in his underwear and forced to walk through a packed Times Square. As he dodges through what is surely the most conspicuous example of mass-commodification and commercialisation in New York City – an advertising arena which itself becomes a spectacle on so many personal social media feeds – the crowd's attention turns to Riggan, and his movements are filmed on a plethora of mobile phones. The footage is soon posted on YouTube and, as if to prove Sam's point, Riggan quickly becomes an online sensation (or a commodified spectacle in Harvey's terms). When she shows him the footage and informs him that he is becoming a 'trending topic', she says, 'Believe it or not, this is power.' The images are quickly deemed newsworthy and appear on *Entertainment Tonight*. In an ironic twist the anchors, so used to the artifice of social media, misread this real event for an elaborate publicity stunt and deride Riggan for creating the spectacle, saying, 'Why do actors have to resort to this? Come on, just put out a good film.'

It is interesting to note that the conflict between Hollywood and Broadway, or inauthentic and authentic art, is not confined to the diegetic world of *Birdman* but is broadly indicative of the film's creation. Iñárritu's directorial career, which started with Spanish language and independent features – films that may pragmatically be referred to as being serious or authentic – has moved more recently towards more commercially viable, Hollywood production company feature films. *Birdman*, which was funded by three production companies – Fox Searchlight, New Regency and Worldview Entertainment – was designed as a low-cost (and low-risk) project for Iñárritu to direct while waiting for timetabling conflicts to be resolved on the much larger production, *The Revenant*.[26] But Iñárritu and his fellow co-writers and producers still struggled to find the fairly modest $18 million needed to finance *Birdman*. The key, it seems, lay in a combination of casting, a short shooting schedule and a fast post-production period. While the simulated long-take style that Iñárritu used – a technique meant to reflect something of an unadulterated, authentic viewpoint for the film's audience – was an artistic risk, it reduced the post-production schedule, and the planned twenty-nine day shoot meant that there was little chance of the budget spiralling out of control. Perhaps most importantly, the ability to produce the film in this short timetabling window meant that *Birdman* could be released in November, just in time for Oscar nominations.[27] But above all of this, and of most value, was the cast. Before the financing was finalised, Michael Keaton and Emma Stone were committed to the film. Edward Norton was soon added, as were Naomi Watts and Zach Galifianakis. The ensemble was buoyed by the collaboration of cinematographer Emmanuel Lubezki – who had won an Oscar for his work on Alfonso Cuarón's *Gravity* (2013) the previous year. Added to this was the media interest surrounding the meta associations of casting Keaton, an actor who formally played Batman, as a washed-up Hollywood actor who formally played a character called Birdman, and Iñárritu's project quickly garnered commercial and critical attention.

And yet – to add another layer – the production of *Birdman*, and the financial associations connected to it, is itself a topic ironised in the film. While Riggan is talking with Jake about who might replace Ralph, their dialogue slips into the hinterland between fiction and reality. Riggan says, 'Just find me an actor, a good actor. Give me Woody Harrelson.' Jake replies, 'He's doing the next *Hunger Games*.' 'Michael Fassbender?' Riggan asks. 'He's doing the prequel to the X-Men prequel', Jake says. Finally Riggan suggests Jeremy Renner. When Jake informs him that he's now an 'Avenger' Riggan says, 'Fuck! They put him in a cape too.' The point of the exchange is unmistakable and rather unsubtle. 'They' refers to the Hollywood studio executives who are producing films that, as Iñárritu said in one interview, 'Don't mean nothing . . . they are just full of explosions and special effects and the superhero in a way as an illusion that doesn't exist.' The cape, of course, is a constant reminder that it was the commercial success of Riggan's own fictional *Birdman Trilogy* that made him the instigator for the present trend of superhero mania in the Hollywood film industry – a fact that now fills him with guilt and drives him to attempt his latest artistic endeavour. The irony of this line of critique (the in-joke we might say) is that the cast of Iñárritu's *Birdman* have found themselves, at one point or another, invested in a major superhero franchise: Michael Keaton in Tim Burton's *Batman* (1989) and *Batman Returns* (1992), Edward Norton as Bruce Banner in *The Incredible Hulk* (2008) and Emma Stone in *The Amazing Spiderman* (2012). Superficially, at least, this appears to be a problematic, even hypocritical, aspect of the film, but the issue is ironised to such an extreme degree that the exaggerated feel fits the canny satire that Iñárritu is attempting to produce. Eric Kohn summarises the situation by arguing that 'the movie functions as a commentary on its own melodramatic excesses', a point reinforced by one of the film's producers who says, 'You can't not look at the casting of Michael Keaton as a former superhero.' In fact, the making-of documentary released with the film's DVD reveals that the film revolves around this meta association. In one prescient moment backstage, Keaton, who is wearing the Birdman costume for rehearsal, reveals to Iñárritu that the costume designer has just told him that they based the design on Keaton's original Batman mannequin, and with a smile says, 'Still fits.' In the film, the reoccurring object of derision is Robert Downey Jr (Iron Man), an actor who, according to Riggan's alter ego, is making 'a fortune in that tin man get up'. Twenty-one years before the production of *Birdman*, Downey Jr inhabited Carver's fictional world when he played Bill Bush, the male protagonist in Robert Altman's adaptation of Carver's story 'Neighbours' in *Short Cuts* (1993).[28]

While Iñárritu uses Riggan and Mike's interpretations of Carver to explore the notion of authenticity in neoliberal culture, the film's clearest intervention with Carver's work itself is the portrayal of Riggan's play. Set in a domestic kitchen in Albuquerque, Carver's story concerns two couples, Mel and Terri McGinnis and Nick and Laura. Narrated by Nick, the story is based on a discussion around the nature and purpose of love. At one end of the pole is Mel, a cardiologist, who subscribes to an idealised, sentimental definition. Summarising Mel's opinion, Nick says, 'I think what you're saying is that love is an absolute.'[29] At the other end is Mel's second wife, Terri, who thinks love is primarily marked by devotion. She recounts a previous relationship she had with Ed, a man so dedicated to her, his passion turned violent. 'He dragged me around the living room by my ankles', she offers as evidence. 'He kept saying, "I love you, I love you, you bitch".'[30] The comparison between Ed's psychopathic love and Mel's sentimentalised affection becomes the central focus of the discussion.

Despite its nonsensical nature, Ed's devotion is stoically maintained by Terri as an example of authentic love. 'Sure, sometimes he may have acted crazy', she explains, 'But he loved me. In his own way maybe, but he loved me.'[31] Dissatisfied with her example, Mel recounts a story that, for him, epitomises the nature of love. He recalls an elderly couple that were involved in a car crash on an interstate highway. Mel, part of the surgical team that operated on them overnight, continued to visit the pair while they recuperated. Both were covered in casts and despite their condition improving the man remained depressed. It was not the accident, he told Mel, but the fact that the casts stopped him from turning his head to see his wife. 'I'm telling you', Mel says, 'the man's heart was breaking because he couldn't turn his goddamn head and see his goddamn wife.'[32] The end of Mel's story marks the conclusion to Carver's narrative, but its lasting impact on the others remains enigmatic. All appear to retreat into a solemn stasis. Laura announces her hunger – like the use of food in Carver's story 'A Small, Good Thing', this, surely, is a symbol of a broader dissatisfaction with life as much as any physical craving – and while Terri offers her some food she fails to move from her chair. Nick is motionless too, and his final line predominantly denotes a Carveresque despair, 'I could hear my heart beating. I could hear everyone's heart. I could hear the human noise we sat there making, not one of us moving, not even when the room went dark.'[33]

The dialogical nature of Carver's story means that any attempt to distil the story's thematic discussion into a neat analysis is frustrated by the multiple anecdotes and assorted viewpoints. Mel is a good example of such equivocation. A medical professional and seminary dropout, he is – on the surface – a character untypical of Carver's fictional world, and yet his mixed professional past is significant, for it is symptomatic of an inner confusion reminiscent of the core of those who inhabit Carver's writing. Stammering for a definition of love at the beginning of the story, Mel only confirms his ideas after Nick proposes his own definition. And yet the definition offered by Nick – that love is an absolute – neatly links with Mel's medical profession, one of scientific understanding and materialistic certainty. Indeed, ought he not know on a definitive level? He is, after all a *heart* doctor. But his self-depreciation later in the story undermines any authority he may have on the issue, 'I'm a heart surgeon, sure, but I'm just a mechanic. I go in and I fuck around and I fix things.'[34] His assertion to 'fuck around' with patients' hearts, of course, interplays with his inability to fully grasp the concept of love, as well as the idea of infidelity and broken relationships present in the story. The idea links to the fluidity of love that Mel argues for elsewhere, that if one of them were to die, 'The other person, would grieve for a while, you know, but then the surviving party would go out and love again.'[35] And yet, Mel's scientific understanding of love is severely undermined by Nick's assessment of him, 'Mel thought that real love was nothing less than spiritual love', an idea that might extend from his time at seminary, although Mel's incomplete theological degree suggests an equally deficient understanding of the story's theme.[36] Meanwhile Mel's ideas are clearly distinct from Terri's, which is fixed to the personal value that she found in Ed's devotion, even if it led to violence. Ultimately, any love that Mel has experienced in his life, with Terri or with his first wife, cannot compare to that exhibited by the elderly couple, and this is the point it seems. Mel's experience of love, in fact, any of the characters' experience of love is deficient, denoting a slipperiness to any offered definition in the story, an idea fundamentally reflected in its title.

Despite the story's complexity it might be tempting to think that the conversational focus and domestic setting of Carver's story makes it the perfect candidate for the kind of kitchen-sink theatrical adaptation that Riggan produces, but Riggan's play does little to interpret or distil the equivocality of Carver's story. In fact, it is not long before Riggan's play has veered so far from Carver's original text that any reader familiar with the original is left – much like the characters – bewildered. The central anecdote about the elderly couple is transferred from Mel and given to Riggan's character,

Nick, and in the process Nick admits to being a cardiologist, leaving Mel's occupational identity unknown. In the transposition, the anecdote is converted from a poignant retelling to a melodramatic monologue delivered away from the quartet towards the audience at the front of stage. Expository monologues are added and backstories invented and the play's plot becomes muddled. At one point Laura (Andrea Riseborough) takes the stage alone for a dream sequence, surrounded by fog and moving trees. The irony of this transposition ought not be lost amongst the chaos of Riggan's adaptation. Its tone is typical of the play and reveals a sentimentality that transgresses the Gardnerian rules of writing that Carver held.[37] Laura says:

> I guess we make choices in life, and we choose to live with them or not. I didn't want that baby, not because I didn't love Nick, and not because I didn't love the idea of it, but just because I wasn't ready to love myself. There's a distance to it all now, a wistful distance, underscored by a gentle breeze and the sound of the birds laughing at the whimsy of it all.

Later, the McGinnises play out a sex scene in the motel room, only to be interrupted by a suicidal Ed. Confusion is further added by the fact that Ed is also played by Riggan, the only visible difference being a denim jacket, an ill-fitting hairpiece and a wispy moustache. The play's finale occurs, not in the fading light of the McGinnises' kitchen, but in their motel room as Ed finally realises that Terri does not love him and commits suicide in front of the pair. Much of the subtlety of Carver's prose is undermined by Riggan's adaptation, and its themes are brought, quite literally, centre stage. Riggan may hold the persona of Carver as an example of artistic authenticity, but his appropriation and treatment of Carver's story reveals little respect for Carver's actual text.

While it is tempting to be critical of Riggan's production on the grounds of fidelity, it would be a mistake to give the inconsistencies too much focus. For, in the first instance, any attempt at a thorough comparative reading is problematised by the oft-interrupted and incomplete portrayal of Riggan's adaptation in the film, but more importantly because Iñárritu appears not to be using Carver's story in an adaptive sense like, say, Altman in *Short Cuts*, but is more interested in the question of artistic authenticity in the neoliberal era. Even so, some critics have been tempted to compare Riggan's adaptation with Carver's text and in so doing criticise the film, and so because these arguments oppose mine, it is worth briefly dealing with them.

A recent article by Jonathan Leaf argues that Riggan's adaptation, and specifically his use of the Lish edited 1981 version of 'What We Talk About When We Talk About Love', is a decision, 'something akin to re-writing Shakespeare'. Leaf's article argues that the choice to use the truncated publication denies the 'deeply human, honest and understated storytelling' that is found in Carver's original manuscript. In one sense Leaf's preference for the unedited version of Carver is not objectionable, but leaving aside the fact that the 1981 version of the story is not only the most widely recognised (and likely most popular) version of the story, his criticism is a misjudgement primarily because it takes Riggan's adaptation at face value – judging it for its inconsistencies – and failing to see the deeper significance of Riggan's misreading.

Francine Prose, in the most comprehensively critical article to date on Carver and *Birdman*, picks up on Leaf's weak argument – admitting her inability to fathom why Iñárritu's choice of the 1981 text should affect our understanding of the film – and posits her own criticism, that 'the scenes from Riggan's drama that we see are the pretty awful stuff of kitchen melodrama ... They lack the delicate subtext that makes so much of Carver's story seem to happen *between* the lines.' As I have already indicated, Prose's analysis is astute. She recognises, for instance, that the 'joke at the heart of the film' is that Riggan's play is (as his alter ego suggests) 'talky, depressing, philosophical bullshit', and yet, like Leaf, she fails to pick up on some of the nuance of Iñárritu's approach. For she speculates about the appropriateness of Carver as model at this time in cultural history, claiming that – in her experience – Carver is rarely read, whereas I am suggesting that the film presents a more nuanced understanding of Carver's influence; that while there may be inconsistencies in Carver's portrayal in the film, it is *exactly* because Riggan views Carver as a prescient artistic model that he adapts Carver's story for his Broadway comeback. Moreover, it is not even necessarily the issue of popularity that makes Carver an important figure for the film, but rather the fact that Riggan's adaptation illustrates, or exemplifies, broader questions about the inherent authenticity of certain art forms in the neoliberal era.

Iñárritu, then, uses Riggan and Mike – and their opinions on Carver – to explore the nature of truth and authenticity in the neoliberal era, and yet their ideas on truth and authenticity are undermined by the film's ironic tone to such an extent that Iñárritu seems to be suggesting that neither character's beliefs embody a solution to the intense commodification and superficiality of art in recent years. Carver, as both a cultural figure and artist, is caught somewhere in the middle, and, in the film, neither his representation as a transcendental touchstone by Riggan or an authentic artist by Mike posit a valid response either. While for Kinder, McInerney and Murakami, Carver becomes a model or figure by which they can negotiate – through a retreat towards craftsmanship – neoliberal culture, for Iñárritu, Carver's influence is rather more ambiguous. In order to fully grasp why Iñárritu positions Carver in this way I want to conclude by taking a closer look at the fractious relationship between Riggan and his Birdman alter ego.

Present at the very beginning through his voice-over, and remaining until the film's conclusion, Riggan's alter ego is a notable addition to the film's aesthetic. The physical embodiment of Birdman, he is the character that launched his career, and the character that, both artistically and psychologically, forever plagues him. Nothing, it seems, can quell the persistent menacing nagging that the voice-over comes to represent. In one significant scene early in the film Riggan attempts to hide a Birdman poster given to him as a gift from the play's crew. He takes the poster off his dressing room wall and walks around the room with it. Neither his bathroom nor his closet is big enough to hide the oversized image, and it spends the rest of the film half-hidden behind the settee, its head poking quite noticeably out the side, reminding Riggan (and the viewer) of its omnipresence. If Riggan's three-by-five motto is designed to pull him towards what he sees as a world of Carveresque longevity, then his alter ego pulls him in the opposite direction. It is at moments of particular psychological weakness that Riggan is tempted to appropriate his Birdman superpowers and slip into a phantasmagoric reality.

Riggan's alter ego then is firmly associated with the superficiality and illusion that Iñárritu sees in neoliberal Hollywood productions – an idea reinforced by the fact that the actor who plays Birdman is uncredited – and operates as a kind of psychological accuser who tempts him back to his commercial past. The internal dialogues that Riggan and his alter ego have throughout the film demonstrate the difficulty that Birdman poses for Riggan. He undermines the validity of Riggan's current artistic endeavour (in the film he says, 'You destroyed a genius book with that infantile adaptation'), and also tempts him with his past commercial success ('You were a movie star, remember?'), and even challenges his future being by asserting his immutable existence ('It's always "we" brother'). As hard as he tries, then, Riggan cannot detach himself from the presence of his debilitating alter ego. The weak repetitive mantra that he mutters to himself when he appears ('Ignore this mental formation, this is a mental formation') has little effect, and his three-by-five motto, while providing him with a distraction in the form of the play, does not afford, as Birdman's persistent presence demonstrates, a consistent enough response.

One suggestion that the film posits, however, is that if Riggan's play can somehow gain critical success then the resulting artistic longevity and posterity would supersede the ephemerality of his early career. And while this solution is not entirely unproblematic – for remember that Riggan is inclined to confuse admiration and love – the key to his success appears to lie with *The New York Times* theatre critic Tabitha Dickenson. Unfortunately for Riggan, Tabitha holds a very clear distinction between the 'serious' art of the theatre stage and the 'superficial' art of the Hollywood studio. Riggan, an actor yoked through his earlier Birdman production to the latter, in her mind, has no place in the former. When they meet in the Rum House, Tabitha outlines her view of Riggan's play:

> I haven't read a word of it, or even seen a preview, but after the opening tomorrow I'm going to turn in the worst review anybody has ever read. And I'm going to close your play. Would you like to know why? Because I hate you, and everyone you represent. Entitled, selfish, spoiled children. Blissfully untrained, unversed and unprepared to even attempt real art. Handing each other awards for cartoons and pornography. Measuring

your worth in weekends. Well, this is the theatre, and you don't get to come in here and pretend you can write, direct and act in your own propaganda piece without coming through me first. So, break a leg.

Tabitha's vitriolic attack on Riggan's past is the most overt critique of the Hollywood film industry in *Birdman*. In positioning Tabitha in this way Iñárritu places his film somewhere on the precipice between what Prose describes as 'justifiable cynicism' and 'idealism', and while of course, Tabitha's critique can easily be levelled at Iñárritu himself – whose own films often reflect that very film industry that he is attempting to criticise – there needs to be, at this point, a certain amount of self-scepticism granted towards Tabitha's comments. As Prose suggests quite appropriately, for this part of *Birdman* to be read correctly there needs to be a certain level of understanding on the part of the audience, for one of the risks that Iñárritu takes with the film is to assume that the audience are 'smart, savvy viewers who can at once appreciate – and see beyond and beneath – its innovative technique, its nested ironies, and its knowing in-jokes'. The question remains, then, how can Riggan overcome Tabitha's scepticism and perform a piece of art worthy of artistic posterity, in turn silencing the superficiality of his Hollywood alter ego? The answer, unsurprisingly, is not exactly straightforward.

A relatively detailed look at the film's finale will help clarify a number of these issues and draw a final conclusion. It begins on the play's opening night. The extraordinary failures of the previews have drawn a large crowd to the theatre, ready for whatever spectacle might confront them. Iñárritu enacts a large temporal compression as day turns to night outside the theatre and the audience emerges during the intermission. The camera zooms through Riggan's dressing room window where he is lying on his dressing table. His ex-wife, Sylvia, enters and the pair finally reconcile, at which point Riggan admits to hearing the voice of his alter ego, as well as a previous suicide attempt when they broke up. Offering little verbal solace, Sylvia kisses Riggan in a moment that seems both lasting and meaningful, and suggests that Iñárritu sees some possibility for love and community amongst the chaos and surface of neoliberalism – even if the act is equivocated by Riggan's subsequent actions. Sylvia leaves and Riggan pulls a gun from a shelf and checks it is loaded. In the bottom corner of the shot is his motto (the last time it is seen in the film), apparently ineffective at stopping what he is about to attempt. As he leaves to make his way to the stage, he telekinetically opens the dressing room door in time with Sanchez's drum score. The combination of the real gun, his willingness to use his superpowers, and the music deliberately builds the film towards its climax, and recalls an earlier proposal by Riggan's alter ego to finish with a grand, sacrificial gesture. Riggan refuses the blood rig and walks onto the stage. Now playing Ed (a disturbed character who suitably fits the psychological distress that Riggan is experiencing) he appeals to Terri, in a speech which might easily be addressed to his daughter, his ex-wife, or even his alter ego, and which therefore conclusively shows the bleeding of the play's fictional onstage reality into Riggan's offstage reality. *'What's wrong with me?'* Riggan says. 'Why do I always end up having to beg people to love me?' Before continuing, 'I just wanted to be what you wanted. Now I spend every fucking minute praying to be someone else. Someone I'm not.' After pointing the gun at Mike, and then the crowd, Riggan eventually turns the gun on himself and shoots.

If his final act on stage was a suicide attempt then, like the suicide attempt by Ed in Carver's story, it failed. The ironic twist is fully revealed later in the hospital when he looks in the mirror and Iñárritu reveals that he has only managed to shoot off his nose – his beak. The aftermath is played out in Riggan's hospital room. Jake visits him and brings with him Tabitha's review. Sylvia reads it aloud:

> Thomson has unwittingly given birth to a new form that can only be described as super realism. Blood was spilt both literally and metaphorically by artist and audience alike, real blood, the blood that has been sorely missing from the veins of the American theatre.

Tabitha's review reveals that Riggan's authentic performance has overturned her opinion. The result, it seems, is that Riggan has finally managed to gain the kind of artistic posterity that he has been searching for. (Jake is ecstatic. 'This play is going to last forever', he says.) Tabitha's review is cleverly assembled. Riggan's authentic 'super realism' – a label reminiscent of those given to Carver's own fiction – deliberately blurs the distinction between offstage and onstage reality, between authenticity and inauthenticity. While his staged adaptation of Carver failed to overcome the superficiality of his early career, his final improvised performance – committed through what Iñárritu depicts as a form of ignorance – portrays a certain level of artistic authenticity. This new reality – or super realism – is far from complete, and its meaning is certainly open to debate (consider the fact that it occurred during a suicide attempt), but it does suggest that Iñárritu thinks that it *is* possible to detach oneself from the influence of neoliberal ephemerality and create a piece of art which communicates some element of what might be called truth and authentic experience. While Tabitha's review, and the film's subtitle, place an emphasis on this idea, it is still a little abstract and underdeveloped by Iñárritu in the film. It perhaps makes most sense in connection to Riggan's relationship with his alter ego, that in the process of letting go or killing his ego, and in turn concerning himself more with others than himself, Riggan is able to achieve a powerful performance of originality and reality.

Carver's role in this process is, considering Riggan's actions, rather equivocal. Iñárritu is far from disavowing Carver as a prescient model for neoliberal negotiation – he is still very much portrayed as an influential artistic figure in the film, after all – but the comprehensiveness of merely taking Carver's work or life and transposing it to a contemporary neoliberal setting is undermined by the fact that Riggan only gains artistic success when he veers from Carver's art. Rather, Carver's influence is found more foundationally in the film's epigraph, Carver's poem 'Late Fragment', which reflects the process by which Riggan's desire for critical admiration – the motivation behind his adaptation of Carver – is replaced by experiential love and community. As the poem puts it, what ought to be desired? Not only to 'call myself beloved' but, more importantly, 'to feel my beloved'.[38] The conflict is ultimately resolved in the film's conclusion, for Riggan finally – and unwittingly – gains critical recognition for his play and in the process restores his filial relationships. At the very end of the film, Sam visits Riggan and the pair reconcile. She leaves momentarily and while she is gone Riggan opens the window, climbs onto the ledge and jumps out.

When Sam returns she runs to the open window and the camera pulls away from her face as she looks up at the sky and smiles. Whether Riggan is flying or not seems far from the point. The moment is more deeply symbolic of his euphoric feeling of love, that, like Carver's poem, he has learnt the distinction between love and admiration.

Notes

1. All references to Iñárritu's film are taken from *Birdman or (The Unexpected Virtue of Ignorance)*, film, directed by Alejandro G. Iñárritu. USA: Fox Searchlight, 2014.
2. Of course this is hardly a unique observation, but even a brief look at the critical material written on Iñárritu's early career confirms a particularly strong connection between art and socio-economics. For examples see Minich, 'Rehabilitating Neoliberalism'; Anker, 'In the Shadowlands of Sovereignty'; Reber, 'Love as Politics'; and Davidson, 'On the Outskirts of Form'.
3. Smith, *Amores Perros*, p. 12.
4. The introduction of neoliberal economics caused a rise in US interest rates. The Mexican government, which had borrowed from US investment banks at low rates, was unable to afford repayments. Neoliberal logic forced Mexico to implement an IMF restructuring programme and the liberalisation of national infrastructure enabled private – nominally American – corporations to buy state apparatus at ultra-low prices. Joseph Stiglitz summarises the ideological basis for IMF restructuring:

   > Decisions were made on the basis of what seemed a curious blend of ideology and bad economics, dogma that sometimes seemed to be thinly veiling special interests. When crises hit, the IMF prescribed outmoded, inappropriate, if 'standard' solutions, without considering the effects they would have on the people in the countries told to follow these policies. Rarely did I see forecasts about what the policies would do to poverty. Rarely did I see thoughtful discussions and analysis of the consequences of alternative policies. There was a single prescription. Alternative opinions were not sought. Open, frank discussion was discouraged – there was no room for it. Ideology guided policy prescription and countries were expected to follow the IMF guidelines without debate ... Inside the IMF it was simply assumed that whatever suffering occurred was a necessary part of the pain countries had to experience on the way to becoming a successful market economy. Stiglitz, *Globalization and its Discontents*, p. xiv.

5. A case study for the Global Report on Human Settlements conducted by University College London in 2003 indicates that the population grew from 8.6 million in 1970 to 17.9 million in 2000. Connelly, 'The Case of Mexico City, Mexico'.

'Why Raymond Carver?' / 179

6. García Canclini, *Consumers and Citizens*, p. 53; Minich, 'Rehabilitating Neoliberalism', p. 977.
7. At the time of writing Mexico has the fifteenth largest economy in the world – worth $1.26 trillion – yet has the second highest wealth disparity among OECD countries: 26 per cent of the country's GDP comes from an informal economy of street-sellers and domestic services; 0.12 per cent of Mexico's economic elite controls almost half of the country's wealth (a proportion that is almost ten times that of the US); 55 million Mexicans – around 46 per cent of the population – are estimated to be living in poverty.
8. For a summary of Mexico's economic prospects see Zarsky and Gallagher. While NAFTA was designed to provide good export and investment opportunities for the Mexican economy, in the neoliberal era capital is dynamic enough to move to the most profitable source. In *A Brief History of Neoliberalism*, Harvey claims that the rise of neoliberalism in countries like China (and their cheap workforce) has led to a decrease of 200,000 jobs in Mexico. Harvey, *A Brief History of Neoliberalism*, p. 138.
9. As Iñárritu explained in an interview with Alice O'Keeffe, 'I also wanted to observe the problem of the borders between the United States and Mexico, and to talk about the millions of Mexicans who live a very harsh reality in America. I was interested in solitude, and deserts . . . urban deserts, where you are surrounded by people but totally isolated.' O'Keeffe, 'Agent Provocateur', p. 36.
10. María Josefina Saldaña-Portillo picks up on a similar idea when discussing NAFTA in relation to Alfonsa Cuarón's *Y tu mamá también*. Cuarón, a contemporary and friend of Iñárritu, released his film a year after *Amores Perros*. Assessing Cuarón's film Saldaña-Portillo writes, 'While NAFTA facilitated the unencumbered movement of goods and capital across the North American continent, it pointedly did not address the third leg of this capitalist triumvirate: labor. NAFTA is strangely mute on the subject of the movement of laborers across national borders . . . although the US economy, from California to New York, is visibly addicted to the importation of cheap, un-documented labor from the south.' Saldaña-Portillo, 'In the Shadow of NAFTA', p. 753.
11. Harvey, *Spaces of Global Capitalism*, p. 68.
12. Harvey, *Spaces of Global Capitalism*, p. 82.
13. In *Spaces of Hope*, Harvey argues that the end result is that the body – that is, humanity – becomes an 'accumulation strategy' for capital, and while this effect is not fully explored in his early films, elements in his more recent work – in *Biutiful* (2010) (through the exploitation of migrant workers) and *Birdman* (through the prevalence of technology and social media) – suggest that Iñárritu is beginning to depict a world in which Harvey's final evaluation is fast becoming the dominant reality. Harvey, *Spaces of Hope*, p. 82.
14. Deleyto and Azcona, *Alejandro González Iñárritu*, p. 49.
15. Kleppe, *The Poetry of Raymond Carver*, p. 168.
16. Carver, *All Of Us*, p. 294.
17. Deleyto and Azcona, *Alejandro González Iñárritu*, p. 75.
18. Riggan admits later on in the film, for instance, the regret he feels over missing

Sam's birth, at the time only video-taping it. 'I should have been there. I should have been in the moment', he confesses to Sylvia.

19. *The Q&A with Jeff Goldsmith*, Podcast, hosted by Jeff Goldsmith. 16 January 2015.
20. It is also worth noting the connection between Carver's story, which emphasises the implication and significance of love, and Iñárritu's early features. *Amores Perros* (translated into English as 'Love's a Bitch') explicitly explores the significance – and even boldly questions the very possibility – of lasting and life-affirming love in the alienated existence created by a neoliberal society. The theme reoccurs in a parallel, but more dramatic, way in *21 Grams*, which portrays Paul Rivers (Sean Penn), a mathematician who suffers from a fatal heart condition, who receives a life-saving heart transplant from Michael Peck (Danny Huston), a husband and father of two, who is killed in a car accident. After the operation, Paul begins a quest to find the owner of his transplanted heart. He meets Michael's widow, Cristina (Naomi Watts), and the two enter into an intense – and despairingly desperate and ephemeral – relationship, as it soon becomes apparent that despite the transplant, Paul's heart condition is quickly deteriorating.
21. Carver, *Collected Stories*, pp. 728–33.
22. Carver, *Collected Stories*, p. 729.
23. Bonetti, 'Ray Carver: Keeping it Short', in Gentry and Stull (eds.), *Conversations with Raymond Carver*, p. 55.
24. Given the ironic tone of the film, it seems significant that the fight unfolds while Mike is holding a copy of Borges – a suggestion by the filmmakers that Mike, despite his pronouncements, broadly stands in for ideas of surface and illusion. Jean Baudrillard's theory of simulacra, for instance, plays on its own reference to Borges's story 'On Exactitude in Science', and argues that contemporary experience is not simply understood as a double or mirroring of reality, but has progressed further to be based on the 'generation of models of a real without origin or reality'. Baudrillard, *Simulacra and Simulations*, p. 2.
25. Harvey, *Seventeen Contradictions and the End of Capitalism*, p. 236.
26. There were two main delays in filming *The Revenant*. The first was that Leonardo DiCaprio, the film's principal actor, was already filming Martin Scorsese's *The Wolf of Wall Street* (2013), and the second was that Iñárritu wanted to shoot his film chronologically through the winter.
27. *Birdman* won four Oscars in 2015, including Best Motion Picture of the Year and Best Achievement in Directing. While success at the Oscars is, in one sense, arbitrary to the study of Iñárritu's film, it did cast a light on Carver's work and placed it in the contemporary popular consciousness. Writing in *Publishers Weekly*, Calvin Reid reported that US sales of *What We Talk About When We Talk About Love* increased by 121 per cent in the three months after the film opened. This was quickly followed by the decision to publish *Beginners*, the unedited manuscript of *What We Talk About When We Talk About Love* (already available in the UK and Japan) in September 2015, while Vintage, Carver's paperback publisher, released e-book editions of both titles for the first time.
28. It is worth briefly mentioning that *Short Cuts* takes a very different approach to

Carver's texts. Altman's multi-protagonist film is a melange – an interwoven and complex narrative – that renders nine of Carver's stories (and one poem) into a feature-length production. The film was approved and endorsed by Tess Gallagher, Carver's widow, and presented as the continuation of Carver's prematurely ended artistic output. For a comprehensive critique of Altman's film in relation to Carver's work see Kasia Boddy, '*Short Cuts* and Long Shots'.

29. Carver, *Collected Stories*, p. 311.
30. Carver, *Collected Stories*, p. 310.
31. Carver, *Collected Stories*, p. 310.
32. Carver, *Collected Stories*, p. 320.
33. Carver, *Collected Stories*, p. 322.
34. Carver, *Collected Stories*, p. 318.
35. Carver, *Collected Stories*, p. 315.
36. Carver, *Collected Stories*, p. 310.
37. As I argued in Chapter 2, John Gardner taught a particularly dogmatic version of literary realism. Talking about what he learned from Gardner in an interview with Hansmaarten Tromp in 1984, Carver said, 'Honesty in writing is one of the things that has remained with me . . . Inexperienced writers often feel compelled to use words which they've picked up here or there, and which "look good" on paper. Or which don't exactly express what the writer intended. Or which express false sentimentality.' Tromp, 'Any Good Writer Uses His Imagination to Convince the Reader', in Gentry and Stull (eds.), *Conversations with Raymond Carver*, p. 78.
38. Carver, *All Of Us*, p. 294.

Conclusion:
Willy Vlautin and Diminished Class Consciousness

Nicolaus Mills opens his critical retrospective of the cultural and political landscape in the 1980s by recalling Nancy Reagan's decision to order a 220-place setting of raised gold paste Lenox presidential china to the tune of $200,000. At another point in history, the First Lady's decision might have caused a large enough political controversy to effect serious, even fatal, political damage. But this was 1981. The US was trying to forget the humiliating 1970s, a decade that had seen presidential resignation, a long-fought and costly war and an economic malaise bought on by the inability of federal economists to overcome the structural flaws of a worn-down Keynesian capitalism. Reagan's campaign, indeed, his two terms in presidential office, were founded on the reverse projection, if not the actual achievement, of cultural triumph, success, power and status. As Mills quite rightly points out, nothing was more important to 1980s culture than its symbols.

What has become clear nearly forty years on, is that much of this culture of triumph was driven and fuelled by an ideological free market libertarianism that promoted vast capital accumulation, the prioritisation of private enterprise and the financialisation of all sectors of society, while simultaneously reducing state intervention and passing unprecedented corporate and personal tax cuts. Charles Murray's *Losing Ground* gave ideological efficacy to the idea that welfare and social security were morally corrupting crutches for the working classes, and the Laffer curve provided the necessary economic proof that an overhaul of the tax system would boost economic efficiency. Addressing the cultural hot-button topic of children's entertainment, and reflecting dominant deregulatory ideology, Mark Fowler, the Federal Commissioner, was reported to have said that it was down to the 'magic of the marketplace' to look after the nation's children. The language of finance – buyout, leverage, acquisition, takeover – became the language of success. Ethics, particularly in the world of business, became irrelevant. Only pessimistic left-wing political activists – a term highly charged with the anti-patriotic undertones of communism – would oppose such a promising cultural enterprise. While history is never an exact science, it is fair to say that in this instance, the 1980s were predictably cyclical. Almost a century earlier, similar legislation had been enacted that ended restrictions on income and inheritance tax to prelude the gilded age. Employing this connection, Mills points out that the late nineteenth-century adage 'conspicuous consumption' had its own 1980s variant: 'flaunting it'. Drawing upon one of the decade's most conspicuous examples of this maxim, he concludes, 'For a figure like real estate mogul Donald Trump, it was not enough to be seen in all the right places. It was essential to brand the world one occupied: to live in Trump Tower, to fly Trump Shuttle, to sail on the Trump Princess.'[1]

Hindsight is – as the aphorism makes clear – twenty-twenty. Even so, it is still remarkable that the very man who, for Mills, epitomised the flaunting-it era, would, in 2016, win the presidential election. What is perhaps more remarkable still, is that his political success was achieved on the back of a wave of grassroots working-class support – a faction of society that has systematically suffered at the hands of neoliberal enterprise. Indeed, while it is inequitable to reduce Trump's election victory to a single cause, recent political analysis has made clear that a major component of his victory was his ability to win a swing of white, working-class voters – the demographic of people without a college degree or regular salaried job. The National Election Pool, a consortium research facility, reported a 14 per cent shift from Democrat to GOP for voters without a four-year college degree, and a 16 per cent shift for those who earn under $30,000 a year. The same poll reported that 78 per cent of GOP voters thought that their family financial situation was worse than in the past; 63 per cent thought it would be worse still for the next generation.² These kinds of figures are best viewed in light of the broader context of contemporary American consciousness. A report jointly commissioned by the PRRI and *The Atlantic* found that the three major factors that appealed to Trump's voters were anxiety about cultural change, immigration and a particular type of economic fatalism born from the realisation that the American dream was as illusory as it had ever been.³ Given this complex weaving of perceived personal economic decline and threatened cultural identity, it is unsurprising that political rhetoric that appealed to the historic values of American exceptionalism had such a purposeful impact.

As I outlined at the very start of this book, just like those who played such a pivotal role in the recent election, Carver was a casualty of faith in the American dream, believing, as he wrote in 'Fires', that if he worked hard enough and did the right things, then the right things would happen to him. For Carver, as I argued in Chapter 1, this meant trying to hold enough part-time jobs to finance his education, and yet, even after graduating with a BA he struggled to hold the kind of white-collar work that he thought would propel him and his family to the middle class. Undone by the personal circumstances of alcoholism and bankruptcy, as well as the macroeconomic impact of shifting capitalist ideology, Carver's early to mid-adult life appears to be synecdochic of many white, working-class Americans during this time. And while Carver may have struggled to make productive sense of his socio-economic situation, it nonetheless affected his life in very pointed and particular ways, trapping him between the conventional American dream of individual freedom and equal opportunity and the reality of inequality and social immobility. Moreover, Carver's late writing embodies a retreat from market-driven neoliberal dominance towards an artisanal form of craftsmanship as a solution to the bewildering world that he saw around him. This muted oppositional alternative is broadly based on residual values and operates outside of the political realm – and is even particularly local to his situation – and yet, is still powerful enough to work beyond its initial historic and cultural moment by becoming a distinctive site of resistance to the hegemonic norms of late capitalism. This, then, is the influential and fundamental tension behind Carver's work –

the desire to return to a residual craftsmanship in a world driven by neoliberal market forces. In this way, Carver's realist authenticity combines with a consolatory craftsmanship that becomes a coping mechanism that offers others a way of navigating a world which seems to exceed the frame of conceptual mapping.

This idea is reinforced by the incongruous fact that despite Carver's portrayal in media and criticism as the 'chronicler of blue-collar despair' there is a conspicuous lack of political discussion, political theory or even trade unionist activity in his fiction. The reason for this reticence is, perhaps appropriately enough, never fully articulated by Carver. While his father was involved in an AFL-sponsored strike when he worked at a Biles-Coleman lumber mill in 1936, Carver, who never fully settled into a long-term labouring career, had no involvement in strike action, a fact that reflects broader trends in the labour sector during his lifetime. Carver's early adult life was marked by industrial decline, particularly in areas reliant on production and manufacturing, and his later years by the quashing of union power under Reagan's administration and the concurrent rise of short-term service sector employment. Exploring this cultural trend while in its infancy, Sennett and Cobb conclude that society's source of social legitimacy comes from 'what a person produces, and it is from this that inferences are drawn about what he essentially *is*'.[4] A young teacher, for instance, who believes their new occupation is valuable because of its role in social education, quickly loses their sense of purpose when they realise that all they are actually doing is helping students pass arbitrary examinations. The same is true, in a different context, for workers who moved from manufacturing to (often temporary) service sector employment, where tasks became increasingly menial and unskilful: mindless waitressing, cleaning endless corridors of hotel rooms and selling stationary supplies. The situation is magnified by the neoliberal state, which represses trade unionist activities, dismantles state welfare and repeals support for secondary industry. The systematic removal of these institutions – all of which help codify a narrative of solidarity for working-class labourers – serves to leave those at the socio-economic base of society in a state of peripatetic alienation.

Carver's writing, which finds its root in this kind of socio-economic experience, therefore reveals the negative space behind the hegemony of neoliberal capitalism. His fiction depicts the waitresses, gas-service attendants, labourers and salesmen that populate the neoliberal service sector; people struggling in temporary employment or unsalaried positions; people who lack the education, opportunity and historic rebellious working-class narratives to challenge neoliberal common sense. In bringing these forgotten people to life, Carver's fiction offers a muted oppositional alternative to neoliberal dominance, and, in turn, sheds light on a particular way of life that, until the 2016 presidential election, found itself sidelined from political discussion. Take Jill, a character in the story 'Boxes'; she is thirty-five and lives in the far reaches of the American Northwest. For the last five years she has groomed dogs for a living. But that is a recent occupational development. Before grooming dogs, she was a full-time housewife and mother, but her first husband ran off to Australia with their kids. She remarried, but her second husband, an alcoholic, left her with a broken eardrum the night he drove their car off a bridge into the Elwha River. He didn't have life insurance and Jill had to take a loan out to pay for the funeral – all before the city sent her the bill for the bridge repair. Or take Sandy's husband, a roofer, who in the story 'Preservation' is sacked on Valentine's Day. The local economy has taken a turn and developers are reducing their quotas. He goes to the employment centre the next day, only to find hundreds of labourers, just like him, looking for work. Or there's Ross, an unemployed aerospace engineer in 'Mr. Coffee and Mr. Fixit'. He's an alcoholic with a gunshot wound from his first wife, who doesn't have the money to pay alimony to his six kids. Or what about Al in 'Jerry and Molly and Sam'? A husband and father who commits to a long-term lease the same month his employer announces a round of lay-offs. Or, the disabled man in 'Viewfinder', whose only way to make a living is to take pictures of people's houses. Or, Holly in 'Gazebo', who imagines an idyllic future with her boyfriend Duane but, in reality, is caught in a web of infidelity, alcoholism and suicidal tendencies while she tries to manage a run-down motel. These are the characters that are the focus of Carver's fiction. They are antecedents of the white working-class voters who, in a period of economic and political disillusionment, cast their lot in with Trump in a last-gasp effort to change the status quo. However, rather than patronise or denigrate, Carver's sympathetic portrayals reveal that these people are causalities of neoliberal libertarianism, and its retraction of public education, social services and health care benefits. While Carver's characters are fiction, they have become presciently synecdochic of contemporary white working-class experience.

Willy Vlautin's novelistic vision continues where Carver's left off and presses into the shadows of contemporary American experience. Born in Reno in 1967, and now residing in Oregon, Vlautin's vocational experience, which ranges from truck driving to warehouse work and house decorating, is as disparate as any early neoliberal working-class career. Inspired to write after hearing Paul Kelly's song 'So Much Water So Close To Home', based on Carver's story of the same name, he searched out Carver's fiction and – just as McInerney and Murakami had done before him – discovered that Carver's work gave purchase to his own reality. Living in his girlfriend's parents' garage at the time and, in his own words, 'beating myself up for what a bum I was', he read Carver for the first time in 1986. 'I swear I thought I understood every line', he said. 'He wasn't better than me, he wasn't from Harvard, he didn't get a scholarship to Oxford, he was just a man from the Northwest trying to hang on.' He concludes in typical self-depreciating manner, 'I was never adventurous or smart enough to be Hemingway or Steinbeck, and Bukowski lived too hard for me, but Carver was just a working-class guy with an edge.'[5] He spent the next two decades touring with his band Richmond Fontaine before publishing his first novel *The Motel Life* (2006), soon followed by *Northline* (2008), *Lean on Pete* (2010), *The Free* (2014) and *Don't Skip Out On Me* (2016). Set amongst the folds of American society, and featuring protagonists without the shelter of clear class or ethnic identities or the defensive narratives of working-class rebellion, Vlautin's fiction, as Carver's did before, gives a glimpse into the experience of the poor white Western – and nominally male – American at the start of this new century.

'I kept running and running', Charley Thompson, the protagonist of *Lean on Pete* says in response and in an attempt to forget the recollection of his father's parental and social failures, 'I was so tired I couldn't think about anything like that . . . It always takes a long time, but it always works.'[6] Much like Carver's, Vlautin's characters tend towards a position of retreat or flight rather than confrontation when threatened with bewildering or incomprehensible situations. This is the fate of Frank and Jerry Lee Flannigan, the brothers in *The Motel Life* who decide to flee Reno for Montana when Jerry Lee accidentally runs over a teenage boy in a snowstorm. It is the fate, in a slightly different way, of Freddie McCall in *The Free*, who works two jobs in an attempt to pay back the mountain of debt bought on by his disabled daughter's health care, and who never confronts or successfully provokes his lazy boss into giving him a pay rise, but rather agrees to allow a friend to store marijuana plants in his basement for extra cash. And it is the fate, also, of Horace Hopper in *Don't Skip Out On Me*, when he leaves his racist Paiute-hating grandmother to reinvent himself as a Mexican boxer named Hector Hidalgo. The concerns that feed this constant flight suggest that the consolatory withdrawal so typical of Carver's fictional world is, for better or worse, as prevalent today as it was at the start of the neoliberal era. This feeling is born out most clearly in *Lean on Pete*, which centres around Charley Thompson, by far the most extreme example of a character who seeks to separate himself from the terrifying and bewildering situation he finds himself in. Abandoned by his mother when he was a year old, and raised by his semi-absent father, Ray, a peripatetic forklift driver and warehouse operative, Charley is forced to live a life of social isolation. He has no knowledge of his roots, and knows little of his mother – other than that she suffered from some kind of mental disability, what Ray calls being 'fucked-up in the head' – and his father, despite his claim that 'I ain't shit but I like being here with you', is more absent than present.[7] The novel opens a week into their arrival at a squat two-bed rental on the edge of Portland after leaving Spokane two days before Charley's school year finished. The reason for their move is never fully revealed – other than that Ray would 'rather go to prison and get the shit kicked out of him every day than spend any more time in a dump like Spokane' – but their move is a complete dislocation for Charley, who is preparing for a second season on his high school football team.[8] It does not take Ray long to hook up with Lynn, a secretary in his company's front office. As they leave for work one day together, Ray reveals to Charley that Lynn is married to a Samoan who, in his words is 'fucking nuts', before giving Charley $10 for food and leaving.[9] Absent for a number of days, Charley is forced to live on the $10 until Ray returns and, one night soon after, Lynn's Samoan husband breaks in and throws Ray through the front window of their rented house. Hospitalised from the injuries, Ray eventually dies while Charley is working a summer job at a local racetrack. Taken by one of the jockeys, Bonnie, to a party on the north-east side of the city only days after his father's death, Charley witnesses Bonnie taking heroine – Vlautin's reference to the opioid epidemic amongst the white working class – and leaves the party and begins running away. As he does so, the image of Bonnie's drug abuse fuels further recollections about his violent and dysfunctional upbringing:

> I'd seen a lot of things. I'd seen my dad do things. I'd seen him having sex with women. I'd seen him bending over our couch and ramming into them and I'd seen them in the kitchen sitting on top of him saying things to him. I'd seen him puking his guts out in the sink and snorting cocaine and smoking weed. I saw a woman passed out in the back of our car in nothing but a bra. I saw her pee on the seat. I saw a guy get a broken beer bottle pushed in his face while we were at a daytime barbeque. I'd seen my dad hit my aunt in the face and call her names when all she did was tell him to come back when he wasn't so drunk and mean. I'd seen him wreck her car and then abandon it. I'd seen him talk to the police. I saw a kid get hit so hard that he began to foam at the mouth and go into seizures and I'd seen a kid shoot a dog in the head with a .22. I'd seen another kid tear the pajamas off his sister just so he could see her down there. She was screaming and crying. And I'd seen a horse break his leg and wobble around on three while the broke one was held on by only skin.[10]

Charley's young experience is not unlike J. D. Vance's in *Hillbilly Elegy*, his acclaimed account of growing up as an Appalachian immigrant in small town Ohio. But where Vance has the covenantal ties of kinship – even if they are patently defective and morally flawed – Charley, who has been constantly moved from one town to another by his father, finds himself alone in the hinterlands of American society, without the safety net of broad family ties or, even, the defensive ethnic identity of hillbilly. If *Lean on Pete* is a kind of coming-of-age novel, then what Charley learns from his experiences, awful as they are, is the importance of this kind of flight and perpetual movement. After the death of his father, Charley begins to squat at the Portland Meadows racetrack, where he works for a failing and cheating racehorse owner called Del Montgomery. When Del threatens to put down Lean on Pete, Charley's favourite horse – or, what he euphemistically refers to as 'sending him to Mexico' – Charley loads Pete into Del's trailer and drives off into the Oregon desert in an attempt to find his estranged auntie who, to the last of his knowledge, was working for a car mechanic in Rock Springs, Wyoming. The odyssey-like journey that Charley takes through the American wilderness brings him into contact with a string of desperate characters living at the edge of American experience; these are citizens in small enclaves of civilisation at the outer extremes of contemporary American life, pushed as far back from the technological and economic hubs of the west and east coasts as possible. When he meets Laurie, an obese girl who is a similar age to him and who is trapped in an abusive home life in which she works as a cook-come-cleaner for her grandfather, Charley asks her why she doesn't leave (his default action when faced with trials), only for Laurie to say, with a definite sense of resignation, 'I don't know where else to go.'[11] The moment is keenly symbolic of a kind of contemporary American experience, one that has had curtailed political engagement in recent times. If, as Harker argues, Carver's texts 'dramatize characters confronting experiences that lie outside the hegemonic stories through which they apprehend the social world', then Vlautin's novel dramatises characters in similar situations but who appear to live without the knowledge that those hegemonic narratives even exist. While Carver's characters might recognise the possibility of the American dream (even if they cannot attain it), Vlautin's characters are removed one stage further and live disconnected from even the idea of upward social mobility and financial self-improvement. In *Lean on Pete*, hegemonic narratives, or any kind of codified existence, are replaced by fruitless experiences that provide only regressive notions of fulfilment. Where Carver's characters might find solace in their relationships – however flawed they may be – the relationships in Vlautin's novel, even those that appear convivial, are disintegrated by the undulating depressive cycles bought on by the pressures of financial and social poverty at both an individual and geographic level and, because of this, his characters are unable to pull themselves towards any kind of notional freedom that might be on offer.

In *Lean on Pete* the difficulties of this kind of conceptual reframing are brought to the fore when Charley lands in Boise, Idaho. Walking through the Boise State University campus one afternoon he watches people – presumably students – swimming in the river and lying in the sun in a park. The next day he returns to the campus because he thinks it is one of the few places he can 'hide without getting caught' and retreats into a university building to wash and drink in a bathroom. The university, with its diverse social encounters, educational promise and, of course, at an institution like Boise State, its collegiate sports, stands in for Charley's missing life. Or, at least, the kind of life that became hegemonic for Carver's generation, but for someone like Charley, drawn from the world of white, working-class poverty two generations on, does not even register. In fact, it is striking how often this kind of situation occurs in the novel. Charley is lonely and lost for much of the narrative, but he is rarely – apart from his foray into the Oregon desert – *alone*. This becomes explicit in Boise as Charley enters the same absolute space as other young people – perhaps only two or three years his senior – who are engaged in a very different and, for Charley at least, incomprehensible lifestyle. Later in the week he returns to the university to sleep under a stairwell – for Charley, the only notable thing about this experience is that 'It was pretty boring in there' – and spends the following day in the library, which, for him, is not a place of independent study and knowledge gathering, but rather just somewhere to meet another wayfarer, 'an old man who only had one arm and lived in an abandoned railcar with his brother'.[12] The role, then, that the university campus plays in illustrating a weakening or, even, failed projection of conceptual freedom from social dysfunction and poverty for an individual from a background like Charley's more broadly reflects a continuation of Carver's own experience as he sought to negotiate his own studies and career in higher education, an idea that, in a roundabout way, brings us back to the opening sections of this book; which is to say, in short, that the importance of Carver's work shows little sign of abating. While a billionaire has been elected to the White House, his presidency has inaugurated the rise of commentary – on both sides of the political spectrum – on the negative impact of neoliberal practice over the past four decades. And while neoliberal trauma has, of course, been the dominant experience for many during this time, there is little doubt that, whatever the political rights and wrongs of the arguments surrounding their experience, the white working class are becoming an increasingly vocal, visible and politically vital demographic; an emphasis that suggests that while he died over thirty years ago, Carver's work will continue to remain influential for the foreseeable future.

Notes

1. Mills, 'The Culture of Triumph and the Spirit of the Times', in Mills (ed.), *Culture in an Age of Money*, p. 13.
2. Huang, Jacoby, Strickland and Lai, 'Election 2016: Exit Polls'.
3. Cox, Lienesch and Jones, 'Beyond Economics: Fears of Cultural Displacement Pushed the White Working Class to Trump'.
4. Sennett and Cobb, *The Hidden Injuries of Class*, pp. 267–8.
5. Vlautin, 'P.S.', in Vlautin, *Lean On Pete*, p. 4.
6. Vlautin, *Lean On Pete*, p. 121.
7. Vlautin, *Lean On Pete*, p. 173.
8. Vlautin, *Lean On Pete*, p. 2.
9. Vlautin, *Lean On Pete*, p. 7.
10. Vlautin, *Lean On Pete*, p. 121.
11. Vlautin, *Lean On Pete*, p. 168.
12. Vlautin, *Lean On Pete*, p. 215.

WORKS CITED

Abrams, Linsey, 'A Maximalist Novelist Looks at Some Minimalist Fiction', *Mississippi Review*, 14.1 (1985), 24–30.
Adelman, Bob, *Carver Country: The World of Raymond Carver* (New York: Quantuck Lane Press, 2013).
Aldridge, John, *Talents and Technicians: Literary Chic and the New Assembly-Line Fiction* (New York: Scribner's, 1992).
Allinson, Gary D., *Japan's Postwar History* (London: University College London Press, 1997).
Amores Perros (Love's a Bitch), film, directed by Alejandro González Iñárritu. USA: Lions Gate Films, 2001.
Anker, Elizabeth S., 'In the Shadowlands of Sovereignty: The Politics of Enclosure in Alejandro González Iñárritu's *Babel*', *University of Toronto Quarterly*, 82.4 (2013), 950–73.
Annesley, James, *Fictions of Globalization: Consumption, the Market and the Contemporary American Novel* (London: Continuum, 2006).
Anon., 'Bear in Mind: Editor's Choice for Particular Interest', *The New York Times Book Review*, 2 December 1984.
Appelbaum, Judith, 'Paperback Talk', *The New York Times Book Review*, 4 September 1983.
Arrighi, Giovanni, *The Long Twentieth Century* (London: Verso, 1994).
Auerbach, Erich, *Mimesis*, trans. Willard R. Trask (Princeton: Princeton University Press, 1953).
Babel, film, directed by Alejandro González Iñárritu. USA: Paramount Vantage, 2006.
Barth, John, 'The Literature of Exhaustion', *The Atlantic*, 2 (1967).
Barthes, Roland, *The Rustle of Language*, trans. Richard Howard (Berkeley: University of California Press, 1986).
Baudrillard, Jean, *Simulacra and Simulations*, trans. Paul Foss, Paul Patton and Philip Beitchman (New York: Sémiotext(e), 1983).
Belsey, Catherine, *Critical Practice* (London: Routledge, 1980).
Birdman or (The Unexpected Virtue of Ignorance, film, directed by Alejandro González Iñárritu. USA: Fox Searchlight, 2014.

Biutiful, film, directed by Alejandro González Iñárritu. Spain: Menageatroz and Mod Producciones, 2010.

Bloom, Harold, *The Anxiety of Influence* (Oxford: Oxford University Press, 1973).

Bloom, Harold, *Bloom's Major Short Story Writers: Raymond Carver* (New York: Chelsea House Publishers, 2002).

Blum, David, 'Hollywood's Brat Pack', *New York*, 10 June 1985, <http://nymag.com/movies/features/49902/> (last accessed 11 April 2019).

Boddy, Kasia, '*Short Cuts* and Long Shots: Raymond Carver's Stories and Robert Altman's Film', *Journal of American Studies*, 34.1 (2000), 1–22.

Bonetti, Kay, 'Ray Carver: Keeping It Short', in Marshall Bruce Gentry and William L. Stull (eds), *Conversations with Raymond Carver* (London: University Press of Mississippi, 1990), pp. 53–61.

Boulter, Jonathan, *Melancholy and the Archive: Trauma, History and Memory in the Contemporary Novel* (London: Bloomsbury, 2011).

Boxer, David and Cassandra Phillips, '*Will You Please Be Quiet, Please?*: Voyeurism, Dissociation, and the Art of Raymond Carver', *The Iowa Review*, 10.3 (1979), 75–90.

Bradbury, Malcolm and Sigmund Ro, *Contemporary American Fiction* (London: Edward Arnold, 1987).

Burn, Gordon, 'Poetry, Poverty and Realism Down in Carver Country', in Marshall Bruce Gentry and William L. Stull (eds), *Conversations with Raymond Carver* (London: University Press of Mississippi, 1990), pp. 117–19.

Campbell, Ewing, *Raymond Carver: A Study of the Short Fiction* (New York: Twayne, 1992).

Carter, E. Graydon, 'Leading the Gliterary Life', *Esquire*, December 1986, pp. 160–6.

Carver, Raymond, *All of Us: The Collected Poems* (London: The Harvill Press, 1996).

Carver, Raymond, *Beginners: The Original Version of* What We Talk About When We Talk About Love (London: Jonathan Cape, 2009).

Carver, Raymond, *Call If You Need Me: The Uncollected Fiction and Other Prose* (New York: Vintage Contemporaries, 2001).

Carver, Raymond, *Cathedral* (New York: Knopf, 1983).

Carver, Raymond, *Collected Stories* (New York: The Library of America, 2009).

Carver, Raymond, *Elephant* (London: Collins Harvill, 1988).

Carver, Raymond, *Fires: Essays, Poems, Stories* (Santa Barbara: Capra Press, 1983).

Carver, Raymond, *Furious Seasons and Other Stories* (Santa Barbara: Capra Press, 1977).

Carver, Raymond, *What We Talk About When We Talk About Love* (New York: Knopf, 1981).

Carver, Raymond, *Where I'm Calling From: New and Selected Stories* (New York: Atlantic Monthly, 1988).

Carver, Raymond, *Will You Please Be Quiet, Please?* (New York: McGraw Hill, 1976).

Connolly, Priscilla, 'The Case of Mexico City, Mexico', *Understanding Slums: Case Studies for the Global Report on Human Settlements 2003*, <http://www.ucl.ac.uk/dpu-projects/Global_Report/pdfs/Mexico.pdf> (last accessed 11 April 2019).

Cornwall, Gareth, 'Mediated Desire and American Disappointment in the Stories of Raymond Carver', *Critique Studies in Contemporary Fiction*, 46.2 (2005), 334–56.

Cox, Daniel, Rachel Lienesch and Robert P. Jones, 'Beyond Economics: Fears of Cultural Displacement Pushed the White Working Class to Trump', <https://www.prri.org/research/white-working-class-attitudes-economy-trade-immigration-election-donald-trump> (last accessed 11 April 2019).

Cushman, Keith, 'Blind, Intertextual Love: "The Blind Man" and Raymond Carver's "Cathedral"', in Keith Cushman and Dennis Jackson (eds), *D. H. Lawrence's Literary Inheritors* (London: Macmillan, 1991), pp. 155–66.

Davidson, Michael, 'On the Outskirts of Form: Cosmopoetics in the Shadow of NAFTA', *Textual Practice*, 22.4 (2008), 733–56.

Davis, Mike, *Prisoners of the American Dream* (London: Verso, 1986).

Dean, Jodi and Mark Fisher. 'We Can't Afford To Be Realists: A Conversation', in Alison Shonkwiler and Leigh Claire La Berge (eds), *Reading Capitalist Realism* (Iowa City: University of Iowa Press, 2014), pp. 26–38.

Deleyto, Celestino and María del Mar Azcona, *Alejandro González Iñárritu* (Chicago: University of Illinois Press, 2010).

Derrida, Jacques, *Of Grammatology*, trans. Gayatri Chakravorty Spivak (Baltimore: Johns Hopkins University Press, 1976).

Durante, Francesco, 'De Minimis: Raymond Carver and His World', in Marshall Bruce Gentry and William L. Stull (eds), *Conversations with Raymond Carver* (London: University Press of Mississippi, 1990), pp. 192–6.

Eagleton, Terry, *Marxism and Literary Criticism* (London: Methuen, 1976).

Edsall, Thomas, *The New Politics of Inequality* (London: Norton, 1984).

Eliot, T. S., *Selected Essays* (London: Faber & Faber, 1951).

Ellis, Bret, *American Psycho* (London: Picador, 1991).

Federman, Raymond, 'Surfiction', in Raymond Federman (ed.), *Surfiction* (Chicago: Swallow Press, 1975), pp. 5–15.

Felski, Rita, 'Nothing to Declare: Identity, Shame and the Lower Middle Class', *PMLA*, 115.1 (2000), 39.

Fisher, Mark, *Capitalist Realism: Is There No Alternative?* (London: Zero Books, 2009).

Fisketjon, Gary, 'Normal Nightmares', *Village Voice*, 18 September 1978.

Foley, Michael, 'Dirty Realist', *London Review of Books*, 2–8 May 1985.

Ford, Richard, 'Good Raymond', *The New Yorker*, 5 October 1998.

Gabriel, Philip, *Spirit Matters: The Transcendent in Modern Japanese Literature* (Honolulu: University of Hawai'i Press, 2006).

Gallagher, Tess, *Soul Barnacles* (Ann Arbor: University of Michigan Press, 2000).

García Canclini, Néstor, *Consumers and Citizens*, trans. George Yúdice (London: University of Minnesota Press, 2001).

Gardner, John, *The Art of Fiction: Notes on Craft for Young Writers* (New York: Random House, 1983).

Gardner, John, *On Becoming a Novelist* (New York: Random House, 1983).

Gardner, John, *On Moral Fiction* (New York: Basic Books, 1978).

Garrett, George, 'American Publishing Today', *The Sewanee Review*, 98.3 (1990), 515–26.

Girrard, Stephanie, '"Standing At the Corner Of Walk And Don't Walk": Vintage Contemporaries, *Bright Lights, Big City*, and the Problems of Betweeness', *American Literature*, 68.1 (1996), 161–85.

Groarke, Steven, 'Raymond Carver and the Banality of Influence', *Talus*, 6 (1991), 174–84.

Habermas, Jürgen, 'The New Obscurity: The Crises of the Welfare State and the Exhaustion of Utopian Energies', trans. Phillip Jacobs, *Philosophy and Social Criticism*, 11.2 (1986), 1–18.

Halpert, Sam, *Raymond Carver: An Oral Biography* (Iowa City: University of Iowa Press, 1995).

Harker, Ben, '"To be there, inside, and not be there": Raymond Carver and Class', *Textual Practice*, 21.4 (2007), 715–36.

Harvey, David, *A Brief History of Neoliberalism* (Oxford: Oxford University Press, 2005).

Harvey, David, *The Condition of Postmodernity* (Oxford: Blackwell, 1990).

Harvey, David, *The Enigma of Capital and the Crises of Capitalism* (Oxford: Oxford University Press, 2010).

Harvey, David, *Seventeen Contradictions and the End of Capitalism* (London: Profile, 2014).

Harvey, David, *Spaces of Global Capitalism: Towards a Theory of Uneven Geographical Development* (London: Verso, 2006).

Harvey, David, *Spaces of Hope* (Edinburgh: Edinburgh University Press, 2000).

Hassan, Ihab, 'The Problem of Influence in Literary History: Notes towards a Definition', *The Journal of Aesthetics and Art Criticism*, 14.1 (1955), 66–76.

Helprin, Mark, 'Small Expectations', *The New York Review of Books*, 24 November 1983.

Hendin, Josephine, 'Fictions of Acquisition', in Nicolaus Mills (ed.), *Culture in an Age of Money* (Chicago: Elephant, 1990), pp. 216–33.

Howe, Irving, 'Stories of Our Loneliness', *The New York Times Book Review*, 11 September 1983.

Huang, Jon, Samuel Jacoby, Michael Strickland and K. K. Rebecca Lai, 'Election 2016: Exit Polls', *The New York Times*, <https://www.nytimes.com/interactive/2016/11/08/us/politics/election-exit-polls.html> (last accessed 11 April 2019).

Ivy, Marilyn, 'Formations of Mass Culture', in Andrew Gordon (ed.), *Postwar Japan as History* (Oxford: University of California Press, 1993), pp. 239–58.

Jackson Lears, T. J., *No Place of Grace: Antimodernism and the Transformation of American Culture, 1880–1920* (Chicago: University of Chicago Press, 1994).

Jameson, Fredric, *Postmodernism, or, the Logic of Late Capitalism* (London: Verso, 1991).

Jameson, Fredric, *The Seeds of Time* (New York: Columbia University Press, 1994).

Kaufmann, David, 'Yuppie Postmodernism', *Arizona Quarterly: A Journal of American Literature, Culture, and Theory*, 47.2 (1991), 93–116.

Kellerman, Stewart, 'Raymond Carver, Writer and Poet Of the Working Poor, Dies at 50', *The New York Times*, 3 August 1988.

Kelts, Roland, *Japanamerica: How Japanese Pop Culture Has Invaded the US* (Basingstoke: Palgrave Macmillan, 2006).

Kinder, Chuck, *Honeymooners* (London: Plume, [2001] 2002).

Kingston, Jeff, *Contemporary Japan: History, Politics and Social Change Since the 1980s* (Chichester: Wiley-Blackwell, 2011).

Kleppe, Sandra Lee, *The Poetry of Raymond Carver* (Farnham: Ashgate, 2014).

Kohn, Eric, 'Why "Birdman" is the First Modern Showbiz Satire', *IndieWire*, 21 August 2014.
Kotzwinkle, William, 'You're Fired, So You Buy a Ferret', *The New York Times Book Review*, 25 November 1984.
Leaf, Jonathan, 'How Birdman Betrays Carver: An Untold Story', *Forbes*, 4 January 2015.
Leavis, F. R., *The Great Tradition* (London: Chatto & Windus, 1962).
Lynd, Helen Merrell, *On Shame and the Search for Identity* (New York: Harcourt Brace, 1958).
McCaffery, Larry and Sinda Gregory, 'An Interview with Raymond Carver', in Marshall Bruce Gentry and William L. Stull (eds), *Conversations With Raymond Carver* (Jackson: University of Mississippi Press, 1990), pp. 98–116.
McCaffery, Larry, Sinda Gregory and Toshifumi Miyawaki, 'It Don't Mean A Thing, If It Ain't Got That Swing: an Interview with Haruki Murakami', *The Review of Contemporary Fiction*, 22.2 (2002), 111–19.
McGuire, Ian, *Richard Ford and the Ends of Realism* (Iowa City: University of Iowa Press, 2015).
McGurl, Mark, *The Program Era* (London: Harvard University Press, 2009).
McHale, Brian, *Postmodernist Fiction* (London: Methuen, 1987).
McInerney, Jay, *Bright Lights, Big City* (New York: Vintage Contemporaries, 1984).
McInerney, Jay, *Brightness Falls* (London: Bloomsbury, 1992).
McInerney, Jay, *Bright, Precious Days* (London: Bloomsbury, 2016).
McInerney, Jay, *How It Ended* (London: Bloomsbury, 2000).
McInerney, Jay, 'I Miss You George', 15 October 2014, <http://www.jaymcinerney.com/blog/170/i-miss-you-george> (last accessed 11 April 2019).
McInerney, Jay, *Ransom* (London: Jonathan Cape, 1986).
McInerney, Jay, 'Raymond Carver: A Still, Small Voice', *The New York Times Book Review*, 6 August 1989.
McInerney, Jay, *Story Of My Life* (London: Bloomsbury, 1988).
Marx, Karl, *Selected Writings* (Oxford: Oxford University Press, 1977).
Matsuoka, Naomi, 'Murakami Haruki and Raymond Carver: The American Scene', *Comparative Literature Studies*, 30.4 (1993), 423–38.
Max, D. T., 'The Carver Chronicles', *The New York Times Magazine*, 9 August 1998.
Meyer, Stephen, *Manhood on the Line: Working-Class Masculinities in the American Heartland* (Urbana, Chicago, and Springfield: University of Illinois Press, 2016).
Mills, Nicolaus (ed.), *Culture in an Age of Money* (Chicago: Elephant, 1990).
Minich, Julia A., 'Rehabilitating Neoliberalism: Disability Representation in the Films of Alejandro González Iñárritu and Guillermo Arriaga', *The Journal of Popular Culture*, 48.5 (2015), 970–89.
Miyoshi, Masao, *Off Center: Power and Culture Relations between Japan and the United States* (London: Harvard University Press, 1991).
Monti, Enrico, 'From "Beginners" to "What We Talk ...": Variations on a Carver Story', in Vasiliki Fachard and Robert Miltner (eds), *Not Far From Here: The Paris Symposium on Raymond Carver* (Newcastle: Cambridge Scholars, 2014), pp. 37–49.
Murakami, Haruki, *After The Quake*, trans. Jay Rubin (London: Harvill Press, 2002).
Murakami, Haruki, *Birthday Stories* (London: Harvill Press, 2004).

Murakami, Haruki, *The Elephant Vanishes*, trans. Jay Rubin and Alfred Birnbaum (New York: Knopf, 1993)

Murakami, Haruki, *Hard-boiled Wonderland and the End of the World*, trans. Alfred Birbaum (London: Hamish Hamilton, 1991).

Murakami, Haruki, 'A Literary Comrade', trans. Maja McGowan, in William L. Stull and Maureen P. Carroll (eds), *Remembering Ray: A Composite Biography* (Santa Barbara: Capra Press, 1993), pp. 130–5.

Murakami, Haruki, *Norwegian Wood*, trans. Jay Rubin (London: The Harvill Press, 2000).

Murakami, Haruki, *Underground: The Tokyo Gas Attack and the Japanese Psyche*, trans. Alfred Birnbaum and Philip Gabriel (London: Harvill, 2001).

Murakami, Haruki, *What I Talk About When I Talk About Running*, trans. Philip Gabriel (London: Harvill Secker, 2008).

Newlove, Donald, 'Fiction Briefs: Review of *What We Talk About When We Talk About Love*', *Saturday Review*, April 1981.

O'Connell, Nicolas, 'Raymond Carver', in Marshall Bruce Gentry and William L. Stull (eds), *Conversations with Raymond Carver* (London: University of Mississippi Press, 1990), pp. 133–50.

O'Keeffe, Alice, 'Agent Provocateur', *New Statesman*, 15 January 2007.

Pinsker, Sanford, 'Soft Lights, Academic Talk: A Conversation with Jay McInerney', *The Literary Review*, 30.1 (1986), pp. 107–14.

Rebein, Robert, *Hicks, Tribes, and Dirty Realists* (Lexington: The University Press of Kentucky, 2001).

Reber, Dierdra, 'Love as Politics: *Amores Perros* and the Emotional Aesthetics of Neoliberalism', *Journal of Latin American Cultural Studies*, 19.3 (2010), 279–98.

Reid, Calvin, '"Birdman" Drives Interest in Raymond Carver Collection', *Publishers Weekly*, 19 February 2015.

Rich, Motoko, 'The Real Carver: Expansive Or Minimal?', *The New York Times*, 17 October 2007.

Ricks, Christopher, *Allusion to the Poets* (Oxford: Oxford University Press, 2002).

Robinson, Marilynne, 'Marriage and Other Astonishing Bonds', *The New York Times Book Review*, 15 May 1988.

Rubin, Jay, *Haruki Murakami and the Music of Words* (London: Harvill, 2002).

Rubin, Jay, 'Murakami Haruki's Two Poor Aunts Tell Everything They Know About Sheep, Wells, Unicorns, Proust, Elephants, and Magpies', in Stephen Snyder and Philip Gabriel (eds), *Oe and Beyond: Fiction in Contemporary Japan* (Honolulu: University of Hawai'i Press, 1999), pp. 177–98.

Runyon, Randolph Paul, 'Beginners' Luck', in Vasiliki Fachard and Robert Miltner (eds), *Not Far From Here: The Paris Symposium on Raymond Carver* (Newcastle: Cambridge Scholars, 2014), pp. 25–35.

Rushdie, Salman, 'Raymond Carver', *Imaginary Homelands: Essays and Criticism 1981–1991* (London: Granta, 1991), pp. 340–2.

Saldaña-Portillo, María Josefina, 'In the Shadow of NAFTA: *Y tu mamá también* Revisits the National Allegory of Mexican Sovereignty', *American Quarterly*, 57.3 (2005), 751–77.

Schumacher, Michael, 'After the Fire, into the Fire: An Interview with Raymond

Carver', in Marshall Bruce Gentry and William L. Stull (eds), *Conversations With Raymond Carver* (Jackson: University of Mississippi Press, 1990), pp. 214–37.
Scott, A. O., 'Raymond Carver's Enigma', *The New York Review of Books*, 12 August 1999.
Seemann, Brian, 'Existential Connections: The Influence of Raymond Carver on Haruki Murakami', *The Raymond Carver Review*, 1 (2007), 75–92.
Sennett, Richard, *The Corrosion of Character* (London: Norton, 1998).
Sennett, Richard, *The Craftsman* (London: Allen Lane, 2008).
Sennett, Richard, *The Culture of New Capitalism* (New Haven: Yale University Press, 2006).
Sennett, Richard, *Respect in a World of Inequality* (London: Norton, 2003).
Sennett, Richard and Jonathan Cobb, *The Hidden Injuries of Class* (Cambridge: Cambridge University Press, 1972).
Shonkwiler, Alison and Leigh Claire La Berge, *Reading Capitalist Realism* (Iowa City: University of Iowa Press, 2014).
Simpson, Mona and Lewis Buzbee, 'Raymond Carver, Art of Fiction No. 76', *The Paris Review*, 88 (1983), <www.theparisreview.org/interviews/3059/the-art-of-fiction-no-76-raymond-carver> (last accessed 8 November 2019).
Sinfield, Alan, *Literature, Politics and Culture in Postwar Britain* (London: Continuum, 2004).
Sklenicka, Carol, *Raymond Carver: A Writer's Life* (New York: Scribner, 2009).
Smith, Paul Julian, *Amores Perros* (London: BFI Publishing, 2003).
Snyder, Stephen and Philip Gabriel, 'Introduction', in Stephen Snyder and Philip Gabriel (eds), *Oe and Beyond: Fiction in Contemporary Japan* (Honolulu: University of Hawai'i Press, 1999), pp. 1–10.
Stearns, Peter N., *Be A Man! Males in Modern Society* (New York: Holmes and Meier, 1979).
Stiglitz, Joseph E., *Globalization and Its Discontents* (London: Norton, 2002).
Strecher, Matthew C., 'Beyond "Pure" Literature: Mimesis, Formula, and the Postmodern in the Fiction of Murakami Haruki', *The Journal of Asian Studies*, 57.2 (1998), 354–78.
Strecher, Matthew C., *The Forbidden Worlds of Haruki Murakami* (Minneapolis: University of Minnesota Press, 2014).
Stull, William L., 'Beyond Hopelessville: Another Side of Raymond Carver', *Philological Quarterly*, 64.1 (1985), 1–15.
Stull, William L., 'Raymond Carver Remembered: Three Early Stories', *Studies in Short Fiction*, 25.4 (1988), 461–9.
Stull, William L. and Maureen P. Carroll, 'The Critical Reception of the Works of Raymond Carver', in James Plath (ed.), *Critical Insights: Raymond Carver* (Ipswich, MA: Salem Press, 2013), pp. 39–55.
Takafusa, Nakamura, *A History of Showa Japan, 1926–1989*, trans. Edwin Whenmouth (Tokyo: University of Tokyo Press, 1998).
Taylor, Ronald, *Aesthetics and Politics* (London: Verso, 1980).
The Q&A with Jeff Goldsmith, Podcast, hosted by Jeff Goldsmith. 16 January 2015.
The Revenant, film, directed by Alejandro González Iñárritu. USA: Regency Enterprises, 2015.

Tolstoy, Leo, *What Is Art?*, trans. Aylmer Maude (London: Collier-Macmillan, 1960).
Tromp, Hansmaarten, '"Any Good Writer Uses His Imagination to Convince the Reader"', in Marshall Bruce Gentry and William L. Stull (eds), *Conversations with Raymond Carver* (London: University of Mississippi Press, 1990).
21 Grams, film, directed by Alejandro González Iñárritu. USA: Focus Features, 2003.
Usery, Stephen, 'A Very Close Deal', *Nashville Scene*, 4 April 2013, <www.nashvillescene.com/nashville/novelist-jay-mcinerney-and-editor-gary-fisketjon-have-been-collaborating-andmdash-and-drinking-jack-daniels-together-andmdash-for-the-last-39-y/Content?oid=3345744> (last accessed 11 April 2019).
Vance, J. D., *Hillbilly Elegy: A Memoir of a Family and Culture in Crisis* (London: William Collins, 2016).
Vlautin, Willy, *Lean on Pete* (New York: Harper Perennial, 2010).
Vonnegut, Kurt, *Slaughterhouse-Five* (London: Vintage, [1970] 2000).
Watt, Ian, *The Rise of the Novel* (London: University of California Press, 1957).
Weber, Bruce, 'Raymond Carver: A Chronicler of Blue-Collar Despair', in Marshall Bruce Gentry and William L. Stull (eds), *Conversations with Raymond Carver* (London: University of Mississippi Press, 1990), pp. 84–97.
Williams, Raymond, *Culture and Materialism* (London: Verso, 1980).
Williams, Raymond, *Problems in Materialism and Culture* (London: Verso, 1980).
Wittman, Lucas, 'Jay McInerney, The Art of Fiction No. 231', *The Paris Review*, 217 (2016), <www.theparisreview.org/interviews/6477/jay-mcinerney-the-art-of-fiction-no-231-jay-mcinerney> (last accessed 11 April 2019).
Woolf, Virginia, 'Mr Bennett and Mrs Brown', in Rachel Bowlby (ed.), *A Woman's Essays: Selected Essays* (London: Penguin, 1992), pp. 69–87.
Wright Mills, C. *White Collar: The American Middle Classes* (New York: Oxford University Press, 1956).
Wriglesworth, Chad, 'Raymond Carver and Alcoholics Anonymous', in Sandra Lee Kleppe and Robert Miltner (eds), *New Paths to Raymond Carver* (Columbia: University of South Carolina Press, 2008), pp. 132–53.
Zarsky, Lyuba, and Kevin P. Gallagher, 'NAFTA, Foreign Direct Investment, and Sustainable Industrial Development in Mexico', *Americas Program Policy Brief*, 28 January 2004, <https://pdfs.semanticscholar.org/a320/643ad3d51cd668838ed90476ca2f43eb07a6.pdf?_ga=2.166404150.924185642.1574235295-347545509.1574235295> (last accessed 19 November 2019).

Further Reading

Anon., 'Honeymooners: A Cautionary Tale', *Publishers Weekly*, 5 July 2001.
Anon., 'NAFTA at 20: Ready to take off again?', *The Economist*, 4 January 2014.
Anzaldúa, Gloria, *Borderlands/La Frontera: The New Mestiza* (San Francisco: Aunt Lute Books, 1999).
Appelbaum, Judith, 'Paperback Talk', *The New York Times Book Review*, 18 September 1983.
Barta, Preston, 'Interview: Director Alejandro González Iñárritu unmasks the *Birdman*', *North Texas Daily*, 23 October 2014.

Barth, John, *The Friday Book* (Baltimore: Johns Hopkins University Press, 1984).
Bellamy, Joe David, 'A Downpour of Literary Republicanism', *Mississippi Review*, 41.1 (1985), 31–9.
Blincoe, Nicholas and Matt Thorne (eds), *All Hail the New Puritans* (London: Fourth Estate, 2000).
Boddy, Kasia, *The American Short Story since 1950* (Edinburgh: Edinburgh University Press, 2010).
Buford, Bill, 'Editorial', *Granta*, 8 (1982), 4–5.
Cartmell, Deborah, *A Companion to Literature, Film and Adaptation* (Malden, MA: Wiley Blackwell, 2012).
Case, Anne and Angus Deaton, 'Rising Morbidity and Mortality in Midlife Among White Non-Hispanic Americans in the 21st Century', *Proceedings of the National Academy of Sciences of the United States of America*, 112.49 (2015), 15078–83.
Cohn, Nate, 'A 2016 Review', *The New York Times*, 28 March 2017.
Duffy, Edward, 'Word of God in Some Raymond Carver Stories', *Religion and the Arts*, 2.3 (1998), 311–36.
Eagleton, Terry, *Ideology: An Introduction* (London: Verso, 1991).
Eagleton, Terry, *Literary Theory: An Introduction* (Oxford: Blackwell, 1983).
Federman, Raymond, 'A Short Note on Minimalism', *Mississippi Review*, 41.1 (1985), 57.
Fisher Fishkin, Shelley, 'Crossroads of Cultures: The Transnational Turn in American Studies: Presidential Address to the American Studies Association, November 12, 2004', *American Quarterly*, 57.1 (2005), 17–57.
Gearhart, Michael W., 'Breaking the Ties that Bind: Inarticulation in the Fiction of Raymond Carver', *Studies in Short Fiction*, 26.4 (1989), 439–46.
Greco, Albert N., Jim Milliot and Robert M. Wharton, *The Book Publishing Industry* (London: Taylor & Francis, 2013).
Green, Emma, 'It Was Cultural Anxiety That Drove White, Working-Class Voters to Trump', *The Atlantic*, 9 May 2017.
Griswold, Daniel, 'NAFTA at 10', *Free Trade Bulletin No 1*, 17 December 2002.
Harvey, David, *The New Imperialism* (Oxford: Oxford University Press, 2003).
Houston, Robert, 'A Stunning Inarticulateness', *Nation*, 4 July 1981.
Imagine: A Wild Sheep Chase: In Search of Haruki Murakami, TV, presented by Alan Yentob. UK: BBC, 2008.
Isenberg, Nancy, *White Trash: The 400-Year Untold History of Class in America* (New York: Viking, 2016).
Kemp, Peter, 'The American Chekhov: Elephant and Other Stories by Raymond Carver', *The Sunday Times*, 7 August 1988.
Kleppe, Sandra Lee, 'Women and Violence in the Stories of Raymond Carver', *Journal of the Short Story in English*, 46 (2006), 2–14.
La Berge, Leigh Claire, *Scandals and Abstraction: Financial Fiction of the Long 1980s* (New York: Oxford University Press, 2014).
Lentricchia, Frank, 'The American Writer as Bad Citizen – Introducing Don DeLillo', *South Atlantic Quarterly*, 89.2 (1990), 239–44.
Lorentzen, Christian, 'Gordon Lish, The Art of Editing No. 2', *The Paris Review*, 215 (2015).

McFarlane, Brian, *Novel to Film: An Introduction to the Theory of Adaptation* (Oxford: Clarendon, 1996).

Mirarchi, Steve, 'Conditions of Possibility: Religious Revision in Raymond Carver's "Cathedral"', *Religion and the Arts*, 2.3 (1998), 299–310.

Murakami, Haruki, *Blind Willow, Sleeping Woman*, trans. Philip Gabriel and Jay Rubin (London: Harvill Secker, 2006).

Murray, Charles, *Coming Apart: The State of White America, 1960–2010* (New York: Crown Forum, 2012).

Nakane, Chie, *Japanese Society* (London: University of California Press, 1970).

Newman, Katherine S., *Falling From Grace* (New York: Pantheon, 1989).

Omnibus: Dreams Are What We Wake Up From, TV, directed by Daisy Goodwin. UK: BBC, 1989.

Parish Flannery, Nathaniel, 'Investor Insight: How Strong is Mexico's Economy?', *Forbes*, 8 September 2015.

Pettifor, Ann, *The Coming First World Debt Crisis* (Basingstoke: Palgrave Macmillan, 2006).

Pettifor, Ann, *Real World Economic Outlook: The Legacy of Globalization, Debt and Deflation* (Basingstoke: Palgrave Macmillan, 2003).

Phillips, Cassandra, 'Accolade-Winning Author Returns to Humboldt', in Marshall Bruce Gentry and William L. Stull (eds), *Conversations With Raymond Carver* (Jackson: University of Mississippi Press, 1990), pp. 3–7.

Prose, Francine, 'A Nightmare on Broadway', *NYR Daily*, <https://www.nybooks.com/daily/2015/01/28/birdman-nightmare-broadway/> (last accessed 19 November 2019).

Reich, Robert and Bill Marsh, 'The Limping Middle Class', *The New York Times*, 4 September 2011.

Roarty, Alex, 'Democrats Say They Now Know Exactly Why Clinton Lost', *McClatchy DC*, 1 May 2017.

Runyon, Randolph Paul, *Reading Raymond Carver* (Syracuse: New York, 1992).

Ryzik, Melena, '"Birdman" y la dualidad que todos tenemos', *The New York Times ES*, 21 February 2015.

Sanborn, Sara, '*The Hidden Injuries of Class*, by Richard Sennett and Jonathan Cobb (Book Review)', *Commentary*, 54.6 (1972), 94–6.

Scofield, Martin, *The Cambridge Introduction to the American Short Story* (Cambridge: Cambridge University Press, 2006).

Scofield, Martin, 'Closer to home: Carver versus Altman', *Studies in Short Fiction*, 33.3 (1996), 387–99

Scofield, Martin, 'Negative Pastoral: The Art of Raymond Carver's Stories', *The Cambridge Quarterly*, 23.3 (1994), 243–62.

Scofield, Martin, 'Story and History in Raymond Carver', *Critique*, 40.3 (1999), 266–80.

Sexton, David, 'David Sexton Talks to Raymond Carver', *Literary Review*, 85 (1985), 36–40.

Stanislavski, Konstantin, *An Actor's Work* (London: Routledge, 2009).

Stiglitz, Joseph E., 'Of the 1%, By the 1%, For the 1%', *Vanity Fair*, 31 March 2011.

Stull, William L. and Maureen P. Carroll, 'Prolegomena to Any Future Carver Studies', *Journal of the Short Story in English*, 46 (2006), 2–5.

Sweeten, Paul, 'Light and Change: Repressed Escapism in *What We Talk About When We Talk About Love*', *Journal of the Short Story in English*, 60 (2013), 2–11.

Tanehaus, Sam and Shayla Harris, 'A Conversation with Jay McInerney', *The New York Times*, 29 April 2009.

Thompson, Anne, 'How *Birdman* Got Made: Fox Searchlight and New Regency Partners Tell All', *Indiewire*, 21 October 2014, available at <www.indiewire.com/2014/10/how-birdman-got-made-fox-searchlight-and-new-regency-partners-tell-all-keaton-norton-stone-videos-190522> (last accessed 19 November 2019).

Vanhan, Peter, 'Top 10 Things to Know About the Mexican Economy', *Agenda for World Economic Forum*, 5 May 2015, <www.weforum.org/agenda/2015/05/top-10-things-to-know-about-the-mexican-economy> (last accessed 19 November 2019).

Villarreal, M. Angeles and Ian F. Fergusson, 'The North American Free Trade Agreement', *Congressional Research Service*, 16 April 2015, <http://fas.org/sgp/crs/row/R42965.pdf> (last accessed 19 November 2019).

Westfall Shute, Kathleen, 'Finding the Words: The Struggle for Salvation in the Fiction of Raymond Carver', *Hollins Critic*, 24.5 (1987), 1–10.

Williams, Raymond, *Marxism and Literature* (Oxford: Oxford University Press, 1977).

Wise, Timothy, 'How Beer Explains 20 Years of NAFTA's Devastating Effects On Mexico', *Public Radio International*, 2 January 2014, <https://www.pri.org/stories/2014-01-02/how-beer-explains-20-years-nafta-s-devastating-effects-mexico> (last accessed 19 November 2019).

Wright Mills, C., 'The Cultural Apparatus', *The Listener*, 26 March 1959.

Wysong, Earl, Robert Perrucci and David Wright, *The New Class Society: Goodbye American Dream?* (Plymouth: Rowman & Littlefield, 2014).

INDEX

Adelman, Bob, 2
  Carver Country, 130
AFL, 185
Albuquerque, New Mexico, 168
alcoholism, 34–5, 55, 75, 98, 127–8, 136–7, 184, 186
Aldridge, John, 50
Altman, Robert, 1, 168, 171
Anderson, Sherwood, 13
Arreguin, Alfredo, 155
Arriaga, Guillermo, 149
Arrighi, Giovanni, 4
Atlantic, The, 184
Atlantic Monthly, 70, 87
Aum Shinrikyo, 131
Azcona, María del Mar, 153, 156

Babel, Isaac, 157
Barraza, Adriana, 151
Barth, John, 71, 73, 74, 76, 88, 89, 157
Barthelme, Donald, 71
Beef Trust, 27, 42–4
Blanchett, Cate, 151
Bloom, Harold, 17, 18, 19, 20
Blum, David, 80
Boise State University, 191
Bonetti, Kay, 162
Borges, Jorge Luis, 163
Boujaily, Vance, 33
Boulter, Jonathan, 133

Boxer, David, 109, 117
Bradbury, Malcolm, 72
Brando, Marlon, 160
Brautigan, Richard, 42, 71
Bretton Woods, 3–4, 110
Broadway, 148, 164, 166, 172
Brodkey, Harold, 91
Bukowski, Charles, 187
Burke-Carver, Maryann, 6–7, 29, 31–3, 35–6, 43–4, 57, 112
Burton, Tim, 168

California State, 33, 34, 40, 44, 45, 49, 50, 74, 115, 151
Campbell, Ewing, 18
Canclini, Néstor, 150
Capra Press, 38, 65
Carney, Art, 48
Carroll, Maureen P., 128
Carver, Raymond
  'A Meditation on a Line from Saint Teresa', 131, 137
  A New Path To The Waterfall, 130
  'A Serious Talk', 62
  'A Small, Good Thing', 84, 137, 169
  'A Storyteller's Shoptalk', 71
  Beginners, 128
  'Bicycles, Muscles, Cigarettes', 45
  'Boxes', 56, 186
  Call If You Need Me, 130

Cathedral, 5, 66, 84
'Cathedral', 19
'Chef's House', 137-8
Elephant, 14
'Fat', 29, 85
'Fires', 6, 75, 78, 97, 111, 184
Fires: Essays, Poems, Stories, 71
Furious Seasons, 65
'Gazebo', 62, 85, 186
'Intimacy', 55, 57, 138
'Jerry and Molly and Sam', 186
'John Gardner: The Writer as Teacher', 63, 74
'Kindling', 12-13, 137-9
'Late Fragment', 1, 177
'Menudo', 13, 56
'Mr. Coffee and Mr. Fixit', 186
'My Boat', 68
'Neighbours', 29, 63, 168
'Night School', 37-9
'On Writing', 15-16, 71, 73, 89, 157-8, 162
'Pastoral', 97
'Preservation', 186
'Put Yourself In My Shoes', 30, 38
'Shiftless', 15
'So Much Water So Close To Home', 30, 43, 106, 187
'The Cabin', 97
'The Projectile', 140
'The Student's Wife', 7-9
'Viewfinder', 186
'Want To See Something?', 62
'What Do You Do In San Francisco?', 115, 126
'What Is It?', 51, 61, 113, 115, 127-8
What We Talk About When We Talk About Love, 47, 62, 66, 74, 84, 128
'What We Talk About When We Talk About Love', 147, 154, 163, 172
Where I'm Calling From, 9
'Where I'm Calling From', 137-8
'Why Don't You Dance?', 85
Will You Please Be Quiet, Please?, 61, 65-6, 112
'Work', 15

Cassill, R. V., 33
Cecily, Diane, 44
Chabon, Michael, 48
Chandler, Raymond, 108
Chekov, Anton, 16-17
Chico State University, 33, 74-6
Cobb, Jonathan, 185
Columbia University, 38, 65
Connell, Evan, 16
Coover, Robert, 71
Cornwall, Gareth, 115
craftsmanship, 3, 12-16, 21-2, 38, 41, 50, 53-4, 56, 70, 78, 98, 110, 137-40, 156, 173, 184-5
creative writing, 16-17, 28, 30-1, 33, 48, 60, 62, 75
Crumley, James, 66
Cuarón, Alfonso, 167

Dean, Jodi, 6
Deleyto, Celestino, 153, 156
DeLillo, Don, 65
Democrats, 3, 183
Derrida, Jacques, 90, 92
Dostoevsky, Feodor, 72-3
Downey Jr., Robert, 168

Easton Ellis, Bret, 80, 85
Edith Mirrelees Fellowship, 40
Eliot, T. S., 17, 72
Entertainment Tonight, 133
Esquire, 12, 28, 63, 70, 137
Establishment, 120, 122, 125, 127, 131-2, 135-6
Evers, Stuart, 1
Everson, William, 29
Experimentalism, 71, 87, 90, 157-8

Farrar, Straus & Giroux, 47
Fassbender, Michael, 167
Faulkner, William, 17, 72-3
Felski, Rita, 36
Fisher, Mark, 6
Fisketjon, Gary, 22, 60-1, 63-8
Fitzgerald, F. Scott, 73, 108
Ford, Richard, 32, 61, 68

Fordism, 3, 117
Fowler, Mark, 183
Fox Searchlight, 166

G. I. Bill, 30
Gabriel, Philip, 135
Galifianakis, Zach, 159, 167
Gallagher, Tess, 19, 64, 68, 129–30, 136–7, 140, 155, 158
García Bernal, Gael, 151
Gardner, John, 15, 33, 35, 63, 71, 74–9, 88–9
Garrett, George, 82
Gass, William, 71, 88, 157
Girard, Stephanie, 65–7, 84
Glass-Steagall Act, 4, 86
Gleeson, Jackie, 48
Goddard College, 35
Goldsmith, Jeff, 156
Goldwater, Barry, 3
GOP, 183
Granta, 70
Graydon Carter, E., 65
Great Depression, the, 4
Greco, Albert, 86
Greenwich Village, 22, 60
Gregory, Sinda, 78
Groarke, Stephen, 9

Habermas, Jürgen, 84
Hall, James, 28–9, 31
Halpert, Sam, 41, 61, 69
Harker, Ben, 9, 16, 111, 190
Harold Strauss Living Award, 35
Harper's Bazaar, 29
Harrelson, Woody, 167
Harvey, David, 7, 11–12, 109–10, 152, 165–6
Hassan, Ihab, 17
Hayes, Helen, 160
Helprin, Mark, 10
Hemingway, Ernest, 13, 16–18, 32, 39, 51, 73, 75, 97–8, 187
Hendin, Josephine, 80–2
higher education, 17, 20–1, 30–3, 35–7, 40

Hobhouse, Janet, 66
Hollywood, 96, 148, 154–5, 157, 160–1, 166–8, 174–5
Hopper, Edward, 8, 188
Howe, Irving, 5–6, 18
Humboldt State University, 33, 112

IMF, 86, 149
Iñárritu, G. Alejandro, 1, 149–51, 153, 156–7, 159–60, 163, 166–8, 171, 173–7
  Amores Perros, 149–50
  Babel, 149–50, 152–3
  Birdman, 22, 148–9, 153, 156, 158, 160, 166–8, 172–5
  The Free, 187–8
  The Motel Life, 187–8
  The Revenant, 152, 166
influence, 1–2, 5, 15–22, 27, 61, 69–72, 83, 95, 107–9, 129, 140–1, 153, 157, 162, 172–3, 177
Institutional Revolutionary Party, 149
International Visitor Program, 22
Irving, John, 34
Ivy, Marilyn, 118
Izanagi Boom, 118

Jakobson, Roman, 72
James, Henry, 72, 90–1, 157
Jameson, Fredric, 6, 81, 92
Janowitz, Tama, 80, 85
Jencks, Tom, 68
Johnson, Denis, 1
Johnson, Lyndon B., 3
Joyce, James, 48, 64, 72

Kaufman, David, 83–5
Keaton, Michael, 148, 167–8
Kelly, Paul, 2, 187
Keynesian economics, 4, 182
Kinder, Chuck, 1, 21, 28, 40–4, 47–8, 68, 173
  Honeymooners, 21, 47–8, 55
  Snakehunter, 40
Kingston, Jeff, 130–1

Kittredge, William, 21, 28-9, 42, 44, 64, 68
Kohn, Eric, 168
Korean War, 118
Kotatko, Andrew, 1

Laffer curve, 182
Lawrence, D. H., 19
Lawrence, Ray, 1
Leaf, Jonathan, 172
Lears, T. J. Jackson, 13
Leavis, F. R., 17
Leavitt, David, 80, 85
LeClair, Tom, 73
Leggett, John, 34
Libertarianism, 5, 182, 187
Life, 51
Lish, Gordon, 28-9, 60, 63, 68, 128-9, 172
Literary Brat Pack, 80
London Review of Books, 10
Lost Decade, The, 130, 136
Lubezki, Emmanuel, 167
Lyotard, Jean-François, 72

McCaffery, Larry, 73, 78, 120
McDonald's, 123
McGraw-Hill, 65
McGuane, Thomas, 66-8
McGurl, Mark, 16-17, 20, 37-8
McHale, Brian, 72
McInerney, Jay, 1, 15, 22, 60-72, 74-5, 79-82, 84-5, 87-93, 95, 98, 173, 187
  'Amanda', 64, 83
  Bright, Precious Days, 61, 87
  Bright Lights, Big City, 22, 63-8, 70-1, 80-3
  Brightness Falls, 22, 71, 85, 87, 89, 98
  'It's Six A.M. Do You Know Where You Are?', 63
  'Jimmy', 70
  'Lost and Found', 70
  Ransom, 70
  'Reunion', 70
  'Smoke', 70, 87-8
  Story Of My Life, 70
  'The Business', 70
  The Good Life, 87
  'The March', 87
  'The Real Tad Allagash', 70
Mailer, Norman, 49
Manhattan, 63, 93, 158
Marshall, Paule, 66
Marx, Karl, 10-11
Mason, Bobbie Ann, 85
Matthiessen, Peter, 66
Max, D. T., 128
Meadows, Audrey, 48
metafiction, 48, 99
Mexico, 149-52, 190
Meyer, Stephen, 41, 44, 50
MGM, 68
Michaels, Lenny, 29, 49
Mills, Nicolaus, 182-3
Minich, Julie, 150
Minimalism, 19
Missouri Review, The, 62
MLA, 42
Modernism, 72-3
Mont Pelerin Society, 4
Montana State, 48, 51, 188
MS, 70
Murakami, Haruki, 2, 20, 22, 61, 68, 106-9, 118-21, 123, 125-8, 131-5, 137, 140-1, 173, 187
  A Slow Boat To China, 108
  'A Slow Boat To China', 123
  A Wild Sheep Chase, 108
  After The Quake, 22, 107, 132-4, 141
  'All God's Children Can Dance', 134
  'Family Affair', 125-6
  Hard-boiled Wonderland and the End of the World, 108
  Hear The Wind Sing, 108
  Norwegian Wood, 187
  Pinball, 1973, 108
  'The Compartment', 138
  The Elephant Vanishes, 22
  'The Second Bakery Attack', 121-2, 126-7

Murakami, Haruk (*cont.*)
   'UFO in Kushiro', 132
   Underground, 131, 133, 135
Murray, Charles, 182

NAFTA, 150, 152
Neoliberalism, 2–3, 5–7, 11–12, 23, 84, 86, 111–12, 141, 150, 152, 156, 175
New Critics, 72
New Regency, 166
New York City, 4, 28–9, 60–4, 68–70, 80, 86–7, 166
New York Review of Books, The, 1, 9
New York Times, The, 10, 163, 174
New York Times Book Review, The, 9, 32, 61, 71, 81, 98
New Yorker, The, 61, 63–4, 81
Newlove, Donald, 128
Newsweek, 82
Nixon, Richard, 3
Norton, Edward, 148, 167–8

Oates, Joyce Carol, 64
Oberlin College, 75
O'Brien, Tim, 64
O'Connor, Flannery, 16
OECD, 4
OPEC Oil Shock, 4, 86
Oscars, 22, 167

Page, Geraldine, 160
Palmer Institute of Authorship, 32
Paris Review, The, 35, 63–4, 70
People, 82
Phillips, Cassandra, 109, 117
Pitt, Brad, 151
Playboy, 80
Playgirl, 43
Plimpton, George, 63–4
Ploughshares, 64, 70
Port Angeles, Washington, 22, 140
Portland, Oregon, 117, 188, 190
Post-Fordism, 3
Postmodernism, 72
Pound, Ezra, 17, 157

Price Fox, William, 34
Princeton-in-Asia Fellowship, 61
Pritchett, V. S., 16
Prose Francine, 172, 175
PRRI, 184
Pynchon, Thomas, 71

Randolph, Joyce, 48
Random House, 60, 64–6
Reagan, Nancy, 182
Reagan, Ronald, 3, 5, 182, 185
Realism, 9, 18, 22, 65, 71–4, 76, 79, 80, 87, 90, 92, 95, 96–7, 99, 107, 128, 157, 176–7
Rebein, Robert, 32
Renner, Jeremy, 167
Reno, Nevada, 187–8
Republican, 3
Ricks, Christopher, 17
Riseborough, Andrea, 171
Ro, Sigmund, 72
Robards, Jason, 160
Robinson, Marilynne, 9
Roth, Philip, 49
Rubin, Jay, 107–8, 120–1, 126, 133, 135–6
Rush, Dan, 1
Rushdie, Salman, 1
Ryan, Amy, 154

San Francisco, 27–8, 48, 50, 115–17
Sanchez, Antonio, 155, 176
Santa Cruz, 27–31, 34, 43
Saudi Arabia, 4
Scientific Research Associates, 28–30, 34, 38
Scofield, Martin, 9
Scott, A. O., 1–2
Seemann, Brian, 109
Sennett, Richard, 11–12, 15, 110–11, 113–14, 138–40, 185
   The Corrosion of Character, 111
   The Craftsman, 12, 15
   The Culture of New Capitalism, 11, 12, 111
Shamos, Jeremy, 159

Silicon Valley, 40, 42
Simpson, Mona, 63-4, 68
Sinfield, Alan, 19-21
Sklenicka, Carol, 42, 62, 74-5, 112, 129
Smith, Adam, 5
Snyder, Stephen, 135
Spokane, Washington, 188
Stanford University, 28-9, 39-43, 48-9, 52
Stegner Fellowship, 27, 29-30, 34, 40, 42-3
Stein, Gertrude, 17
Steinbeck, John, 187
Steinhardt, Annie, 29
Stieglitz, Alfred, 133
Stone, Emma, 156, 167-8
Strecher, Matthew, 120
Stull, William L., 97-8, 128
Surrealism, 106
Syracuse, 60, 62-4, 67, 69-70, 79, 148
Syracuse University, 22, 35, 64

Telvisa, 149
Tolstoy, Leo, 76
TriQuarterly, 62
Trump, Donald, 183-4, 186
Trurow, Scott, 42

University of California, Berkeley, 29, 108
University of California, Davis, 43-4
University of California, Santa Barbara, 35
University of California, Santa Cruz, 27

University of Iowa Writers' Workshop, 21, 28, 36
University of Montana in Missoula, 29
University of Texas, El Paso, 35

Vance, J. D., 189
Village Voice, 65-6
Vintage Contemporaries, 22, 47, 64, 66-7
Vlautin, Willy, 1, 23, 61, 187, 189-90
  Don't Skip Out On Me, 187-8
  Lean on Pete, 187-91
  Northline, 187
  The Free, 187-8
  The Motel Life, 187-8
Volcker, Paul, 5
Vonnegut, Kurt, 71, 73, 108

Watts, Naomi, 159, 167
West Coast Fiction, 106
Western Humanities Review, 97
WFM, 149
Williams, Raymond, 11, 20
Williams College, 60
Wolff, Geoffrey, 73, 157
Wolff, Tobias, 64, 66-8
Woolf, Virginia, 72
Worldview Entertainment, 166
Wright Mills, C., 14
Wriglesworth, Chad, 129-30

YouTube, 164-6

Zeta Films, 149

EU representative:
Easy Access System Europe
Mustamäe tee 50, 10621 Tallinn, Estonia
Gpsr.requests@easproject.com

www.ingramcontent.com/pod-product-compliance
Lightning Source LLC
Chambersburg PA
CBHW070354240426
43671CB00013BA/2503